Lives of Fort de Chartres

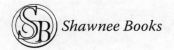

Shawnee Books

Lives of Fort de Chartres

COMMANDANTS, SOLDIERS, AND CIVILIANS IN FRENCH ILLINOIS, 1720–1770

DAVID MACDONALD

Southern Illinois University Press
Carbondale

Southern Illinois University Press
www.siupress.com
Copyright © 2016 by the Board of Trustees,
Southern Illinois University
Printed in the United States of America

19 18 17 16   4 3 2 1

Cover illustrations: Exterior of the reconstructed stone
Fort de Chartres (foreground image), courtesy of Joseph Gagné;
Governor Kerlérec's commission of the Cherokee chief
Okana-Stoté, February 27, 1761 (background image, detail),
U.S. National Archives.

Library of Congress Cataloging-in-Publication Data
MacDonald, David, 1943– author.
Lives of Fort de Chartres : commandants, soldiers, and
civilians in French Illinois, 1720–1770 / David MacDonald.
pages cm. — (Shawnee books)
Includes bibliographical references and index.
ISBN 978-0-8093-3460-5 (pbk. : alk. paper)
ISBN 978-0-8093-3461-2 (e-book)
1. Fort de Chartres Site (Ill.)
2. French—Illinois—History—18th century.
3. French—Illinois—Biography.
4. Illinois—History—To 1778.
5. Frontier and pioneer life—Illinois. I. Title.
F544.M33 2016
977.3'01—dc23   2015027260

Et ceux qui ne font rien ne se trompent jamais.
—Théodore Faullain de Banville

Contents

Figures

Preface

MODERN HISTORICAL WRITING is deeply shaped by the concerns and insights of the social sciences and is largely problem centered, attempting to analyze the causes and effects of specific historical factors on change and continuity through time. Narrative history and biography, especially the biographical sketch, are largely regarded as obsolete and lesser forms of history. Yet it is good to remember that all history is ultimately the history of individuals, and it is on this level that we can most immediately and intimately comprehend the past. The sources on eighteenth-century French Illinois seldom permit deep insight into the personalities of the men and women who lived there, but still they allow an appreciation of their humanity and the world in which they lived.

Most of the biographical sketches presented here are of men. Evidence for the lives of individual women, Indians, Africans, and African Creoles is scarce and rarely consists of more than a few bare facts and perhaps an anecdote or two. Strong and important individual members of these groups did exist, but those for whom one can find sufficient evidence of anything approaching a true biography—such as Elizabeth Montour or Madame Chouteau—usually fall outside the geographic or temporal range of this work. Collective biography offers fuller and more nuanced appreciation for these groups,[1] but that approach exceeds the scope of this work.

L. C. Dean and M. K. Brown's microfilm collection of documents titled Kaskaskia Manuscripts, 1714–1816: A Calendar of Civil Documents in Colonial Illinois is fundamental to the history of French Illinois. The Kaskaskia manuscripts directly concerned with the village that formed around Fort de Chartres are gathered together with some manuscripts from other sources and translated in M. K. Brown and L. C. Dean's *The Village of Chartres in Colonial Illinois, 1720–1765.* Also important are Brown and Dean's *The French Colony in the Mid-Mississippi Valley* and Brown's *History as They Lived It: A Social History of Prairie du Rocher, Ill.*

C. J. Ekberg's classic works *Colonial Ste. Genevieve: An Adventure on the Mississippi Frontier*; *French Roots in the Illinois Country: The Mississippi Frontier in Colonial Times*; and *Stealing Indian Women: Native Slavery in the Illinois Country* are essential for understanding the nature of French culture in Illinois. His recent work with S. K. Person, *St. Louis Rising: The French Regime of Louis St. Ange de Bellerive*, has been eagerly awaited and fundamentally alters understanding of early St. Louis.

France's Forgotten Legion: Service Records of French Military and Administrative Personnel Stationed in the Mississippi Valley and Gulf Coast Region, 1699–1769, by C. A. Brasseaux, is a guide to the careers of French marines and administrators who served in Louisiana. For those who came from or served at some time in Canada, information can often be found in the *Dictionary of Canadian Biography/Dictionnaire biographique du Canada*. Also basic is the *Alphabet Laffilard*, a ledger of the career of military officers and civil administrators serving in the French colonies from 1627 to 1780. H. W. Mumford's *The French Governors of Illinois, 1718–1765* provides sanitized biographies of the commandants of Fort de Chartres. New material and perspectives have appeared, however, in the fifty years since its writing.

Many original documents in translation may be found in R. G. Thwaites's *The Jesuit Relations and Allied Documents: Travels and Explorations of the Jesuit Missionaries in New France, 1610–1791*; T. C. Pease's *Anglo-French Boundary Disputes in the West, 1749–1763*; T. C. Pease and E. Jenison's *Illinois on the Eve of the Seven Years' War, 1747–1755*; and D. Rowland and A. G. Sanders's *Mississippi Provincial Archives*, volumes 1–4. For the last decade of the French era, the Vaudreuil papers, abstracted in B. Barron's *The Vaudreuil Papers: A Calendar and Index of the Personal and Private Records of Pierre de Rigaud de Vaudreuil, Royal Governor of the French Province of Louisiana, 1743–1753*, contain valuable information.

Basic modern works are M. Giraud's five-volume *Histoire de la Louisiane Française* [A history of French Louisiana]; N. M. Belting's *Kaskaskia under the French Regime*; M. de Villiers du Terrage's *The Last Years of*

French Louisiana; and R. D. Edmunds and J. L. Peyser's *The Fox Wars: The Mesquakie Challenge to New France*.

Rather than cite these works repeatedly, I have confined endnotes to specific original documents to which reference is made in the text, controversial interpretations, and sources less often used than those mentioned above.

Acknowledgments

EVERY STUDY OF French Illinois is immensely indebted to Margaret Kimball Brown. Her works are monumental, and her courtesy and kindness are profound. Carl J. Ekberg's works dealing with French Illinois are both basic and revolutionary. He has never stinted in his help and generosity, sharing sources and insights. Sharon Person has saved me from many errors and assorted blunders. I humbly thank her. Joseph Gagné is emerging as a leader in the new generation of scholars of Nouvelle France and French Louisiana. I thank him for his endless help with manuscripts and unfailing pleasant and uplifting friendship.

Errors remain, of course, my responsibility.

Lives of Fort de Chartres

PART ONE

French Illinois

THE SPANISH WERE the first Europeans to see the Mississippi, perhaps Alonso Álvarez de Pineda in 1519 and certainly Hernando de Soto in 1541, but French explorers from Canada were the first Europeans to explore the great river. Louis Jolliet and Father Jacques Marquette descended the Mississippi to the mouth of the Arkansas in 1673, but when they learned the river emptied into the Gulf of Mexico rather than the Pacific, they returned north. In 1682, René-Robert Cavelier de La Salle traveled down the Illinois River to the Mississippi and then followed that river to its mouth, naming the Mississippi River valley La Louisiane in honor of King Louis XIV. La Salle later attempted to colonize the mouth of the Mississippi, but the expedition miscarried, ending in Texas, where disgruntled followers killed him and Indians destroyed the colony.

In 1699, Pierre Le Moyne d'Iberville established the first tentative French settlement in southern Louisiana at Biloxi. In the following years, the French established other settlements, first on the Gulf coast and then increasingly centered on the Mississippi River. Meanwhile, French fur traders and missionaries from Canada moved down the river systems south of the Great Lakes into the areas of modern Illinois, Michigan, and Indiana. In 1696, missionaries first arrived at Cahokia, home of one of the tribes of Illinois Indians, on the eastern side of the Mississippi near modern St Louis. There they found fur traders, mainly unlicensed *coureurs des bois* (literally, "woods runners"), living among the Indians in the American Bottom.

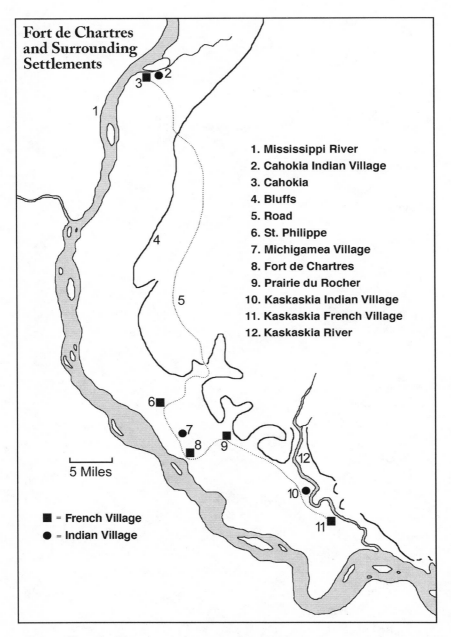

Fort de Chartres and Surrounding Settlements

1. Mississippi River
2. Cahokia Indian Village
3. Cahokia
4. Bluffs
5. Road
6. St. Philippe
7. Michigamea Village
8. Fort de Chartres
9. Prairie du Rocher
10. Kaskaskia Indian Village
11. Kaskaskia French Village
12. Kaskaskia River

5 Miles

■ = French Village
● = Indian Village

Fig.1.1. Fort de Chartres and surrounding settlements. Map derived from Thomas Hutchins, "A Plan of the Several Villages in the Illinois Country with Part of the River Mississippi &c.," in Thomas Hutchins, *A Topographical Description of Virginia, Pennsylvania, Maryland, and North Carolina* (London: Printed for the author and sold by J. Almon, 1778). Hutchins's map is a copy of an anonymous French manuscript map of the 1760s now in the Archives de la Marine at the Château de Vincennes in Paris.

THE LAND

THE FRENCH ILLINOIS Country, le Pays des Illinois, was an imprecisely defined area centered on the American Bottom in the middle Mississippi valley (fig. 1.1), a floodplain bordering the eastern side of the Mississippi River from Alton, Illinois, in the north to the Kaskaskia River in the south.[1] The northern portion from Alton to Cahokia is less fertile and in places narrowly confined by limestone bluffs. The French did not settle there during the colonial period. The southern section, from Cahokia to Kaskaskia, was the heartland of French settlement in the Illinois Country. Bluffs border the American Bottom, with steep vegetation-clad hills in the vicinity of Cahokia, sheer cliffs well over a hundred feet in height near Fort de Chartres, and low hills near the Kaskaskia River (figs. 1.2 and 1.3). A few streams have carved steep ravines that give access to and from the plain beyond the bluffs. The width of the bottomland between river and bluffs varies, being greatest near Cahokia and decreasing as one moves south. In the area of Fort de Chartres, the bottomland is about three miles wide.

The soil of the American Bottom consists of river deposits, often containing a significant amount of clay, but generally fertile and moist. Unless drained, the bottom has swamps, and periodic shallow lakes appear in wet years. The bottom is hot and humid during the summer and

Fig. 1.2. Bluffs near Fort de Chartres. Photo David MacDonald.

Fig. 1.3. Bluffs from the vicinity of Fort de Chartres.
Photo David MacDonald.

often flooded when the Mississippi rises, even today despite large levees near the river. Wood decays quickly in this environment.

The Illinois Country in its broadest definition also included the lower valleys of the Missouri, Illinois, Ohio, and Wabash Rivers and extended on the Missouri side of the Mississippi some distance inland to the lead-mining district around the modern towns of Old Mines and Potosi. These areas were less fertile and less densely settled by the French.

NATIVE PEOPLES

WHEN THE FRENCH arrived late in the seventeenth century, the native people of the American Bottom were the Illinois, whose name also appears in a number of other forms, such as *Illiniwek, Liniouek, Aliniouek, Alimiwec, Ilinioüek,* and *Irini8ak,* the symbol *8* indicating a sound similar to "ou" or "w." *Illinois* was the collective term for an alliance of four populous tribes—the Cahokia (consolidated with the Tamaroa), Michigamea, Kaskaskia, and Peoria—and a number of smaller tribes that over the course of the eighteenth century largely disappeared, merging into the larger tribes (fig. 1.4). The Illinois tribes shared an identical culture and a common language of the Algonquian group, and their members often intermarried. The name *Illinois* seems to be derived from the Algonquian, meaning approximately "he or she speaks correctly."[2]

Fig. 1.4. Member of the Kaskaskia tribe. Vignette from map.
G. Bois St Lys and J. J. Boudier, "Carte générale du cours de la
rivière de l'Ohio . . . le tout dessiné sur les lieux par Joseph Warrin
. . . pour servir à l'intelligence des voyages du général Collot dans
l'année 1796." Bibliothèque nationale de France, département
Cartes et plans, CPL GE A 664.

During the first half of the seventeenth century, the Illinois were
dominant in a broad area stretching approximately from southern Wisconsin in the north to the Ohio River and down the western side of the
Mississippi into Arkansas in the south, and from the Wabash River
basin in the east into eastern Iowa across the Mississippi in the west.

Hunting parties sometimes roamed even beyond these limits in Kentucky, Missouri, and Iowa. Early European population estimates vary greatly, but the most reliable estimate is that there were once about 10,500 Illinois.[3]

The Illinois Country was rich and other tribes coveted it, but the Illinois seem to have been able to hold their territory until the arrival of Europeans. Then, far to the east of Illinois, European enthusiasm for beaver skins led in the seventeenth century to the Beaver Wars and their wide-ranging effects. European traders profited greatly from exchanging European goods for beaver skins, and tribal peoples quickly became dependent on European manufactures, such as cloth and guns. The eastern tribes soon exhausted the beavers in their own territory and pushed into the lands of other tribes, forcing them into still more conflict with tribes farther to the west. Tribes also attempted to control the flow of European trade to other tribes, both to profit from that trade and to deny European guns to enemies. Tribal conflicts increased in frequency and ferocity. The Illinois suffered disproportionately. In the second half of the seventeenth century, the Iroquois made bloody attacks on Illinois villages. The Fox, Sauk, Kickapoo, Miami, and Mascouten encroached on the Illinois from the north; the Shawnee moved into east-central Illinois; the Osage and Missouri pushed the Illinois out of northern Missouri and southeastern Iowa; and the Quapaw seized their territory in Arkansas.[4]

During the eighteenth century, until the end of the French regime, the Illinois were generally able to prevent further encroachment on their territory, undoubtedly aided by their alliance with the French and ready access to French guns and munitions. To the north, hostilities continued with the Fox (*Mesquakie* or *Meskwaki* in their own language, *Renards* to the French, Fox to the English) and their usual allies, the Mascouten, Sauk, and Kickapoo, but these typically took the form of endemic Indian warfare, being homicidal raids rather than attempts to acquire territory. In 1730, however, the Fox were crushed by the French and a broad alliance of tribes, but even that failed to do more than diminish violence between the Illinois and Fox. Relations with still other northern and northeastern tribes, such as the Wea and Piankashaw, varied with time and circumstances. Eastern tribes such as the Huron, Delaware, and Iroquois also ventured into the area occasionally, swept up in the continual antagonism between the English and French, and came into contact with the Illinois and Illinois French, with whom their relationships also fluctuated.

To the south, from the 1730s until the virtual dissolution of the Illinois late in the eighteenth century, the English-allied Chickasaw, often along with the Cherokee, bedeviled the Illinois, who only occasionally were able to mount effective retaliation. The Shawnee were sometimes allies, other times enemies of the Illinois. Along the Mississippi, the Quapaw of Arkansas became friendly trading partners with the Illinois, and trade goods from tribes even farther south, such as the beautiful pottery of the Caddo and Tunica, were prized by both Illinois and French alike.

To the west, other tribes, such as the Missouri and Oto, generally enjoyed friendly relations with the Illinois and frequently traded with them and at Fort de Chartres. The Osage and Sioux occasionally visited Fort de Chartres, but in general they were too far to the west to be constant callers. The Sioux occasionally allied with the Fox, and by the end of the French regime, the Osage became more troublesome and grew increasingly so in the last decades of the eighteenth century.

The French praised the Illinois above neighboring tribes. In 1674, the Jesuit Father Marquette proclaimed that the Illinois had "an air of humanity that we have not observed in the other nations that we have seen upon our route."[5] André-Joseph Pénicaut, a carpenter and chronicler of early eighteenth-century Louisiana, wrote with some considerable exaggeration that "the Kaskaskia Illinois nation is Catholic" and that "this nation is highly civilized."[6] In 1720, the year Fort de Chartres was built, the Jesuit Father Marest, missionary to the Kaskaskia, wrote:

> Our Illinois are very different from these [pagan] Savages, and from what they themselves were formerly. Christianity, as I have already said, has softened their fierce habits, and they are now distinguished for certain gentle and polite manners that have led the Frenchmen to take their daughters in marriage. Moreover, we find in them docility and ardor in the practice of Christian virtues.[7]

Such comments are not entirely candid. The Jesuits were eager to depict their missionary activities as successful, and they were at pains to justify marriages between Indians and Frenchmen, which were under attack by the authorities in New Orleans and France.[8] In contrast, the French officer Bernard Diron d'Artaguiette in 1723 wrote, "The Jesuit fathers who have for more than thirty years been among them, have up to the present failed in their attempts to make them understand that God had made himself man and died for us." He further observed that the Indians' native beliefs seemed unchanged.[9] At the end of the French colonial period, there were still many who had not been baptized among the Kaskaskia, and the rate of conversion was even less among other Illinois tribes, particularly the Peoria, who remained the least assimilated. One may also question the degree to which even the baptized Illinois actually abandoned or even significantly modified their indigenous attitudes and cultural norms, but evidence bearing on such questions is largely inadequate.

Despite generally cooperative relations between the French and the Illinois, tensions and suspicions existed, as one would expect between any two different cultures. Early in the eighteenth century, the Illinois sometimes hunted free-ranging French livestock as if they were wild animals, and the French were always fearful the Illinois would submit to English blandishments or the appeals of other tribes hostile to the French.

There were also tensions among different groups of the French in regard to the Indians. Missionaries frequently denounced the traders and voyageurs as immoral and dissolute, responsible for debauching the Indians and leading them in wicked ways. The missionaries were particularly appalled by what they saw as sexual immorality, but their condemnations are often vague and seem exaggerated and rhetorical. Traders and voyageurs were usually indifferent to missionary activity and enjoyed freedom from traditional European manners and morals among the tribes, often contracting marriages with Indian women according to native customs rather than the rites of the church. The clergy members seem to have been equally infuriated by the traders' failure to grant them the deference and obedience traditional in Europe. It can hardly be doubted that the traders were often coarse, heavy drinkers and sometimes violent, but it can be debated whether it was missionaries or traders and voyageurs who disrupted Indian societies more.

Prior to 1719, French traders, missionaries, and increasingly farmers lived in the same villages with the Illinois at Cahokia and Kaskaskia, but in that year the French and Indian communities separated, although the French settlements and the Indian villages were only a few miles apart. The missionaries urged this separation to isolate the Indians from the corrupting influences of voyageurs, and Pierre-Sidrac Dugué de Boisbriand, recently arrived to build Fort de Chartres, may have also felt that the separation would minimize conflicts between the French settlers and the Illinois.

Despite the establishment of separate communities, interactions between the two groups continued to be frequent, and the Illinois adopted many aspects of French culture. Even before the arrival of the first French in the Illinois Country, the tribe had already begun to use European cloth, obtained by trade from other tribes. After the establishment of the French, the Illinois became increasingly dependent on farming by the French model, cultivating their fields with French plows and raising cattle, pigs, and chickens. Excavations of Illinois sites from the eighteenth century have revealed a wide variety of French goods.[10]

SETTLERS

IT IS TOO simple to designate the people who came to Illinois simply as French. The French who settled in Illinois were, for the most part, different from the French of France. Most came from Canada, not directly from the settled, stable area in the St. Lawrence River valley, but rather after having lived for some time in the western regions of Canada, le Pays d'en Haut ("Upper Country," referring to the Great Lakes region). There they made their way as traders and voyageurs in a rugged and often dangerous land. Free in large part from the conventional restraints of hierarchical French society, government, and church, these men and women became more self-reliant, resolute, and individualistic, and at the same time, their respect for authority diminished. The French coming from France and Louisiana saw these "Canadian" traits as typical and enduring characteristics of the inhabitants of Illinois. For example, in 1752, Pierre-François de Rigaud de Vaudreuil de Cavagnial, marquis de Vaudreuil, the governor of Louisiana and later governor of Canada, wrote to the new commandant of Fort de Chartres, Jean-Jacques de Macarty Mactique, in Illinois:

> I am very glad to observe to you also avoid all insub-
> ordination on the part of the [French] inhabitants and
> never find yourself in such a situation with respect to
> them, that you should exact nothing of them save after

much thought, approaching them with gentleness,
though always with firmness. You will do better so than
by harshness. The Canadian is high-spirited, as you
know; but he is brave and enterprising. All that is necessary is to take them on the side of honor and reason to
bring easily to your wishes.[11]

In addition to the Canadian majority in Illinois, others came to Illinois
from Louisiana in the south. Some were Creoles, born and raised in
Louisiana, while others were natives of France who came to Illinois as indentured servants, soldiers, officers, administrators, and missionaries. Both
those from France and the Louisiana Creoles may have initially felt themselves more sophisticated and more truly French than the Illinois Canadians,
but they all blended into the society of Illinois without substantially diluting
what others saw as the essential character of the Illinois French.

SLAVERY

INDIAN SLAVERY EXISTED in Illinois before the arrival of Europeans. Intertribal warfare produced captives. Captive men unlikely to submit easily
to slavery were often killed, but if they proved tractable, they might be
adopted into the captors' tribe or kept as slaves. Male Indian slaves could
be useful to the French for heavy farm work or lead mining, but they could
prove difficult to control and found it easy to escape. Women and children
were more likely than men to be adopted into the tribe or kept as slaves.
Initially, Indians presented Indian slaves, most often women or children, to
the French as part of reciprocal gift and favor exchanges. The French found
Indian women useful as domestic servants and desirable as concubines and
sometimes marriage partners. Indian slaves, particularly women, quickly
became objects of commerce. Indian slavery continued throughout the
French colonial period and even afterward, but African and African Creole slaves, simply called *blacks* by the French, outnumbered Indian slaves.

A few black slaves were brought to Louisiana in the earliest years of
the colony, generally from the French colonies in the Caribbean, but it
was only in 1719 that slaves were first imported in significant numbers,
directly from Africa to southern Louisiana. From there, the black slaves
were brought to Illinois, probably by the Jesuits, in the early 1720s. In

contrast to the Indian slaves, more black slaves were male and, far from their homeland, they found it harder to escape. They were much in demand as laborers and soon came to constitute a significant portion of the population in Illinois, although the supply of African slaves was never as great as the demand.

Few censuses of French Illinois exist, and none of those that do is fully comprehensive and accurate, but two, for the years 1732 and 1752, suffice to indicate the approximate proportion of slaves to the free population. According to the 1732 census, of 284 adult males, 56 percent were French, 24 percent were black slaves, and 20 percent were Indian slaves. The percentages are almost identical when the total population is considered: 56 percent French, 25 percent black slaves, and 19 percent Indian slaves.[12] The census officially did not include the garrison of Fort de Chartres, with about 100 men, although some individual officers and troops who were married and lived in the village of Chartres were counted. The 1752 census lists 578 adult males (including the youths capable of bearing arms), of whom 57 percent were French, 33 percent black slaves, and 10 percent Indian slaves. When the total population is included, the results are scarcely different: 58 percent French, 32 percent black slaves, and 10 percent Indian slaves.[13] Again, the census did not include the garrison of Fort de Chartres, which numbered about 300 in 1752, although a few officers and men who lived in the village were counted. This was probably a much smaller percentage of the garrison than in the 1732 census, since about 200 of the troops had arrived very recently. The degree of continuity between the two censuses is remarkable, the one significant change being the relative decline in Indian slavery and proportionate increase in black slavery.

Black slavery in Louisiana and Illinois was officially regulated by the Code Noir, promulgated in 1724.[14] Slavery as envisioned in the Code Noir was less inhumane in a number of aspects than that generally practiced in the British colonies, although the authorities often found it inconvenient, impractical, or impossible to ensure adherence to the code. Nevertheless, the reality of slavery in Illinois was somewhat less onerous than English slavery, and strangers coming to the Illinois Country in the eighteenth and early nineteenth centuries expressed surprise at the relatively mild situation of the slaves there. Despite that, Illinois French slavery was still slavery, with all slavery's inherent ills and inhumanity.

Male black slaves sometimes established personal relations with Indian women slaves. Rarely, however, did black and Indian slaves form common cause in larger numbers. In a few instances in southern Louisiana, escaped black slaves formed communities that included fugitive Indian slaves. Such groups were mainly small refugee camps of little threat to the French, but the French viewed all such alliances with horror and trepidation that far outweighed their real significance. Such "maroon" communities seem absent in the Illinois Country.[15] A few fugitive black slaves found asylum with Indians, and in Missouri during the early 1750s, an escaped black slave briefly led a group of Indians that raided lead miners,[16] but even this was exceptional.

Slaves, both Indian and black, were occasionally emancipated. Most often an elderly slave owner would make provisions that upon his or her death, one or more slaves would be freed. These were usually slaves with whom the owner had particularly close relations, such as trusted household servants, concubines, or illegitimate children. A few black and Indian freedmen were found in Illinois, the earliest already in the 1720s.

THE FRENCH SETTLEMENTS

THE LARGEST SETTLEMENT in the American Bottom was Kaskaskia, officially Notre Dame de Cascasquias. There the Kaskaskia tribe settled in 1703 along the river that also received their name. Indians had inhabited the site, near the juncture of the Kaskaskia River with the Mississippi, at least intermittently for centuries. Settled along with the Kaskaskia initially were Jesuit missionaries and a few French traders who had married into the tribe. In 1719, the French separated from the Kaskaskia Indians, who established their own village a few miles north. French Kaskaskia grew to become a predominantly agricultural settlement, the largest town in the Illinois Country, and eventually the first capital of the state of Illinois. In the nineteenth century, the Mississippi changed course, took over about ten miles of the lower course of the Kaskaskia River, and washed away the town. Now the land around Kaskaskia is a bit of the state of Illinois isolated on the west side of the Mississippi, reachable only through Missouri.

In 1719–20, the French established Fort de Chartres about sixteen miles north of Kaskaskia, and around the fort a village grew up, known simply as Chartres or Nouvelle Chartres. To the north about three miles was a village of Michigamea Indians, one of the Illinois tribes, and a few miles beyond that was the small French village of St. Philippe, more formally St. Philippe du Grand Marais (St. Philip of the Great Marsh). Two miles south of the fort and near the sheer rock bluffs lay the village of Prairie du Rocher. The French villages were predominantly agricultural, but they were also homes to craftsmen, traders, and retired soldiers. Today only the village of Prairie du Rocher remains.

About 1750, the Illinois French settled a new village on the west side of the Mississippi, north of Kaskaskia and south of Fort de Chartres. At first it was nicknamed Misère (misery), presumably because of the initial poverty of the site, but soon the village, under its proper name Ste. Geneviève, prospered agriculturally. The villagers first built along the bank of the Mississippi, but then late in the eighteenth century, they gradually shifted the settlement several miles inland to higher ground to escape the periodic Mississippi floods. Today Ste. Genevieve contains the largest group of French domestic structures in the United States.

Cahokia, officially Sainte Famille de Kaoquias, is at the northern limit of the area of the American Bottom inhabited by the French, slightly south of modern St. Louis but on the eastern, Illinois, side of the river. During the French regime, settlers built a prosperous French village there, home to both farmers and merchants, who supplied traders who went up the Mississippi, Missouri, and Illinois Rivers to trade with Indians for furs and hides. The Seminary of Foreign Missions (Séminaire des Missions Étrangères) developed a substantial estate at Cahokia, its slaves tending the fields and herds. The Cahokia Courthouse and the nearby Church of the Holy Family are fine examples of the traditional French *poteaux sur sole* vertical-log construction.

Just as the French Kaskaskia separated from the Kaskaskia Indian village, so at the same time did the French Cahokia separate from the Indian Cahokia, who built a new village a few miles to the west along the small Cahokia River, on the site of the long-abandoned great Mississippian center. Seminary missionaries established a church on the principal mound of the abandoned village, known today as Monks Mound.

Just at the end of the French colonial era, a new settlement, at first nicknamed Pain Court, literally, "Short of Bread," grew up on the western

side of the Mississippi just north of Cahokia. Its formal name has prevailed: St. Louis.

The core area of the American Bottom is connected to the outlying
areas by the rivers that formed the communication network for French
Illinois. To the northeast is the Illinois River, on which was Pimetoui
(today Peoria) at the southern end of "Lake Peoria," a wide pool of the
river. Pimetoui was the home of the Peoria, the most independent and
fiercest of the Illinois tribes, and there the French founded the small Fort
St. Louis and a trading post. Pimetoui eventually developed into a small
but prosperous French village. Suspicious English-speaking Americans
burned down the village and drove out the inhabitants during the War
of 1812. The Americans took the land and rebuilt the village, no longer
French in language or culture. Still farther to the north on the Illinois
River lay Fort St. Louis, also known to the French as Le Rocher (now
Starved Rock). There La Salle and Henri de Tonty first established a small
fort in 1682–83. The fort did not last long, but the French reoccupied the
site briefly on several occasions.

To the northwest of the American Bottom lies the Missouri River,
allowing penetration deep into the West. For many years, traders traveled
up the Missouri to barter for furs and hides with the western tribes, and
on this river the French founded Fort d'Orléans in 1723. It survived for
some years. Then in 1744, they built a new trading post farther up the
Missouri, near what is now Fort Leavenworth. This post was initially
called Fort de La Trinité and then renamed Fort Cavagnial. Both names
continued in use. The appellation of Missouri applied to the river only,
for the territory west of the Mississippi River and north of the Arkansas
was always deemed to be a part of Illinois during the colonial era.

To the west on the Ouabache (Wabash) River, the French established
a small fort and trading post in 1732, and a modest French village grew
up around the fort. It was called by several names, including the Wabash
Post and St. Ange (after a commandant who served there for many years),
but finally the name Vincennes prevailed, after a commandant killed in
the Chickasaw Wars soon after the village's foundation.

The Wabash River flows more or less from north to south, joining the
Ohio, which flows into the Mississippi south of the American Bottom.
For the French, the Wabash seemed the main stream, so the lower Ohio
was also called the Wabash or simply La Belle Riviére (the Beautiful

River). Late in the French colonial period, the French established Fort Massiac on the lower Ohio at the site of modern Metropolis, Illinois, almost across the river from where Paducah, Kentucky, later developed.

MILITARY AND CIVILIAN ADMINISTRATION

IN THEORY, THE king of France was an absolute monarch, the ultimate authority whose will stretched down to the humblest fusilier (infantryman) and colonial clerk. Reality was far different. The king stood rather at the head of a vast inefficient bureaucracy, the parts of which were headed by ministers. Louis XV met with each of his chief ministers once a week, but the king was never noted for assiduous attention to government or original thought. He officially made all policy decisions and appointments, but in practice he generally followed the guidance of the individual ministers. There was little coordination in planning or action among the separate ministries, and in matters of promotion, the influence of courtiers and high-ranking aristocrats could override even ministerial decisions.

From the first French settlement in Louisiana in 1699 until 1714, Louisiana was a royal colony. It then became a proprietary colony from 1714 to 1731, administered by the French merchant Antoine Crozat from 1714 until 1717, and then by the Compagnie d'Occident from 1717 to 1719. Scottish businessman John Law reorganized the Compagnie d'Occident into the Compagnie des Indes, which ran the colony from 1719 to 1731. Louis XV's royal government then reassumed direct control of the colony. While Louisiana was a proprietary colony, it found itself with two masters: king and proprietor. Even under proprietary rule, the king had a representative in the colony, and the royal government received constant reports. In a sense, the proprietor was free to do as it wished, provided its wishes conformed to royal policy. Soldiers and civilian officials in this period were in a very real sense employees of the proprietor, who assigned them duties and paid them, but at the same time they were in the service of the king, who granted promotions and ultimately controlled the course of their careers. Symbolic of this dual relationship, troops in this period continued to wear royal uniforms, but they were bought and issued by the proprietary government.

The troops who served at Fort de Chartres and elsewhere in Louisiana were members of the Compagnies Franches de la Marine, the *marine* in this sense referring to the Ministry of the Marine. The minister of the marine was directly responsible for the administration of the French Navy, merchant marine, overseas colonies, and colonial troops. He and his staff of clerks supervised the expenditure of funds, recruitment of personnel, and supply of materials sent to the colonies. Provincial officials sent a steady stream of communications to the minister, and the minister generated a similar stream of orders flowing back to the colonies, but transit took months in times of peace and sometimes much longer in times of war. Loss or interception of communications was always a possibility. Moreover, there was no adequate means to check that the provincial officials were reporting fully and truthfully. Indeed, chronic feuding within the ranks of provincial officials virtually guaranteed that the minister commonly received contradictory, immoderate, and even libelous accounts of events.

Next in the command chain was the governor of Louisiana. Officially, the governor of Louisiana was subordinate to the governor of Nouvelle-France (Canada), but each governor communicated independently with the minister of the marine, and the governor of Louisiana was de facto almost entirely independent of Canada, much to the Canadian governor's disgust. The official title of the governor of Louisiana varied over time, but role of the office remained much the same. The governor had a wide variety of ill-defined administrative, judicial, legislative, and military responsibilities and usually held the rank of lieutenant general, although he seldom exercised direct military command except in rare major campaigns. Louisiana governor Jean-Baptiste Le Moyne de Bienville's famous expeditions against the Chickasaw were exceptions, not the rule.

A member of the governor's staff with the title of lieutenant of the king, also called the royal lieutenant, commonly oversaw military affairs in the province. Early in the eighteenth century, the governor of Louisiana relied on a single royal lieutenant, but by the end of the French regime, there were three: one each for New Orleans, Mobile, and Illinois. The lieutenant of the king for the Illinois Country was also the commandant of Fort de Chartres. Three city majors, again one each for New Orleans, Mobile, and Fort de Chartres, were adjutants of the king's lieutenants. Their duties originally consisted of disciplining troops and overseeing the local militia. The use of the military terms *lieutenant* and *major* for these administrative posts leads to easy confusion with actual military ranks. Thus a captain may at the same time have been a royal lieutenant or even the major of New Orleans.[17]

In the latter half of the French colonial period, the commandant of Fort de Chartres was often also the major of New Orleans, and along with the title, he received a substantial and deserved supplement to his salary. Distance prevented the Illinois commandant from taking an active role there, but he commanded a military contingent distant from New Orleans and sometimes second in size only to that of the city. The commandant also had many demands on his pocket, such as hospitality to visiting officers and prominent Indians.

An independent counterpart of the governor was the *commissaire-ordonnateur*. Like the governor, the *ordonnateur* had a variety of loosely defined responsibilities, in his case mainly financial and judicial, and his official title differed somewhat over time. The *ordonnateur* represented royal financial interests in the colony. He supervised royal properties, dispersed royal funds, issued royal supplies, and collected taxes and tariffs. The *ordonnateur* was also the colony's chief judicial officer, the first judge of the Superior Council of Louisiana, and members of his staff filled lesser judicial roles throughout the colony. In essence, the *ordonnateur*'s role emulated the office of *intendant* in Canada and the provinces of France.

In France, the bipolar bureaucracy of governor and *intendant* worked well enough. There the social status of governors was usually high enough to overawe *intendants*, and the royal government was present to control conflicts that did arise. In distant colonies, however, the social statuses of governor and *ordonnateur* were usually similar, and the absence of close supervision by the central government allowed conflicts to flourish. For example, the governor was the head of the military, but all expenditures of funds and issues of supplies for the military had to be approved by the *commissaire-ordonnateur*. There was no way to resolve disagreements other than slow appeals to distant France, and disagreements often flared into extraordinarily bitter feuds.[18]

By 1717, the Compagnie d'Occident felt it advisable to establish a military post in Illinois to regulate, exploit, and protect the growing French settlement there. Fort de Chartres, first built in 1719–20, served, in four successive versions, as the military and administrative center of Illinois for the next half century. In Illinois, the commandant of Fort de Chartres was both the commander of the marine troops stationed there and the head of the region's government. A successful commandant had to be a resilient officer who could be relied on to follow the orders and conform to the policies set forth by the governor of Louisiana and yet function independently when local circumstances and crises required it. In theory, he wielded great powers, but in reality, he had to earn respect and learn to exercise his authority with tact and sensibility. He had to be able to deal simultaneously with troops, civilians, and Indians, each of whom presented particular challenges. It is not surprising that the commandants of Fort de Chartres had strong, even colorful personalities. It is surprising that they succeeded as well as they did.

The administration of Illinois consisted of both military officers and civil judicial and financial officials, some appointed by the *ordonnateur* in New Orleans. Military officers, too, particularly the commandant, exercised a variety of judicial and regulatory roles. Some officials had no military role, but even those functioned regularly in concert with military officers. There was no separation of powers in this eighteenth-century colonial world. Military, civilian, church, royal, provincial, and local all blended together in a seamless if sometimes conflicted and inefficient whole.

In lower Louisiana, the chief judicial authority was the Superior Council, but distance made it impractical as a court of first resort for the inhabitants of Illinois. So in 1718, the Compagnie, with the king's approval, established the Provincial Council as the judicial authority for Illinois. The membership and function of the Provincial Council changed somewhat through time, though it generally included the commandant of Fort de Chartres and several other high-ranking officers, a judge, a chief clerk, and the *garde-magasin*. Civil litigation was handled by a committee composed of a judge (who sometimes was also the chief clerk) and two other suitable citizens, regularly members of the Provincial Council. For criminal cases, the judicial committee consisted of five, the additional two generally military officers, one of whom was usually the commandant of Fort de Chartres if the case was at all significant. No lawyers were permitted in Louisiana. The clerk recorded all cases, and appeals could be made to the Superior Council, which customarily reviewed all important decisions.

Other important officials included the *garde-magasin* (storehouse keeper) and the notary. The *garde-magasin* received and dispersed goods sent upriver from New Orleans for the troops, Indians, and settlers. He also received and forwarded products, such as flour and lead, to be sent to New Orleans. A considerable portion, although not all, of the imports and exports of the Illinois Country passed through his hands. The notary drew up all legal papers, such as bills of sale, leases, marriage contacts, partnerships, employment contracts, and wills, for small fees. He signed all legal documents and kept detailed registers of such documents. The *huissier* was an assistant to the notary, serving subpoenas and aiding with estate and other sales.

Illinois was frequently short of ideal candidates for these posts. The *garde-magasin* was regularly a civilian, but on occasion, a military officer filled the post. When a qualified notary was not available, anyone with basic literacy, such as a clerk, *habitant* (resident landowning farmer), militia officer, or priest, might serve. There were also a number of minor officials. The commandant hired the *interprète*, interpreter or translator of Indian languages, almost always a civilian. A good *interprète* not only translated words but also served as an intercultural ambassador and mediator. The royal *armurier* (gunsmith) repaired guns for the troops, militia, and friendly Indians for a salary and might take on private work as well.

On the local level, each village elected a syndic annually, with the approval of the commandant. The syndic presided over village meetings about matters of common local interest, such as maintenance of roads and the fences to exclude animals from the common fields. The syndic might also serve to enforce the decisions of the village assembly. Other local officials were the *marguilliers*, or church wardens, chosen locally to administer the material aspects of the parish, which was identical to the village. The *marguilliers* were concerned with matters such as building maintenance and management of the graveyard. They functioned usually in cooperation with, but occasionally in opposition to, the local priest. Militias were also raised locally, although the commandant of Fort de Chartres appointed the local militia captain, customarily from an important local family, whose status was further enhanced by the appointment. Social prestige and group dynamics shaped local governance more than formal offices and bureaucratic rules.

In France, commissioned military officers were regularly recruited from the younger sons of the gentry or occasionally from bourgeoisie with important family or social connections among the nobility or government bureaucrats. Officers in Louisiana generally came from the same sorts

of families, although often of somewhat lower aristocratic status or less
wealth than those who secured posts in France. Some *roturiers* (common-
ers) did become marine officers in Louisiana, and they attempted to do
whatever possible to elevate their status, such as seeking marriages that
brought with them seigniorial titles from Canada or France or simply
adding pseudoaristocratic elements to their names. Such claims were
rarely challenged. It would have been difficult to check the legitimacy,
and any implication to the contrary would be likely to provoke a duel.
Within the officer corps, promotion in rank was slow, uncertain, and often
possible only if a vacancy was created by death, resignation, or transfer
out of Louisiana. Louisiana was for many an undesirable post. Many
newly appointed officers simply refused to go, and officers who did come
from France to lower Louisiana frequently sought transfers elsewhere,
anywhere, but seldom obtained them.[19]

In some instances, officers were placed on half pay. Originally, marines
received full pay when at sea and half pay when on land. Marines in
Louisiana, however, were permanently stationed ashore, and new con-
ventions applied. Half-pay status implied the officer was in some manner
underemployed, between assignments, assigned to a post with a garrison
much smaller than usually appropriate for his rank, or retired. A deserving
officer might receive promotion in rank with half-pay status as a reward
if his assignment would not otherwise qualify him for promotion.

The basic military unit in Louisiana and Illinois was the company,
theoretically of fifty men. In the early eighteenth century, a lieutenant
commanded a company; later in the century, a captain held that post.
A captain had subordinate officers: one lieutenant (first or second), one
enseigne en pied (full ensign), and two second ensigns. The garrisons of
large forts consisted of many companies. Fort de Chartres at its largest
had six. Small posts were manned by a single company or a detachment
as small as half a dozen men commanded by a sergeant. A surgeon was
frequently stationed at large posts, but the medical knowledge of a provincial military surgeon was usually rudimentary, generally restricted to
providing obvious first aid, dispensing nostrums of dubious value, and
barbering. In the eighteenth century, a surgeon was a simple artisan who
had learned his trade by apprenticing with another surgeon, much inferior
in status to a doctor, who had formal academic training. Doctors generally
could be found only in New Orleans. Occasionally, the governor might

send an engineer-surveyor from New Orleans to a post when a special need arose. For lesser occasions, an officer who had some knowledge of *génie*, the term generally used for military engineering, might suffice.

Virtually every company also contained one or more cadets, who were young men in training to become officers. Cadets served in the ranks with common soldiers, though they were marked out from the first for eventual promotion. Bright, ambitious cadets might be assigned to study engineering. The higher the status of a cadet's family or the greater the influence of an official willing to intervene on his behalf, the shorter the time the cadet was likely to spend before commissioning, provided there was a vacancy to fill. A cadet might serve only a few months before promotion or more than a decade. The usual term was about three to six years. There were two types of cadets. The *cadet de l'aiguillette* was so called because he wore an *aiguillette*, a shoulder cord. *Cadets de l'aiguillette*, also referred to as "gentlemen cadets," were of higher social status and usually receive earlier promotion than the cadets of lesser status, who were designated simply as *cadet soldats*. Cadets were frequently sons of officers.

In addition to the commissioned officers and cadets, each company theoretically consisted of two sergeants, three corporals, two drummers, and forty-one fusiliers (infantrymen). The common soldiers most often came from France, particularly early in the eighteenth century. As the century wore on, more of the soldiers were Creoles, born and raised in the colony, often sons of former soldiers, but majority of common soldiers were always French-born. The life of a common soldier in the eighteenth century was uninviting, and the majority of men who entered into service did so out of desperation born of the lack of other opportunities. Desertion was frequent, and deserters were often punished harshly if captured. If a common soldier was able, diligent, and lucky, he might become a noncommissioned officer, but he had almost no chance of rising to become a commissioned officer.

Militias were organized in each of Louisiana's administrative districts. In Illinois, all able-bodied men between the ages of twelve and fifty, with the exception of officials, were obligated to serve, but these rules seem to have been interpreted pragmatically rather than literally. Militia officers were appointed by the commandant of Fort de Chartres and were subordinate to him. The Illinois militia mustered for local Indian troubles; occasionally served during distant campaigns against Indians, notably

during the Fox and Chickasaw Wars; and played a significant role in
the French and Indian War, both convoying supplies and occasionally
participating in campaigns against the English. The royal government,
however, was generally reluctant to employ the Illinois militia. Most
Illinois militia members were *habitants*, and their agricultural production
was generally more important than militia service.

Of some military significance were the Illinois Indians. Already in
the early eighteenth century, they were reputedly less warlike than the
Northern Woodland tribes, and this tendency seems to have increased
over time as the Illinois came more and more under French cultural and
religious influences. Alcohol and European diseases certainly weakened
their military effectiveness and diminished their numbers. Yet there were
always some who were willing to join French military expeditions. They
were valued for their abilities to track and to move quickly and quietly,
as well as their endurance.

Other Indian tribes sometimes fought alongside the marines of Fort
de Chartres. For example, in the attack and slaughter of the Fox in
1730, a great array of tribes supported the French: Illinois, Miami, Wea,
Piankashaw, Huron, Potawatomi, Sac, Kickapoo, and Mascouten. The
last four tribes had previously been allied with the Fox, and the Kickapoo
and Mascouten had in the past raided into Illinois along with the Fox. In
1756, when François Coulon de Villiers attacked Fort Granville, he and
his French troops from Fort de Chartres were accompanied by Illinois,
Delaware, and Shawnee tribesmen. At various times, the marines at Fort
de Chartres found themselves allied with or opposed to Indians from virtually every tribe residing between the Alleghenies and the Great Plaines.

THE FOUR FORTS DE CHARTRES

IN 1717, KING Louis XV's government transferred control of the Illinois
Country from Canada to Louisiana, administered from 1719 to 1731 by
the proprietary Compagnie des Indes. The Compagnie sent Pierre de
Boisbriand to Illinois to establish and protect its economic interests.
Boisbriand constructed the first Fort de Chartres there and became the
first commandant of the Illinois Country.[20]

Boisbriand named the fort after Louis, duc de Chartres, son of the
regent of France. The site chosen was roughly sixteen miles north of

Kaskaskia, the largest French settlement, and a little over forty miles south of Cahokia. The commandant of Fort de Chartres administered a number of smaller posts at various times: Fort Cahokia on the Mississippi, Fort St. Louis at Pimetoui (Peoria) on the Illinois River, Forts d'Orléans and Cavagnial on the Missouri River, Fort Vincennes on the Wabash River, and Fort Massiac on the Ohio River. Generally, an officer commanded each of these posts with a small detachment of soldiers.

The commandants of Fort de Chartres ranged from a lieutenant in its early days, to a captain later on, to a major in the last years of the French regime, when the commandant was assisted by an adjutant. The size of the garrison at Fort de Chartres differed at various times, depending on the circumstances. When first established in 1719–20, there were less than a hundred soldiers. The normal strength until shortly before the French and Indian War was two companies, which then increased to six companies. The actual number of soldiers in service was usually well below the theoretical level, not only at Fort de Chartres but throughout French Louisiana. In 1754, for example, Louisiana units were fully a third understrength. In that year, Fort de Chartres mustered 285, probably the largest number in the history of the fort.[21]

The first Fort de Chartres, square with two bastions at opposite corners, was erected near the riverbank. The walls of the fort were constructed of wood posts set vertically in the ground. The fort enclosed several buildings, probably including a magazine containing the garrison's supplies and the trade goods of the Compagnie des Indes, a barracks for the small garrison, and perhaps separate buildings for cooking, a guardhouse, and quarters for the commandant and other officers.

In 1725, a second fort replaced the first, probably on the same location. The moist soil of the American Bottom rots wood quickly, but it is more likely that Indian threats led to the construction of the new, stronger fort. The administration of Canada bitterly resented the loss of the Illinois to Louisiana and did nothing to discourage the bloody raids of the Fox, Kickapoo, and Mascouten, which killed French and French-allied Illinois alike.[22]

Within the fort, one building served as a storehouse and residence for the commandant and the *garde-magasin*. Other buildings were a barracks, a house of unspecified use, a guardhouse, and a powder magazine. Just two years after construction, a flood badly damaged the second fort, so

much so that a letter written at the time characterizes it as destroyed.[23]
A few years later, another document describes it as "falling into ruins,
in one spot only held up by a prop."[24] It is likely that the Mississippi has
now washed away all traces of the first two forts.

In 1731, the Compagnie des Indes relinquished control of Louisiana to
direct Crown control, and although the documentary evidence is slight,
it now seems probable that the fort was reconstructed in 1732 at some
distance from the river. A document from 1734 mentions that the fort
had been "reestablished" two years earlier, but that the piles were already
partly decayed.[25] Margaret Kimball Brown and Robert Mazrim suggest
that this rapid deterioration may be due to the reuse of timbers from the
second fort. It is this third fort, square with bastions at each corner, that
Brown and Mazrim revealed in test excavations in 2012.[26]

The "reestablished" fort of 1732 continued in use until the early 1750s.
Every year, the inhabitants and voyageurs had to provide sufficient timbers
to replace one of the curtain walls. In 1747, the commandant moved most
of soldiers to Kaskaskia, primarily because of Indian problems. Only a
small detachment remained at the fort. Late in 1751, Macarty, the newly
appointed commandant, noted that while the frames of the buildings
within the fort were good, the buildings needed other significant repairs
and one was close to collapse.[27]

In 1752, after considerable debate and consideration of alternate locations, Macarty and the engineer François Saucier decided to rebuild Fort
de Chartres in stone only a few hundred yards from its original location
(fig. 1.5). It proved an expensive undertaking, and at one point the royal
government in France ordered the project terminated, but the governor
in New Orleans pointed out that a great portion of the cost had already
been expended, and construction went forward. The English officer Philip
Pittman, writing in about 1764, provides an excellent description of this
fourth Fort de Chartres:

> It is built of stone and plastered over, and it is only designed
> as a defense against the Indians, the walls being two feet two
> inches thick, and pierced with loop-holes at regular distances,
> and with two post-holes for cannon in the faces, and two in
> the flanks of each bastion; the ditch has never been finished;
> the entrance of the fort is through a very handsome rustic gate:

within the wall is a small banquette, raised three feet, for the men to stand on when they fire through the loop-holes. The buildings within the fort are, the commandant's and commissary's houses, the magazine of stores, corps de garde, and two barracks; these occupy the square. Within the gorges of the bastion are, a powder magazine, a bakehouse, a prison, in the lower floor of which are four dungeons, and in the upper rooms, and an out-house belonging to the commandant. The commandant's house is thirty-two yards long, and ten broad; it contains a kitchen, a dining-room, a bed-chamber, one small room, five closets for servants, and a cellar. The commissary's house (now occupied by officers) is built in the same line as this, its proportions and distribution of apartments are the same. Opposite these are the store-house and guard house, they are thirty yards long and eight broad; the former consists of two large store-rooms (under which is a large vaulted cellar) and a large room, a bed-chamber, and a closet for the store-keeper; the latter, of a soldier's and officer's guard-room, a chapel, a bed-chamber and closet for the chaplain, and artillery store-room. The lines of barracks have never been finished; they at present consist of two rooms each, for officers, and three rooms for soldiers; they are good spacious rooms of twenty-two feet square and have betwixt them a small passage. There are spacious lofts over each building which reach from end to end; these are made use of to lodge regimental stores, working and entrenching tools, &c. It is generally allowed that this is the most commodious and best built fort in North America.[28]

No battle was ever fought at the stone fort, but men stationed there went forth to play significant roles in the French and Indian War, took part in several significant victories, and suffered greatly in the Battle of La Belle Famille. At the end of the Seven Years' War, all French territory on the western side of the Mississippi was ceded to Britain. The British took possession of Fort de Chartres in 1765. They renamed it Fort Cavendish, although the name never gained general currency, even among the British.

Before the British arrived, the Mississippi was already cutting away the riverbank by the fort. Efforts to halt the erosion proved futile, and in

Fig. 1.5. Exterior of the reconstructed stone Fort de Chartres.
Photograph courtesy of Joseph Gagné.

1771 the English abandoned the fort, moving their troops to Kaskaskia. Shortly thereafter, in 1772, the wall of the fort facing the river collapsed into it. Having driven the British from the fort, the Mississippi altered course again, ceasing to threaten the rest of the fort.

The abandoned fort was soon overgrown with brush, vines, and trees. In the course of the nineteenth century, the region's inhabitants found the fort to be a convenient source of building stone. They carted away the walls and building until only the foundations and the powder magazine, constructed of extremely durable stone and mortar, remained. Forest debris buried the ruins.[29] In 1913, the state of Illinois purchased the site of the old fort and designated it a state park. Over the following decades, the state had the powder magazine consolidated and the gate and two principal buildings reconstructed. Systematic excavations in the 1970s and 1980s discovered details of construction preliminary to the reconstruction of the land wall and bastions and portions of the side walls. Conservationists pointed and capped with cement the original foundations to preserve them and "ghosted" several buildings by using large timbers to reconstruct only their framework (fig. 1.6). Just outside the fort are a shed and garden, both of colonial French style.

Today Fort de Chartres is managed by the Illinois Historic Preservation Society. One reconstructed building houses a chapel, chaplain and officer's quarters, storage attic, and guard room. The other contains the park offices, a small but excellent museum, and a library that can be used by visitors. Fort de Chartres was recognized as a national historic landmark in 1966 and included in the National Register of Historic Places in 1974. It is the site of a wide variety of local and regional activities and is open to visitors all year.

CONVOYS

FRENCH AMERICA WAS held together by water. The first French came to Illinois through the Great Lakes and rivers, and the water connections between Canada and the Mississippi River watershed remained of great significance well into the nineteenth century.[30] The Mississippi naturally led from Illinois to the Gulf coast, and the course of the Mississippi was the object of early French exploration. When Illinois was removed from Canadian administration and assigned to the Louisiana colony in 1717, the route down the Mississippi grew in importance.

The government in New Orleans supplied Fort de Chartres through a convoy system.[31] Two official government convoys were scheduled to travel both ways every year in the spring and autumn, but occasionally conditions forced their cancellation. The official convoys consisted of bateaux, large plank-built boats built in several styles, pointed or square at both ends (fig. 1.7). Early bateaux were flat-bottomed, although the term was also applied to the keeled boats that eventually became common. Bateaux varied in size. A typical example would have been forty feet long, nine

Fig. 1.6. Reconstructed, frame-ghosted, and consolidated foundations of original buildings of Fort de Chartres. Photograph courtesy of Joseph Gagné.

feet amidships, and able to carry about fifteen thousand pounds, though larger bateaux could carry twice as much. Bateaux carried a mast and sail that could be quickly erected if the wind was favorable, but on the winding Mississippi, men usually had to row. When moving upstream against heavy current, the crew sometimes had to punt the bateau, propelling it with poles, or go ashore and tow it with a rope, called a *cordelle*.

Pirogues varied in size from small dugout canoes that could carry no more than one or two men to giants forty or fifty feet long and about four or even five feet wide, hollowed out of enormous Louisiana cedars, Illinois cottonwoods, or other trees that grew along the Mississippi. Such huge pirogues carried four tons of goods propelled by twenty or thirty paddlers. Small pirogues were useful for scouting ahead of the main body of bateaux and pirogues, dispatching men to hunt for game, or carrying messages. Bark canoes, common in le Pays d'en Haut, were rare in Illinois and Louisiana. The appropriate bark to build and maintain such canoes did not grow there.

The numbers of bateaux and pirogues in a convoy varied with the occasion. They were usually heavily loaded. For example, the 1751 autumn

Fig. 1.7. River bateau in *Evening Bivouac on the Upper Missouri*, by Karl Bodmer. From Maximilian, *Prinz von Wied, Reise in das innere Nord-America in den Jahren 1832 bis 1834*, 2 vols. (Coblenz: J. Hoelscher, 1839–41).

convoy from New Orleans transported over two hundred men and supplies to Fort de Chartres in just six bateaux and a number of pirogues.[32]
The men who crewed the bateaux and pirogues were a diverse group:
soldiers, black and Indian slaves, and hired voyageurs. Some voyageurs
were born in France; others were American-born French Creoles, Métis
(those born of the union of French and Indian), Indians, and free blacks.
Voyageurs were commonly allowed to transport a modest amount of their
own goods on the boats as part of their salaries.

Choosing the right moment for departure was essential. Departure
dates varied, depending on such factors as the arrival of materials from
France at New Orleans, the level of the Mississippi, and the inevitable
delays in organizing any large undertaking. If a spring convoy left New
Orleans too early, it would have to fight high water, fast currents, and
cold weather. If it left too late, temperatures would be high and the water
low, requiring extensive maneuvering of the heavy boats, exhausting the
men and inviting sickness. If an autumn convoy left New Orleans too
early, water levels would be low and the trip slow and grueling. If it left
too late, poor weather might force the convoy to delay at length or even
spend the winter at the small Arkansas Post, which offered little shelter
and often little food. It was not unusual for New Orleans convoys to take
three or four months to reach Fort de Chartres.

In Illinois, if a spring convoy departed too early, it would face poor
weather, high water, and strong currents. If it left too late, the water
might be low, making progress slow, and the Indians, having returned
to their large camps after the winter hunt, could easily menace the
convoy. If an autumn convoy from Illinois left too early, it would face
similar problems, and if it started too late, it could encounter poor
weather and rough water. If an Illinois convoy left when water conditions were good, it could normally reach New Orleans in as little as
three to four weeks.

In addition to water and weather conditions, the number of boats and
weight of the loads carried dictated the speed of the convoy. A convoy
could progress only as fast as the slowest boat, a large convoy would likely
require long pauses for hunting, and heavily laden boats traveled more
slowly than lightly loaded ones. A particular convoy might travel much
slower or faster than usual. Diron d'Artaguiette departed New Orleans
for Illinois in a small bateau on December 22, 1722, accompanied for most

of the voyage by two pirogues. He finally reached Kaskaskia on April 17, 1723, after a long, miserable winter voyage.[33] In contrast, the small spring convoy of 1761, carrying only Indian trade goods, traveled from New Orleans to Fort de Chartres and returned to New Orleans in just sixty-seven days.[34]

The government boats in the convoys from New Orleans carried a wide variety of manufactured goods destined for the royal *magasin* at Fort de Chartres, and from there the goods would be distributed to the troops or sold or traded to settlers and allied Indians. Some goods were designated as gifts to be given to Indians to reinforce alliances. Many officers and some enlisted men supplemented their meager salaries as small traders, and they used service on a convoy as an opportunity to transport their own merchandise. This was officially permitted on a modest basis, but the privilege was often abused. For example, in 1735, several officers were accused of off-loading a vital supply of gunpowder so they could transport their own goods.[35] On another occasion, in 1762, a *commissaire* assigned to Illinois left New Orleans with so much baggage that the convoy had to add an extra bateau, at royal expense.[36] Often privately owned boats attached themselves for protection to the official convoys from either New Orleans or Illinois. Those coming from New Orleans carried goods similar to those in the official boats, but for private consumption or use in the Indian trade.

Convoys from Illinois carried a variety of regional products, both those that had been traded to the government *magasin* and privately owned merchandise. The government bateaux returning to New Orleans from Illinois seem to have frequently had room for privately owned merchandise. The following notice, probably typical, was posted in May 1737:

> Notice to everyone who wishes to go down to the sea [*à la mer* in the original, meaning to New Orleans] and to send their goods in the King's boats, to appear by Monday the sixth of May at Fort de Chartres to give an account of the goods which will be sent in the said boats to Mss. de La Buissonnière and de La Loëre Flaucour.[37]

The most important export of Illinois was wheat flour, which would not grow in southern Louisiana. Antoine-Simon Le Page du Pratz claims, perhaps with some exaggeration, that in the spring of 1748, eight hundred thousand pounds of flour were shipped downriver from Illinois.[38] Other agricultural products commonly shipped to New Orleans were dried peas, onions, and medicinal herbs, such as ginseng. Also shipped south from Illinois were hams, both pork and bear, as well as dried and salted buffalo tongues and flanks, beef, venison, and tallow. Bear oil from Illinois was popular in New Orleans, judged as good as or better than fine olive oil. Lead was exported in quantity, but production and profits were limited by a shortage of labor and transportation expenses.[39]

Traders shipped furs and hides to New Orleans in large numbers. Deer skins were a major export, and skins of bears, otters, wildcats, foxes, and wolves were also sent downriver. The fur of Illinois beavers was inferior to that from colder regions to the north, but it found a market, and some higher-quality beaver pelts were brought down to Illinois from the Missouri River and Great Lakes region. The fear that the Mississippi route to New Orleans would divert fur trade from Canada was a major source of contention between Canada and Louisiana. The market for buffalo hides in Europe was relatively small in the eighteenth century, although they were often used in Illinois.

In addition to the official convoys, private convoys plied the waters between Illinois and New Orleans. They varied in size and composition from one or two pirogues of modest size to groups of large bateaux and pirogues traveling together. On occasion, swift small pirogues carried out special missions, such as transporting messages or important passengers. Under absolutely ideal conditions, such boats could make remarkably rapid round-trips between New Orleans and Illinois.

Convoys also traveled to and from other places. Convoys from Fort de Chartres regularly supplied the posts on the Missouri, Illinois, and Wabash Rivers, and during the Seven Years' War, Fort de Chartres dispatched large convoys to supply the Ohio River valley forts. Surviving Illinois voyageur contracts reveal that while New Orleans was the most common destination, voyageurs were also hired to go up the Missouri River, to Michilimackinac (modern Mackinaw City, Michigan), Detroit, and Canada to trade with the Wea and even with the usually hostile Fox, and also frequently to hunt for the hides and meat that constituted a significant portion of the exports from Illinois.[40]

THE END OF FRENCH ILLINOIS

THE SEVEN YEARS' War was a disaster for France. In Europe, a powerful coalition of enemies defeated France, crippled by governmental inefficiency and corruption. English dominance of the sea severely hampered French efforts in North America and the Caribbean. Crop failures in Canada and Illinois on the eve of the war and during it exacerbated the supply situation, and the mismatch of populations, between sixty thousand and eighty thousand French in Canada and Louisiana compared with over a million in the English colonies, doomed French efforts in North America. Given the profound disadvantages, it is remarkable that the French did so well during the early years of the war and endured as long as they did.

Québec fell to the English in the autumn of 1759. Negotiations to end the war soon began, but they were not concluded until 1763. France surrendered all of its holdings in North America. Britain acquired Canada and all of Louisiana east of the Mississippi, except New Orleans and the territory immediately surrounding it. France ceded New Orleans and its land claims west of the Mississippi to Spain.

The British did not occupy Fort de Chartres, the last French post, until 1765, delayed not by French action but rather by Pontiac's uprising and the resistance of other Indian groups who remained hostile to the coming of the English and mourned the departure of the French. The last French commandant of Fort de Chartres acted in accord with his orders, handing the post over to the British with proper decorum and professionalism, but the French civilians of Illinois did not welcome the British, who had long been the enemy. French men from Illinois had died in battle against the British, and even during periods when England and France were nominally at peace, the British had attempted unceasingly to turn the Indians against the French. The Illinois French also initially feared persecution of Catholicism under the rule of the Anglican British. Although the British in fact did at least nominally respect Catholicism in Illinois, in other matters British rule frequently proved heavy-handed and corrupt.

A number of the Illinois French left the area rather than live under the British, some before the British arrived, others soon after. Still others left after the influx of Americans in the early nineteenth century. Some returned to France, while others moved to the western, Spanish side of the Mississippi, settling in Ste. Geneviève or St. Louis. The Spanish king, Carlos III, was a Bourbon, cousin to Louis XV and a Roman Catholic. Many remained in Illinois, however, and significant numbers of French Canadians moved to Illinois and Missouri after the end of French sovereignty. French culture endured on both sides of the Mississippi, and French connections persisted from Canada to New Orleans, shaping the area in many ways, from settlement patterns to sense of identity. There are still those throughout the region who bear French family names familiar in the eighteenth century, and the influences of those eighteenth-century lives remain, shaping ours. Those early inhabitants of Illinois in all their humanity demand our attention.

PART TWO

Commandants of Fort de Chartres

FRANCE ANNEXED THE Illinois Country to its Louisiana colony in 1717, and in 1719–20, it established Fort de Chartres there as the civil and military administrative center. Illinois was so far from New Orleans, the capital of the colony from 1722, that government convoys carried men and material to and from Illinois only twice a year. Yet Illinois was no isolated, unimportant post. It was the link between Canada and Louisiana, a center of vital food production, and home to small but vigorous French communities, the largest of which became the first capital of the state of Illinois. Twelve men served as commandants of Fort de Chartres and the Illinois Country between 1720 and 1765, when Fort de Chartres was turned over to the British. Two men served as commandants twice.

The commandants of Fort de Chartres bore many responsibilities, chief among which was the establishment and maintenance of alliances and friendly relations with the various Indian tribes in the area. From the early eighteenth century, the French had close, peaceful relations with the Illinois and a number of more distant tribes. However well established and long enduring these relations, tensions and difficulties did sometimes arise, and it was the duty of the commandant to resolve disagreements and maintain Indian alliances. In order to do this, they needed to foster and exhibit cultural respect and sensitivity, which no formal training could provide. In dealing with those tribes hostile to the French, the commandant had to be a military leader in a sort of warfare much different than the European norm, and danger was real. Two of the commandants were killed in Indian wars.

Another constant source of concern to every commandant was those French who were not settled on the land but rather formed a constantly shifting, changing population of voyageurs, hunters, Indian traders, and vagabonds. These free spirits often associated closely with the Indians and paid little regard to traditional French cultural order and values. The Jesuits in particular frequently denounced them as libertines and drunkards who undermined efforts to proselytize the Indians. Commandants had to pay constant attention to policing and regulating these itinerants to avert the potential disruption they could bring to the communities of Illinois.

Commandants, in addition to their military role, exercised broad executive, judicial, and legislative powers and even played a role in the religious life of the French communities. Yet if they were to be successful, commandants could not behave autocratically. Most of the Illinois French had come from or were descendants of people who had come from western Canada. Even before arriving in Illinois, they had long since left behind much of the hierarchical world of the French *ancien régime* and had necessarily developed habits of self-reliance and independence. These traits were further accentuated in Illinois, where traditional structures were much weaker than in France or even in the long-settled areas of eastern Canada. If commandants were to be successful in Illinois, they had to demonstrate competence, earn respect, and lead rather than order. Most succeeded admirably; only one, an interim commandant relieved after a few months, failed badly. Their stories are a major part of the history of early Illinois.

FIRST COMMANDANT:
PIERRE-SIDRAC DUGUÉ DE BOISBRIAND
(1718–24)

Early Life

Pierre-Sidrac Dugué de Boisbriand was born in Montréal in 1675. He was a cousin of the Le Moyne brothers, two of whom, Pierre Le Moyne d'Iberville and Jean-Baptiste Le Moyne de Bienville, had great influences on Boisbriand's career. He joined the colonial troops in 1691 as a half-pay ensign and in 1694 was promoted to full ensign. In 1696–97, he served with d'Iberville against the English in Newfoundland and Hudson's Bay.

Following a brief visit to France, Boisbriand went to Louisiana with d'Iberville in 1699. He then held the rank of captain.[1] When Mobile was founded in 1702, Boisbriand received a land grant there. Boisbriand served as an aide major to Bienville, who entrusted Boisbriand with important missions. In 1703, Boisbriand made a trip to Pensacola to borrow supplies from the Spanish. The following year, he commanded twenty-five French soldiers escorting seventy Chickasaw through Choctaw territory to a peace conference between the two tribes at Mobile. The Choctaw, however, attacked and massacred the Chickasaw and severely wounded Boisbriand in the melee. The Choctaw exhibited their remorse by sending three hundred warriors to accompany Boisbriand's stretcher to Mobile, where Marie-Françoise de Boisrenaud nursed him slowly back to health. The two developed feelings for one another and wished to marry, but as an officer, Boisbriand needed the permission of the governor, his cousin Bienville. Bienville, however, prevented the union because Marie-Françoise was prominent in the faction opposing him. Boisbriand never married.

In 1713, Antoine Crozat, heading the new proprietary company, appointed Antoine Laumet de La Mothe Cadillac governor, replacing Bienville, who remained in Louisiana as the king's lieutenant, the officer charged with representing the king's interests. Cadillac was vain, arrogant, condescending, and quarrelsome, and Bienville proud, irritable, and equally quarrelsome. Factions developed around each man. Boisbriand naturally supported his relative Bienville and drew the ire of Cadillac when, in 1716, he took the side of Lieutenant Vitrac de La Tour in a quarrel with Cadillac.

Shortly after arriving in Louisiana, Vitrac de La Tour married Bienville's cousin. This tied La Tour to the Bienville faction and enraged Cadillac; the ruling elite in French Louisiana was small, but the amount of bitter partisan infighting was enormous. When La Tour applied for permission to travel to Mobile to visit his ill mother-in-law, Cadillac questioned the legitimacy of his request. La Tour felt insulted and exchanged words with Cadillac, who charged La Tour with insubordination and ordered his arrest. Infuriated, La Tour threatened violence but finally allowed himself to be arrested, breaking his sword over his knee rather than surrendering it. Cadillac wanted La Tour recalled and dismissed, but Bienville and Boisbriand drew up reports condemning Cadillac's behavior and excusing La Tour's. Cadillac complained bitterly to France that Bienville and Boisbriand were undermining his authority.[2]

Ultimately, little came of the quarrel. Before the end of 1716, the proprietary company recalled Cadillac and again appointed Bienville governor. Along with Bienville, Boisbriand returned to prominence, and La Tour was quietly reinstated.[3] Louisiana was also about to experience major changes.

The Illinois Country

In 1717, Antoine Crozat relinquished his proprietorship of Louisiana to the Compagnie d'Occident, which the Scottish banker John Law reorganized as the Compagnie de Indes. The royal government transferred the Illinois Country from Canada to Louisiana,[4] and in 1718, the Compagnie appointed Boisbriand first commandant of Illinois.

The journey up the Mississippi was difficult. Boisbriand began the voyage in December, but the convoy got no farther than the post on the Arkansas River before halting to spend the winter. Boisbriand and his party of soldiers, *engagés* (indentured servants and laborers engaged on contract), and miners, who were to prospect for mineral wealth, finally arrived at Kaskaskia in May 1719. There he found a mixed village of Kaskaskia Indians, French traders, a few farmers, and a Jesuit mission.[5]

After examining possible sites in the American Bottom, Boisbriand decided to establish a fort about sixteen miles north of Kaskaskia. He named it after the duc de Chartres, the son of the regent of France during the minority of Louis XV. Fort de Chartres was both a military facility and the administrative center of the Illinois Country. Three officers who served under Boisbriand later became commandants of Fort de Chartres: Claude-Charles Dutisné, Jean-Charles de Pradel, and Pierre d'Artaguiette d'Itouralde.

As commandant, Boisbriand was responsible for the military administration and also played an important role in the newly established Provincial Council, which dealt with criminal cases, requests, complaints, donations, contracts, and land grants. The Compagnie granted Boisbriand a large tract of land, known as *la belle prairie du rocher*, which would become the village of Prairie du Rocher, today one of the oldest continually inhabited towns in Illinois.[6] He conveyed this grant to his nephew, Lieutenant Jacques-Gaspard de Ste. Thérèse de L'Angloiserie, who passed on much of this land to other settlers in 1734 when he left the area to become the commandant of the Arkansas Post.

Philippe Renault and St. Philippe

The Compagnie de Indes hoped and expected to find considerable mineral wealth in the Illinois Country, silver and copper as well as lead, and to that end, the Compagnie sent Philippe Renault to Illinois as director of mines.[7] Little is known of Renault before his arrival in Louisiana except that he was ironmaster from Maubeuge in northern France. Renault may have accompanied Boisbriand to Illinois, but the first explicit mention of Renault in surviving documents dates from 1722. Renault first spent some time investigating the lead deposits west of the Mississippi at and near the mine that former governor Cadillac supposedly located during a prospecting trip. Renault then prospected for copper along the Illinois River, but the copper does not exist in Illinois in workable deposits. It is merely a component of debris carried by glaciers from the north.

Finally, Renault decided to mine lead from a deposit on the Meramec River, a small river that flows into Mississippi from the west, north of Fort de Chartres and south of the future site of St. Louis. Boisbriand provided a sizable land concession to Renault on the eastern bank of the Mississippi a few miles north of Fort de Chartres. On this land in the early 1720s, Renault established a small settlement called St. Philippe and built a little fort, garrisoned by small detachment from Fort de Chartres. Renault was designated director of the concession in documents, so he may have managed the land for the Compagnie rather than owned it. Whatever the situation, he had the authority to grant lands to settlers at St. Philippe. The lead mine and St. Philippe did well initially, but Fox Indian raids forced the temporary abandonment of the settlement in 1725. It seems to have been reinhabited about 1728 and continued as a small village throughout the French regime in Illinois. Lead mining also continued, but in the long term it failed to live up to hopes. Labor was scarce, the specter of Indian threats never entirely disappeared, and the expense of shipping lead to New Orleans and exporting it left little profit. Renault remained in Illinois after the Compagnie surrendered its proprietorship and Louisiana again became a royal colony, until he was finally recalled about 1743.

Indian Affairs

Much of Boisbriand's attention was occupied with Indian affairs, maintaining good relations with the friendly Illinois and guarding against hostile tribes that threatened both the French and the Illinois. Physically unimpressive, small and with a hunched shoulder, Boisbriand nevertheless managed to impress the Illinois, addressing them in their own language and style of rhetoric. To lessen friction between the Kaskaskia Indians and the French settlers and sometimes rowdy voyageurs, Boisbriand persuaded the Kaskaskia to move their village several miles north of the French settlement. About the same time, the Cahokia Indians also built a new village separate from French Cahokia.

From its beginning, Fort de Chartres played an important role in efforts to secure the Midwest for France and develop a center for trade with Indians on the Missouri River and into the West. In 1713–14, the audacious French explorer Étienne de Véniard de Bourgmont established relations with the Missouri Indians. In 1719, Spain went to war with France, and that same year Claude-Charles Dutisné, operating out of Fort de Chartres, undertook the first of two daring explorations that began by moving up the Missouri and then proceeding to visit tribes as distant as Kansas. At the same time, another French explorer, Jean-Baptiste Bénard de La Harpe, moved up the Red River from Louisiana to visit western tribes. The Spanish, alarmed by the French penetrations into the Great Plains, sent an expedition in 1720 commanded by Pedro de Villasur from Santa Fe through Colorado into Nebraska. The Pawnee and Oto were apprehensive of Spanish attentions, hostile to the Spanish-allied Padouca (Plains Apache), and desirous of ingratiating themselves with the French. They attacked and wiped out most of Villasur's party. Boisbriand learned of the massacre through confused second- and third-hand reports carried by French traders and Indians who came to trade with the French. The Spanish would never again send an expedition so far north and east, but that was unknown at the time, and the French and Spanish in America remained wary and antagonistic even after the two mother countries made peace.[8]

In 1723, Bourgmont returned to Illinois with a royal commission designed to assert French influence on the Missouri River. The royal government directed him to establish a post as close to the Spanish as possible to develop trade with them, to make peace between the Padouca and the tribes allied with the French to facilitate trade, to situate his post with attention to its defensive ability, and to arrange a visit to France by chiefs of important tribes to impress them with French power.

Both Bienville and Boisbriand were unenthusiastic about the project. A hurricane had ravaged New Orleans in 1722, and the town still lay largely in ruins. Supplies of every sort were scarce both in Lower Louisiana and the Illinois Country. Moreover, it seemed unlikely that Bourgmont, whose personal history was disreputable, could fulfill the wildly ambitious objectives of this royal commission. Despite their reservations, Bienville and Boisbriand obeyed the royal commission, and Boisbriand dispatched men and supplies to build Fort d'Orléans, a fortified trading post.[9] Bourgmont did succeed in creating alliances with several remote tribes, and Fort d'Orléans operated successfully for some years, maintaining French alliances with the Indians of Missouri.

Northern tribes, the Fox, Kickapoo, and Mascouten, frequently raided deep into Illinois. The hostility of the Canadian administration exacerbated the situation. Canada still protested the reassignment of the Illinois Country to Louisiana and was unwilling to take any effective measures to curtail the raids. In 1721, the Fox raided as far south as Kaskaskia. In 1722, Boisbriand led a force to relieve the Peoria whom the Fox and their allies had besieged. The Fox broke off the attack and retreated before Boisbriand's forces arrived. In 1723, a small Fox war party killed a soldier near the gate of Fort de Chartres and two traders on the Illinois River. The following year, a war party killed five French traders on the Illinois River south of Pimetoui (modern Peoria), and during 1724–25, hostile raiders so threatened the settlers in the American Bottom that they could not plant their crops. In 1725, a prominent resident of Kaskaskia, who had served as head church warden, was killed by the Fox "two steps from the village."[10] In that same year, the royal government in France finally ordered in strong terms that the Canadian administration take action against the Fox and their allies, but by then Boisbriand had left Illinois for a new role in New Orleans.

Interim Governor of Louisiana and Recall

In 1724, Boisbriand helped Bourgmont arrange for a group of Indians to visit France,[11] a trip Boisbriand intended to accompany, but other events intervened. Late that year, Bienville was recalled to France, accused of corruption, mismanagement, and factionalism by his enemies, and Boisbriand traveled from Fort de Chartres to New Orleans to serve as acting governor of Louisiana. He occupied the office for three years, during which time factionalism continued unabated. Boisbriand complained bitterly about the anti-Bienville forces to France, and they complained about him. With the arrival in 1727 of the new governor, Étienne de Périer, the enemies of Bienville and Boisbriand were completely in control.

Boisbriand returned to France the following year, where he was censured and dismissed from royal service, though he was awarded a modest pension in 1730. He must have taken some solace in Bienville's reappointment as governor in 1733, but Boisbriand never returned to Louisiana. He died in France in 1736. Jean-Bernard Bossu, who spent time at Fort de Chartres a generation later, wrote that Boisbriand was remembered with respect and affection by the Illinois Indians.[12]

SECOND AND FIFTH COMMANDANT:
CLAUDE-CHARLES DUTISNÉ
(1724–25, 1729–30)

Claude-Charles Dutisné was perhaps the most colorful character to command at Fort de Chartres.[1] He was born in Paris about 1681. There are two versions of how he came to Canada and was promoted to ensign, one prosaic and the other bizarre. Evidence for either case is less than decisive, and that is somehow appropriate for Dutisné, who was himself something of an enigma.

According to the first version, Dutisné was commissioned ensign while still in France and traveled to Québec in 1705 with half a dozen new recruits. This is implied but not specifically stated in a letter from the governor of Canada, Philippe de Rigaud Vaudreuil, to the minister of the marine.[2]

The second version claims that Dutisné entered the colonial marines because he was too short to join the regular French Army. Shortly after arriving in Québec in 1705, he took part in an expedition to visit and trade with a distant, unspecified Indian tribe. Dutisné, who was to prove himself an able linguist, quickly acquired enough of the local language to understand that the Indians were planning to kill him and seize the trade goods. A childhood affliction had left him partially bald, and he habitually wore a wig. At a crucial moment, he told the natives that if they wanted his scalp so much, they could have it, pulling off his wig and throwing at their feet. According to the story, the natives, thoroughly cowed, ceased to threaten him and cheaply traded their skins to the French. Returning to Québec amid the cheers of his comrades, Dutisné was commissioned an ensign.

The best source for the second version is Antoine-Simon Le Page du Pratz in his *Histoire de la Louisiane*, based on his observations made in Louisiana between 1718 and 1734. Du Pratz published his account many years later, first in installments in the *Journal Economique* from 1751 to 1753, and then in three volumes in 1758. Du Pratz knew Dutisné in the 1720s and recorded that after he heard the story about Dutisné's adventure from several Canadians, he asked Dutisné himself about it, who confirmed the tale. Yet Du Pratz heard the story long after the event, it was confirmed by a man not adverse to self-promotion, and Du Pratz liked a good story.[3]

Despite his unprepossessing appearance, Dutisné was quick-witted and charming. In 1708, he made an advantageous marriage to Marie-Anne Gaultier de Comporté, widow of Alexandre Peuvret de Gaudarville and heir to the seigneury of Champigny and Gaudarville. He could now style himself as Sieur Dutisné, an advance in status. Before her death in 1711, Marie-Anne bore him three sons, but only the eldest, Louis-Marie-Charles, seems to have survived to maturity. After the death of Dutisné's first wife, he was able to make an advantageous second marriage, to Marguerite Margane de Lavalterie, in 1713.

In 1714, Dutisné commanded an expedition of twelve Canadians to the Wabash River. There he was supposed to meet reinforcements and together build a fort to discourage English penetration of the area. When no other troops materialized, he went to the Mississippi, visited Kaskaskia briefly, and then went down the Mississippi and finally to Mobile, the capital of the colony at that time. Seeing new opportunities, Dutisné resigned his Canadian commission and took service in Louisiana.

Dutisné was involved in an odd incident at this time. On the way to Mobile, he obtained a sample of ore at Kaskaskia, which he gave to the governor of Louisiana, Cadillac. Cadillac had the sample analyzed and declared it to be high-grade silver ore. Shortly thereafter, Cadillac undertook a sudden exploration trip up the Mississippi as far north as Kaskaskia in the Illinois Country and west into the Missouri lead-mining district. When he returned to Lower Louisiana, he proclaimed that he had indeed found a very rich source of silver. There was, however, very little silver in the lead deposits near the Mississippi mined by the French. A little silver was mined in modern times near modern Fredericktown in Madison County, close to the French lead-mining district, but the ore is poor and probably would not have even been recognized as such in the early eighteenth century. Cadillac did not reveal the location of his purported discovery, giving a weak excuse,[4] and there was no attempt to pursue his find. Cadillac's silver may not have existed at all. He was a man who could never admit personal failure.

A mystery remains. How did Dutisné produce an ore sample apparently rich in silver when the Illinois-Missouri region contained no such deposits? It has been suggested that the silver sample actually came from Mexico and people in Kaskaskia sought to perpetrate a hoax on Cadillac.[5] Cadillac, who had spent his career in Canada before coming to Louisiana, was a thoroughly dislikable person, and most of the inhabitants of Kaskaskia were Canadians, some likely to have harbored ill feelings toward Cadillac. When Cadillac reached Kaskaskia, he was treated with such hospitality as the little settlement could offer, but that may have simply been part of the joke. If it were a hoax, was Dutisné an unsuspecting tool of the pranksters or a coconspirator? Did he too dislike Cadillac in 1714,[6] or might he have done it out a sense of whimsy? Questions abound; evidence is absent.

There is perhaps a simpler explanation. Chemical analysis in the eighteenth century was difficult and often uncertain when conducted by less than the most highly trained chemists, and such skillful technicians were unlikely to be found in early Louisiana. Perhaps the analyst was wrong about the content of Dutisné's ore sample, whether through simple error or self-deception, expecting to find silver in the rock.

Despite the silver ore fiasco, Dutisné was promised promotion to lieutenant late in 1714, although the actual promotion seems not to have taken place until early the next year. Early in 1716, Dutisné led a convoy up the Mississippi to build a fort at Natchez. He arrived at a Tunica Indian village near Natchez just after Natchez warriors had looted a group of French traders and killed four of them. A missionary informed Dutisné and the leader of another convoy that happened to be in the area that four Natchez were visiting the Tunica village. The two French officers planned a demonstration to intimidate the Natchez. They had their men fire off all their guns and make it seem as if a much larger French force had arrived. The ruse succeeded, and the Natchez remained quiet until Bienville arrived with more troops, at which point Dutisné, along with another officer, was sent to the Natchez to begin negotiations. The Natchez submitted, for the time being, executing those who had killed the French traders and permitting the construction of Fort Rosalie. Dutisné briefly served at this fort as second in command until he became commandant of a post he established at Natchitoches on the Red River to counter Spanish interest in the area. He served there for two years.

In 1718, Governor Bienville called Dutisné down to Mobile and assigned him to serve under Boisbriand, who was to go to Illinois in 1719.[7] Before joining Boisbriand, Dutisné traveled on foot with fourteen companions from Mobile to Québec to bring his family south. Lacking any map, he guided the journey with only a compass. He returned to the Illinois Country with his family by the Great Lakes.

Bienville sent Dutisné as commander on an expedition up the Missouri River in 1719. The expedition had a number of objectives, not all of which were entirely consistent. Dutisné was supposed to pass beyond the friendly Missouri Indians to reach the Wichita and Padouca (Plains Apache) farther west. He was to establish cordial relations with these tribes, promote peace among them, forestall Spanish influence in the area, prospect for precious metals, and open a route for trade with the outlying Spanish settlements to the southwest. Dutisné's party reached the main Missouri village on the Missouri River a little to the west of the junction with the Grand River. The Missouri gave him a friendly reception, but they did not want him to go farther to trade with the neighboring Wichita. This was a common stance of Indian tribes, who did not want to lose their own advantage in trading with tribes not directly in contact with Europeans and particularly did not want potentially hostile tribes to obtain firearms. Dutisné returned to Illinois.

Determined to reach the Wichita, Dutisné embarked on a second trip, on foot with a single companion, first to the little Saline River near Kaskaskia. This river flowed from the interior of Missouri eastward to the Mississippi. From the Saline, Dutisné traveled west to the village of the Great Osage on the Osage River in far western Missouri. The Osage also received him hospitably, but they, like the Missouri Indians, did not want him to deal with the Wichita. It was only by threatening the Osage with Bienville's anger that he managed finally to get to the Wichita, traveling overland for some forty leagues (about 120 miles), into modern Kansas. The Osage, however, attempted to sabotage relations between Dutisné and the Wichita by sending a runner claiming that Dutisné intended to enslave them.

Initially, the Wichita were hostile, twice threatening to brain Dutisné, but he won them over with his boldness. Dutisné had few trade goods with him, some of which he exchanged for two horses and a mule with a Spanish brand. He wished to travel farther to the Apache tribes and perhaps even the outlier Spanish settlements, but the Wichita did not allow that. Acquiring more horses through trade, and once again relying only on a compass, Dutisné navigated his way back from Kansas to Illinois. Bienville sponsored his promotion to captain. Dutisné spent the next few years in Illinois, where he commanded a company.

In 1723, Dutisné accompanied Boisbriand and the other company commander, Pierre d'Artaguiette, on an expedition to relieve the Fox siege of the Peoria, though the Fox withdrew before the French arrived. Also that year, the Compagnie des Indes decided to recall Bienville. Boisbriand replaced Bienville as governor, and Dutisné replaced Boisbriand in Illinois. Before that happened, however, Dutisné suddenly resigned his commission. His father had died in France and he traveled there, apparently to take up his inheritance.

Dutisné returned to Louisiana in 1724, where he was restored to his former rank. When Boisbriand became governor in New Orleans that same year, Dutisné did become commandant of Fort de Chartres in his place, but only briefly. Dutisné requested replacement early in 1725, ostensibly because of illness. After Dutisné's departure, Jean-Charles de Pradel served briefly as interim commandant. Still in 1725, Boisbriand, now interim governor, appointed Dutisné commandant at Natchez and Pierre-Charles Desliette, the former Natchez commandant, commandant at Fort de Chartres.

In late 1726, the Capuchin priest Father Raphaël accused Dutisné of misconduct with young men at both Fort de Chartres and Natchez, as well as with harsh and cruel behavior toward the colonists at Natchez.[8] The accusations should not be taken at face value. Father Raphaël was a censorious personality, often at odds with military officers and given to accusation and feud. He frequently railed against sexual misbehavior, often with little or no apparent grounds other than his own fervid imagination.[9] His main grievance with Dutisné seems to have been that the commandant did not support the missionary effort at Natchez, but Dutisné had barely enough to sustain his small garrison and no authorization to support the missionary. Moreover, Dutisné's supposed tyrannous behavior may have been no more than attempts to rein in the activities of the French settlers that contributed to the revolt of the Natchez Indians and the massacre of French settlers there a few years later. In any event, Dutisné was relieved of command there late in 1726, even before Father Raphaël's letter was sent.[10]

Desliette died in 1729, and Dutisné again became commandant at Fort de Chartres. There is no indication that his appointment created any indignation or scandal in Illinois, such as we might expect if Father Raphaël's accusations had any substance. The Fox Wars were at their height, and during that same year, a Fox wounded Dutisné in the cheek.[11] The treatment he received was inept, and he died of the wound in 1730. Dutisné's son, Louis-Marie-Charles Dutisné, continued to serve at Fort de Chartres after his father's death.

THIRD COMMANDANT:
JEAN-CHARLES DE PRADEL
(INTERIM 1725)

Jean-Charles de Pradel, who served briefly as acting commandant at Fort de Chartres in 1725, had an undistinguished military career in Louisiana, although he later prospered as a civilian. Pradel was born in France in 1692. His father held a number of important offices and attained the rank of lieutenant general. Jean-Charles was a younger son, and in 1713 he joined the marines. It was a difficult time to begin a military career. When the War of the Spanish Succession ended in 1710, the French military forces were partially demobilized and many officers discharged. The marines provided one of the few opportunities in royal service, and that led the young Jean-Charles de Pradel to Louisiana in 1714. He went with the expectancy of the rank of ensign, but all positions were initially filled, and Pradel had to wait until 1716 to be commissioned. The following year, he was accepted as an ensign by the Compagnie d'Occident, which had assumed proprietary control of the colony following Crozat's withdrawal as proprietor. In the next few years, Pradel received rapid promotion, to second lieutenant in 1717, full lieutenant in 1719, and captain in 1720.[1]

During 1723, Pradel went to Illinois and participated in an expedition headed by Étienne de Véniard de Bourgmont to establish a fortified trading post, Fort d'Orléans, on the upper Missouri River in the general vicinity of Marshall, Missouri. The aristocratic Pradel and Second Lieutenant François Simars de Bellisle attempted to undermine the command of the commoner Bourgmont, tried to profiteer fraudulently on the provision of meat for the expedition, traded illegally in slaves and horses, demeaned Bourgmont to the Indians when he was absent, and showed themselves to be insubordinate and insolent in his presence. Finally, Bourgmont wrote about their behavior to Boisbriand, the commandant at Fort de Chartres. Boisbriand recalled both and sharply rebuked them. Bellisle was reassigned to New Orleans. Pradel remained at Fort de Chartres, in command of a company.[2]

When Boisbriand left Fort de Chartres in 1724 to become the governor of Louisiana, Claude-Charles Dutisné became commandant, but he resigned the post after a very short time. Pradel served as interim commandant at Fort de Chartres for a short time in 1725 but did not perform satisfactorily. This was a difficult time in Illinois. The raids by the Fox and their allies were frequent, and the inhabitants had to be on constant guard. Moreover, Pradel compared poorly with the popular Boisbriand in the opinion of the French inhabitants of the area. He got into a dispute with a man from Prairie du Rocher, Antoine Plé (*dit* La Plume). The nature of the dispute is not clear in the surviving records, but Pradel arrested Plé, provoking a local popular disturbance and complaints to New Orleans. Pradel was relieved of his command and sent down to New Orleans. It was apparent that Fort de Chartres required a more experienced and thoughtful officer. Pradel was replaced by Pierre-Charles Desliette, who wrote on Pradel's behalf to the governor in New Orleans. Charges were dismissed, and Pradel was reinstated in his rank but not returned to Illinois.[3]

In 1729, Pradel was waiting for a commission from France to replace the corrupt and venal Commandant Chopart of Fort Rosalie at present-day Natchez, when the Natchez Indians rose and massacred the garrison and many of the civilians at that post. After the defeat of the Natchez, Pradel served as commandant there.

Soon after arriving in Louisiana, Pradel, like so many other officers, became a part-time merchant. In a letter to a brother, Pradel wrote that trade was the only way of becoming rich in Louisiana. Pradel returned to France frequently, in 1720–22, 1727–28, and 1730–31. The first two trips were purely in furtherance of his commercial ventures, with Pradel often pestering his brothers for loans. During the last trip to France, he also introduced his bride to his family.

In 1730, Pradel married a daughter of Jacques de La Chaise, the royal *commissaire* and first councilor of the Superior Council of Louisiana. La Chaise was an ally of the new governor, Étienne de Périer, and an enemy of Bienville, who had been governor of Louisiana twice before and would be again. Pradel was among the few officers who allied themselves with Governor Périer. Both Périer and La Chaise, who died shortly after Pradel's marriage, had been instrumental in Bienville's removal in 1724, and in 1733 Bienville returned to replace Périer. Pradel also made an enemy of Edmé Gatien de Salmon, the powerful *commissaire-ordonnateur*, whom he accused of libel in 1734. Salmon later fell out with Bienville, but in 1734 the two were allies.

Périer had treated Bienville's followers poorly and had even driven officers who supported Bienville out of the service. Now Bienville did the same to Périer's followers, including Pradel. Bienville found fault in Pradel's apparent disregard of his duties as an officer of the marines so that he had time for his commercial ventures. At some time in the 1720s, Pradel had fallen victim to what sources call *flux*, probably dysentery, a malady that afflicted him periodically for the rest of his life, but Bienville accused Pradel of using *flux* as an excuse to shirk his duties. Bienville claimed that Pradel had feigned illness to avoid taking command of the convoy to Illinois in 1733 and had not attended properly to his duties for several years. Bienville wrote that Pradel also refused to resume his duties nominally because he had requested retirement but actually because he wanted to remain close to New Orleans, where wine was abundant. When Bienville offered Pradel command of the Natchitoches Post, Pradel initially accepted but then refused and resigned from the marines. That was the end of Pradel's military career, although in 1743 he petitioned the minister of the marines for appointment as major of New Orleans, which was denied, and in the 1740s he repeatedly petitioned to be awarded the Cross of Saint Louis, until he was pointedly informed that the award would not be approved.

While his military career floundered, Pradel's widespread commercial ventures flourished. He imported large quantities of merchandise from France, including wine, cheese, and lace. He was not above using ruses to avoid customs, which he bragged about in his letters. Smuggling brought many poor men to Louisiana in chains, but apparently Pradel felt it was a legitimate source of gain for one of his status. As early as 1729, Pradel brought two *sabotiers* from France to make wooden shoes for sale in Louisiana and also became a partner in a cabaret in New Orleans, maximizing the profits from his wine imports. Pradel also acquired land and slaves, first having his slaves harvest the timber on the land for sale, and then having them develop the land into a profitable plantation.[4]

Pradel's concern with acquiring wealth may have been motivated at least in part by the demands of his family. His wife was accustomed to the finer, or at least more expensive, things in life. His son was a degenerate gambler, whose substantial debts Pradel paid after his son's early death, and it was expensive to support his daughters in France and then later in New Orleans in a style appropriate to their status and his hopes for their marriages.[5] Despite these expenses, Pradel became fabulously wealthy and built an opulent chateau, which he named Monplaisir, across the Mississippi opposite the Place d'Armes and the St. Louis Cathedral (modern Jackson Square). There he died in 1764 from the *flux* that had so long afflicted him. Jean-Charles de Pradel contributed little to the development of Illinois during his short tenure in command of Fort de Chartres, but his biography reveals much about opportunities in French colonial Louisiana for an acute if somewhat ruthless personality.

FOURTH COMMANDANT: PIERRE-CHARLES DESLIETTE (1725–29)

The Desliette family was numerous and prominent in French Canada. Contemporary documents usually employ just a form of the family name in referring to individuals, undoubtedly coherent enough at the time and in the particular context, but today it is often difficult and in instances impossible to distinguish which person was meant. The name was originally Italian, di Lietto, the family having moved to France probably with the Tontys in the mid-seventeenth century. As it was adapted to French, the name assumed many forms, such as Desliette, Des Liette, Desliettes, De Liette, Deliette, Delisle, De Lisle, and De L'Isle.

A Desliette was the commandant of Fort de Chartres from 1725 to 1729, and his career immediately before and during that time is unusually clear, as it is recorded in the *Alphabet Laffilard*,[1] an alphabetic list of colonial military officers and bureaucrats from 1627 to 1780, but it remains a matter of controversy whether the commandant was Charles-Henri-Joseph de Tonty Desliette or Pierre-Charles Desliette.

Charles-Henri-Joseph de Tonty Desliette was born in Canada in 1697 to Alphonse de Tonty and Marie-Anne Picoté de Belestre. He was one of four brothers who pursued military careers. His uncle was Henri de Tonty, the companion of La Salle and an important figure in early French America in his own right. Charles-Henri-Joseph's early career is obscure, but a "Delisle" was commissioned as second lieutenant in Louisiana in 1720, and this is one of the several possible spellings of the name Desliette. Delisle, however, is a perfectly good name in its own right and need not have had anything to do with Desliette. According to Brasseaux, this "Delisle" returned to France in 1726 and left the service.[2] He cannot have been Charles-Henri-Joseph de Tonty Desliette.

Late in 1724, Boisbriand left Fort de Chartres to become governor of Louisiana, and after the short interim term of Pradel, the new commandant arrived in 1725. At that time, Charles-Henri-Joseph was only twenty-eight years old, and it is most unlikely that such a junior officer would have been appointed commandant of Fort de Chartres, particularly with the older, far more experienced, and well-regarded higher officers Pierre-Charles Desliette and Pierre d'Artaguiette already serving at the fort. Moreover, the Desliette who was commandant at Fort de Chartres died in 1729, but Charles-Henri-Joseph seems to have been the Desliette who was second in command at Baie des Puants (today Green Bay, Wisconsin) in 1737 and commandant there in 1738. Baie des Puants, "Bay of Stinks" or "Bay of Stinkers," was supposedly so named because of the odor of decaying algae in the stagnant water at the end of the bay, or possibly after an unflattering term for the Winnebago. Charles-Henri-Joseph probably also served briefly as commandant of Fort Frontenac (present-day Kingston, Ontario) in 1746 and died in Montréal in 1749.[3] Charles-Henri-Joseph's entire career may have been spent entirely in the Canadian command, and he appears to have survived for twenty years after the death of the Desliette who was commandant of Fort de Chartres.

A much more likely candidate is Pierre-Charles Desliette, but Father Pierre-François-Xavier de Charlevoix wrote that he died in 1721. The ecclesiastical historian is, however, now generally recognized to have been in error. Pierre-Charles was probably born about 1672–74.[4] He likely migrated to Canada in 1685 with his cousin Alphonse de Tonty.

From 1687 to 1702, Pierre-Charles Desliette served under his more famous cousin, Henri de Tonty. Early in this period, Pierre-Charles lived for a period with the Illinois and Miami, hunting, trading, and learning their language and customs. He served as commandant at Fort Saint-Louis from 1690 until the post was abandoned in 1692. Between then and 1702, when Tonty and his partner François Dauphin de La Forest abandoned their trade concession, Pierre-Charles served at various times as interim commandant at Chicago and at Pimetoui (Peoria). He was probably the commandant at Pimetoui when the conflict flared about Marie Rouensa-8cate8a's marriage to Michel Accault (see the chapter on Marie Rouensa-8cate8a in part 3). From 1702 until 1711, Pierre-Charles Desliette remained the sole representative of the French government among the Indians in the area. He returned to Montréal in 1711 but was almost immediately dispatched back to Illinois. War had broken out between the French and the Fox, and Desliette was sent to establish peace between the Illinois and the Miami, prevent an alliance between the Miami and Fox, and counter English trade ventures in the area. Despite reversals, by 1715 Desliette had dealt with the situation successfully. He again traveled briefly to Canada and quickly returned to reestablish Fort Saint-Louis at Starved Rock, where he commanded until 1718, when Illinois was transferred from Canada to Louisiana.[5]

During one of his brief intervals in Montréal, Pierre-Charles Desliette wrote the so-called "De Gannes Memoir." This lengthy document is signed by someone named De Gannes, perhaps a scribe, but the contents clearly indicate that Desliette composed it. The document is an important account of Desliette's early career and the Illinois and Miami Indians. It is also one of the most appealing, personal, and informative accounts of French activity among the Indians ever written.[6]

In 1717, the royal government in France removed the Illinois Country from the jurisdiction of Canada and gave it to Louisiana. The *Alphabet Laffilard* indicates that a Desliette transferred from Canada to Louisiana.

This same man was commissioned as a captain in 1720, but he soon resigned his commission. He was quickly reactivated and in 1721 appointed commandant of the Wabash district. The *Alphabet Laffilard* reports that this Desliette was commandant at Natchez from 1723 to 1725 and then in 1725 became commandant of the Illinois Country.[7] Pierre-Charles, mature and long experienced among the tribes of the area, was surely more likely to have become the commandant of Fort de Chartres than his young nephew. The resignation and quick reactivation may have been because of yet another of Pierre-Charles Desliette's visits to Montréal, perhaps to take care of personal matters.

One of Desliette's immediate concerns was the replacement of the first Fort de Chartres by a second fort, also built close to the riverbank, the planning and construction of which had probably begun before his assumption of command. The first fort had deteriorated to some extent during its five years in the moist, warm environment of the American Bottom, but it is likely that the construction of the new, stronger fort was undertaken mainly because of raids by the Fox Indians. Just two years later, in 1727, the second fort was so badly damaged by a flood that a contemporary document describes it as destroyed.[8] After the flood, Desliette moved most of the garrison from the fort to Kaskaskia, probably more to guard against Fox raids than because of the condition of the fort. While at Kaskaskia, Desliette entrusted Fort de Chartres to his second in command, Robert Groston de St. Ange. Although damaged and in poor condition, the second fort remained in use until 1732.

During the 1720s, the Fox continued to raid into Illinois virtually every year, attacking and killing Illinois and French alike, and for most of the decade the Canadian administration did little to relieve the situation despite frequent complaints from Illinois and New Orleans. Finally, a stern directive from Paris and a new governor in Canada changed the course of the Fox Wars. In 1727, Charles de Beauharnois de La Boische, the governor of Canada, planned a major campaign intended to destroy the tribe. Beauharnois appointed Constant Le Marchand de Lignery to command the enterprise, and French troops and allied Indians from the western Canadian forts were to gather under Lignery's command in the summer of 1728. Although Desliette and the Illinois Country were part of Louisiana rather than Canada, Desliette was to take his forces to Chicago and join Lignery's expedition.

As Desliette led a party of twenty French and several hundred Illinois warriors north toward the designated rendezvous, near Chicago they encountered and attacked a hunting camp of Fox along with some Kickapoo and Mascouten. The Fox and their allies suffered twenty killed and fifteen captured. After the battle, the Illinois returned home, despite Desliette's pleas. R. David Edmunds and Joseph L. Peyser suggest that the Illinois may have been disheartened by their casualties in the battle, although the sources do not mention any losses.[9] Native attitudes toward war differed from the European, and Indians often simply felt it was sufficient to make a single attack before retiring. European concepts about war did modify native attitudes to some extent over time, but even the French who lived in close connection with native peoples often seem to have been unable to persuade native allies to continue a campaign beyond an initial successful engagement.

Lignery's campaign failed, though the absence of Desliette and the Illinois had little impact. Lignery's forces, which consisted of almost 1,650 men, were too conspicuous, moved too slowly, consumed too much, and accomplished little except burning Fox and Winnebago villages and crops.

Governor Beauharnois, however, was determined to destroy the Fox and pursued that end ruthlessly until the French and Indian allies gathered in Illinois in 1730 to inflict a defeat on the Fox that nearly annihilated the tribe. Before that, however, Desliette died suddenly in May 1729, and a few months later, a new Indian crisis arose that would long convulse the Illinois Country and Louisiana.

SIXTH COMMANDANT:
ROBERT GROSTON DE ST. ANGE
(1730–33)

Robert Groston was born in humble circumstances in France about 1665.[1] The date at which he migrated to Canada and joined the marines is not known, but by 1686 he had attained the rank of sergeant, the highest rank to which a man of his social status could expect to achieve. At some point he acquired the nickname "St. Ange," which, as in so many similar instances, was gradually transformed to "de St. Ange," conveying an air of aristocracy and perhaps providing evidence of higher aspirations. Through most of his life, Robert Groston was called simply St. Ange.

In 1688, Robert married Marguerite-Louise Crevier. The couple had eight children before her death in 1707. Ten years later, Robert married again. At that time, he was still a sergeant and still living in Canada. By 1721, St. Ange was serving at Fort St. Joseph, a post of the Canadian command on the St. Joseph River in southwestern Michigan, at a location that today is on the outskirts of Niles, Michigan. Fort St. Joseph was of some importance, but in 1721 it housed only a small garrison.

At Fort St. Joseph, St. Ange met the Jesuit author Father Pierre-François-Xavier de Charlevoix and became the commander of his escort to the Illinois Country.[2] St. Ange, about fifty-five years old and stuck in the rank of sergeant, apparently recognizing that there were opportunities in the Illinois Country, decided to remain there and transferred to the Louisiana command. The next year, St. Ange led forces against the Fox, severely defeating a war party that was raiding in Illinois. The commandant at the time, Pierre de Boisbriand, must have been favorably impressed with the old soldier and played a significant role in an extraordinary event, the promotion in 1722 of St. Ange to ensign, the lowest rank of commissioned officers. In the eighteenth century, officers were recruited from the younger sons of the aristocracy or nouveau riche with aristocratic connections. Promotion from the ranks was rare. Before the end of 1722, St. Ange was further promoted to lieutenant.

In 1723, St. Ange met Étienne Véniard de Bourgmont, probably at Fort de Chartres, where Bourgmont conferred with Boisbriand. In the previous decade, Bourgmont and others had extended French knowledge of the West. In 1713–14, Bourgmont had explored up the Missouri River, where he had been well received by the Missouri Indians. After traveling to France to promote his plans, Bourgmont returned to America with a royal commission to establish a post on the Missouri.

St. Ange joined Bourgmont and played a large role in the expedition. Bourgmont was so well regarded among the Missouri that they sent a band to Fort de Chartres to welcome him and escort him up the Missouri River, where before the end of 1723 the expedition built Fort d'Orléans. St. Ange served along with two other officers, the younger, educated, and aristocratic Jean-Charles de Pradel and François Simars de Bellisle. In December 1723, Pradel and Bellisle drafted a letter condemning Bourgmont's management of the enterprise. They persuaded or intimidated the illiterate St. Ange into signing the letter, but as soon as St. Ange got away from the pair, he reconsidered. He went to Bourgmont and repudiated the letter; the two were fully reconciled. When Boisbriand received news at Fort de Chartres of the behavior of Pradel and Bellisle, he immediately recalled and censured them.

In the spring of 1724, Robert St. Ange moved his family to Fort d'Orléans on the Missouri River. Along with his second wife, Elisabeth Chorel, came his two sons, who served under their father, Ensign Pierre de St. Ange and Cadet Louis Groston de St. Ange de Bellerive. During that year, Bourgmont led two expeditions westward onto the plains in search of the Padouca. Louis accompanied the first, in June, which returned without success when Bourgmont fell ill. Bourgmont's second expedition, in October, after an arduous journey did reach a major encampment of the Padouca in central Kansas. After a mutual exchange of gifts, the Padouca agreed to peace with the French and French-allied tribes. In November, the expedition returned in triumph to Fort d'Orléans.

Late that same month, Bourgmont gathered a group of Indians and departed from Fort d'Orléans for France by way of Fort de Chartres and New Orleans.[3] Bourgmont, whose health had suffered in Missouri, did not return to Fort d'Orléans, but rather retired in France. Robert St. Ange and his sons remained in charge on the Missouri.

From Bourgmont's departure late in 1724 until 1727, there is little information about the activities of St. Ange and his family. Complaints and incidents produce documents, and the very absence of such records is evidence of their success. The family ran the fort with a minuscule garrison, engaged in trade with the western tribes, and maintained the peace, though at times the Fox threatened the traffic on the lower Missouri and on the Portage des Sioux, an overland trail from the Mississippi to the Missouri River that avoided the difficult mouth of the Missouri. In 1729, the Louisiana governor Étienne de Périer planned to close Fort d'Orléans, feeling it was too expensive to maintain and no longer necessary since the western tribes were at peace.[4] The Natchez crisis intervened, however, and the proposal was forgotten. The fort seems to have remained active at some level, perhaps seasonally, until 1736.

In 1727, Pierre-Charles Desliette called St. Ange down from Fort d'Orléans to serve as second in command in the Illinois Country and to command at Fort de Chartres when Desliette moved most of the garrison to Kaskaskia. St. Ange probably also remained behind at de Chartres when

Desliette led a war party against the Fox in 1728. It was customary to leave the second in command at the fort during the commandant's absence.

In May 1729, Desliette suddenly died. Claude-Charles Dutisné was appointed to succeed him, his second term as commandant. St. Ange remained as second in command. Before the year was over, however, Dutisné had been shot by a Fox, and in 1730 he died a lingering death from the wound.

St. Ange now became commandant of Fort de Chartres. He was about sixty-five years old and had served for more than forty years. Detractors discounted him as "an old idiot," sneering at his illiteracy, but the more perceptive Father Tartarin, the priest at Kaskaskia, thought him a good man and deserving of promotion to captain.[5] St. Ange soon showed himself still active, able, and decisive.

The Fox were St. Ange's immediate concern.[6] By 1730, the combination of French diplomacy and the Fox's own imprudent actions, which alienate even traditional allies, reduced the tribe to despair. Isolated and unable to resist the forces arrayed against them, the Fox resolved to move from their home territory on the Fox River in Wisconsin to seek refuge among the Iroquois, some eight hundred miles away to the east. The Iroquois had been friendly to the Fox in previous years and were so far away that they were not involved in the hostile alliances against the Fox. Fox messengers approached the Seneca, the Iroquois tribe settled near Niagara, who seemed willing to receive the Fox but would send no forces to aid their migration.

The Fox, about three hundred warriors and six hundred women and children, moved south along the Fox River to the Illinois River near Le Rocher (Starved Rock), the site of an abandoned French fort. They crossed to the south bank of the Illinois River and camped there to rest and hunt. They did not know that the Cahokia, one of the tribes of the Illinois, had established a village in the vicinity, much farther north than they had ventured in many years. Hunting parties of the two tribes clashed. As the word spread of the encounter, the Fox sought to escape by moving south deep into the Illinois prairie. Cahokia, Potawatomi, Kickapoo, and Mascouten converged on the Fox, who found it impossible to continue their travel. They took refuge in a grove, which they fortified with trenches and a hastily constructed palisade.

When word of the Fox reached the Illinois Country, about three hundred warriors from the villages near Fort de Chartres set out immediately, joined shortly by St. Ange leading nearly a hundred French soldiers and militia and about a hundred more tribesmen. From Fort Ouiatanon on the Wabash came twenty-eight French and about four hundred Wia and Piankashaw, and from Fort St. Joseph in southern Michigan, about three hundred Sauk, Potawatomi, and Miami. The Fox had extensively intermarried with the Sauk and Wea, and now the Fox asked these tribes to arbitrate with the French, but the wars had gone on too long and enmities were too deep. Led by St. Ange, the French and their allies would accept no compromise.

The siege of the Fox camp stretched on through the last half of August and into September. A small contingent of Illinois returned home, but nearly two hundred Huron, Potawatomi, and Miami arrived to reinforce the besiegers. Starving, the Fox broke out at night under the cover of a thunderstorm. The French and allied tribes followed the next morning, and the result was a massacre in which about five hundred Fox were killed. Many others were taken prisoner, some of whom were tortured and burned to death. Only a remnant of the tribe survived, though a little more than twenty years later they would again confront the Illinois.

A few months after Desliette's death, the Natchez Indians, far to the south of Illinois, rose against the French, killing over two hundred and holding still more women and children captive. Rumors of a general Indian uprising convulsed Louisiana and alarmed settlers even in the Illinois Country. There was no general uprising, and the French forces in southern Louisiana defeated the Natchez so decisively that the tribe was essentially destroyed, the survivors reduced to scattered refugees. When, however, Natchez survivors found refuge with the Chickasaw, the French and Chickasaw went to war, a conflict that would have profound effects in the Illinois Country, although that would come to pass only under St. Ange's successor.

Back at Fort de Chartres, the stockade walls of the fort were in poor condition, and in 1730, St. Ange had them repaired at his own expense. Still, it was apparent that the second Fort de Chartres was approaching the end of its useful life. In 1732, the fort was rebuilt for the third time, a reconstruction only poorly documented in the surviving sources. The new fort stood somewhat farther from the river than the previous ones. It covered one square arpent (36,802 square feet) and had bastions at each corner. No wood fort could escape the effects of the warm, moist soils of the Mississippi floodplain, and within two years it was showing signs of deterioration. Eventually, it became necessary to replace one of the four curtain walls every year.[7]

In 1731, the Compagnie des Indes, tired of losses and shaken by the Natchez massacre and resultant flight of settlers from Louisiana, surrendered its proprietorship of Louisiana to the Crown. Louisiana would henceforth be a royal colony. Bienville returned once more as governor, and Edmé Gatien de Salmon became *commissaire-ordonnateur.* Salmon was a man with definite opinions, and although he had never traveled there, his opinion of Illinois was not good. He did not approve of the sort of laissez-faire social order that prevailed in the Illinois Country:

> A sort of freedom obtains there [Illinois], for no stern officer maintains law and order. Sieur de St. Ange is a good officer, and he deserves credit for his service in the last war [against the Fox]. All the officers in the colony speak well of him, but he is not really in command, and everyone there is his own master.[8]

In 1733, Robert Groston de St. Ange, close to seventy years old, stepped down as commandant of Fort de Chartres. Salmon's criticism probably had little to do with his retirement. The impending war against the Chickasaw would predictably be difficult, and the forces from Fort de Chartres would need a physically vigorous commandant. As a reward for his many years of service, St. Ange was promoted to captain on half-pay status in 1736, the same year his son Pierre was killed in the Chickasaw War. St. Ange continued to live near Fort de Chartres, where he died in 1740. He had risen from humble enlisted status to become a respected officer and commandant of the Illinois Country. His son Louis would also become a commandant of Fort de Chartres and play a major role in the founding of St. Louis.

SEVENTH COMMANDANT:
PIERRE D'ARTAGUIETTE D'ITOURALDE
(1733–36)

Pierre d'Artaguiette d'Itouralde was born in France in 1698, the youngest of three brothers who came to Louisiana. The eldest brother, Jean-Baptiste-Martin d'Artaguiette d'Iron, appears in Louisiana documents as simply Diron d'Artaguiette or even just as Diron.[1] He was appointed *commissaire general* of Louisiana in 1707 and ordered to investigate charges brought against Governor Bienville. His criticism of Bienville's actions was mild, and the governor retained his post. Henceforth, the d'Artaguiettes were generally counted among Bienville's supporters. Diron d'Artaguiette departed for France in 1711 and did not return to Louisiana.

The middle brother, Bernard Diron d'Artaguiette, rarely used his first name and appears in most documents as Diron d'Artaguiette, Diron, D'Artaguiette, Dartaguiette, or Dartaguette, leading to confusion with his older and younger brothers.[2] He probably traveled to Louisiana with his older brother in 1707. He served under Boisbriand briefly in 1718 but returned to New Orleans in 1719 as inspector general of the troops in the province. In this capacity he kept a diary, a valuable source for early Louisiana and the Illinois Country.[3] For instance, he recorded organizing the first militia at Kaskaskia in 1723. Later, he became the king's lieutenant in Louisiana and then the commandant in Saint-Domingue, where he died in 1742.

The youngest brother, Pierre d'Artaguiette d'Itouralde, appears in documents generally just as D'Artaguiette, Dartaguiette, or Dartaguette. The last part of his name, D'Itouralde, was seldom used, and when it was used it was often misunderstood, such as "D'Houralde" or even "dit Ouralle," indications that despite the plethora of documents for which French bureaucracy was known, the culture was still largely oral.

Pierre d'Artaguiette may not have come to Louisiana until 1717, a decade after his brothers. He went with Boisbriand to the Illinois Country in 1718 as an ensign and there received rapid promotion to captain, commanding a company. In 1722, Boisbriand led an expedition to relieve the Peoria, who were under siege by the Fox. The two captains who served under him, Dutisné and D'Artaguiette, accompanied him. The Fox retreated before the French force arrived.

In the mid-1720s, Pierre d'Artaguiette was reassigned to New Orleans. In 1729, Chopart, the corrupt and arrogant local French commandant of Fort Rosalie (where the city of Natchez later arose), attempted to force the Natchez Indians to give up the site of their principal village so he could take the land as his personal plantation. The Natchez rose up and massacred about two hundred French, mostly men, and took many women and slaves captive. The governor of Louisiana, Étienne de Périer, launched retaliatory campaigns against the Natchez in 1729 and 1730, during which D'Artaguiette distinguished himself. When a French outpost was overrun, D'Artaguiette saved the situation by leading a furious counterattack with only five men. Governor Périer praised D'Artaguiette as valorous, brave, and conscientious. The French forces defeated the Natchez decisively. Many Natchez were killed in the fighting, and others were captured and sold into slavery in Saint-Domingue. Relatively few escaped, and the Natchez tribe never recovered. After the defeat of the Natchez, D'Artaguiette briefly commanded the new fort at the site, holding the rank of captain but performing the duties of a major.

In the aftermath of the Natchez massacre, the king recalled Périer and sent Bienville to replace him, the fourth time Bienville had been named governor. When a remnant of the Natchez found refuge with the Chickasaw, war broke out between that tribe and the French. Antagonism between the French and Chickasaw actually long predated the Natchez uprising. The Chickasaw were allied to the English, their chief trading partners, and enemies of the Choctaw, chief allies of French Louisiana. Hostilities between the two tribes constituted a long proxy war between the English and the French.

In 1732, Bienville appointed D'Artaguiette major of New Orleans and the next year made him commandant of the Illinois Country, where he replaced the aging Robert de St. Ange. Also in 1733, Bienville wrote in his evaluation of officers that D'Artaguiette was "prudent, judicious, and fair-minded and has proven valiant in every instance."[4] These characteristics were needed in Illinois, where the Illinois Indians, particularly the Cahokia, had grown more independent and difficult since the elimination of the Fox threat. When D'Artaguiette arrived, he refused to meet with tribal leaders until they improved their behavior. The crisis soon passed, and the Illinois resumed cordial relations with the French. The resolution of the crisis is usually attributed to the personality of D'Artaguiette, but the two companies of troops and four cannons he had brought with him to Illinois may have played a more important role. D'Artaguiette had a small fort erected at Cahokia to ensure continued tranquillity.

The wooden Fort de Chartres was once again deteriorating in the moist warmth of the American Bottom, and D'Artaguiette proposed to abandon it and build a new fort near Kaskaskia, high on the bluffs east of the Kaskaskia River. Bienville asked the opinion of D'Artaguiette's second in command, Alphonse de La Buissonnière, who was knowledge-able about fortification and advised that the site lacked sufficient water, was poorly suited to defend the French settlements, and would be very expensive to construct. D'Artaguiette replied that he knew of no bet-ter site. Plans went forward slowly and then were canceled far short of completion, as there were other, more pressing crises.

Outbreaks of Indian violence in the Missouri valley led D'Artaguiette to send several small, punitive parties of troops there under Pierre de St. Ange and Louis Dutisné, sons of previous commandants of Fort de Chartres. Louis Dutisné was wounded on one of the operations.[5]

By 1734, Governor Bienville began preparations for a large-scale cam-paign that he intended to eliminate the rest of the Natchez, break the power of the Chickasaw, damage English trading interests, and guarantee Choctaw dependence on the French. Bienville planned a complex two-part campaign, to take place in 1736. In the South (fig. 2.1), he mustered troops from the garrisons at New Orleans, Natchitoches, and La Balize (a small fort at the mouth of the Mississippi); volunteers and militias from New Orleans and Mobile; and a contingent of armed slaves led by free black men, for a total of 544 men, not counting officers. In addition, the Choctaw promised to send a large force of warriors. The plan was to gather the forces at Mobile, travel up the Tombigbee River, and advance to the Chickasaw and Natchez villages in the area that later became Tu-pelo, Mississippi, where they intended to meet a force moving down from the north and together attack the Natchez and Chickasaw.[6] According to Bienville's report, composed after the campaign, he sent an order to D'Artaguiette in December 1735 to gather his forces and meet Bienville in the vicinity of the Chickasaw villages at the end of March. (There is reason to doubt the veracity of this report; see this chapter's appendix.)

The northern force, commanded by D'Artaguiette, was composed of 8 officers and 27 soldiers, 110 civilian militia members and volunteers from the French Illinois settlements, and 326 Indians, consisting of 100 Illinois, 160 Miami, 38 Iroquois, and 28 Arkansaw (Quapaw). The Ar-kansaw were an advance guard of a larger group that did not arrive in time to participate in the campaign.[7] D'Artaguiette left behind his second in command, Captain La Buissonnière, with soldiers to guard Fort de Chartres and the French settlements, and Ensign Jean-François Tisserant de Montcharvaux, commandant of the small fort at Cahokia, to gather

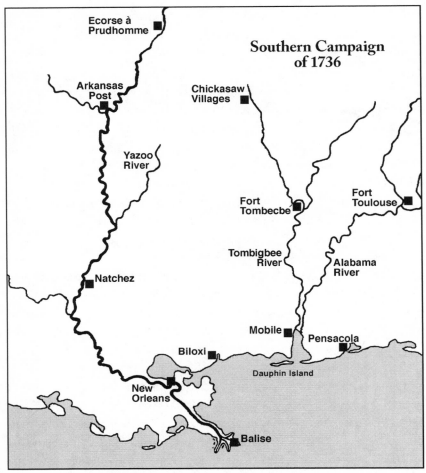

Fig. 2.1. Southern Campaign of 1736

and follow with an additional 180 Illinois Indians who were still dispersed on the winter hunt.

Bienville's complex plan quickly began to come apart. The means to transport his men and supplies were supposed to have been ready in October, but they were still not complete in mid-January. Provisions from France, salt and artillery, failed to arrive on schedule at the beginning of February. A ship did bring salt at the end of the month, but no artillery. Contrary winds delayed troops moving by sea to the camp by the Tombigbee River. A ship from New Orleans bearing rice for the army encountered bad weather, and half its cargo was spoiled. To make up for the shortfall, Bienville ordered ovens to be constructed and bakers brought from Mobile to the camp to bake biscuits for the army, consuming yet more time.

Bienville sent a messenger from Mobile ordering D'Artaguiette to delay leaving Illinois until the end of April. It is not apparent from Bienville's narrative exactly when he dispatched this second message, but given the unpredictability of travel time from Mobile to Illinois, it should have been apparent that the message might not arrive before the Illinois forces departed. Bienville did not leave Mobile until April 1, and the journey up the Tombigbee River toward the Chickasaw villages proceeded slowly.[8]

In Illinois, D'Artaguiette and his troops left Fort de Chartres on February 22, 1736, moving down the Mississippi to Ecorse à Prudhomme, a little north of what today is central Memphis, where he arrived on February 28 (fig. 2.2). There he built a small fort and left twenty-five men, leaving the river on March 5 to move overland southeast toward the Chickasaw villages about 120 miles away. The force advanced very slowly, arriving in the vicinity of the Chickasaw villages on March 24. A day or two earlier, D'Artaguiette finally received Bienville's message that he could not meet the northern force at the scheduled date (see the appendix at the end of this chapter). By that time provisions were running out, and in a council of war, the Iroquois advised D'Artaguiette to attack the Chickasaw camp in the hope of finding food and a defensive position where they could await the coming of Bienville and the southern force.

In the early hours of March 25, D'Artaguiette established a depot for his baggage and ammunition, guarded by an ensign, five soldiers, and fifteen militia members. The Jesuit Father Antoine Senat also remained there. D'Artaguiette then arranged his forces for battle: the French, seventy-three officers, soldiers, and militia, in the center; Iroquois and Miami on the left; and the Arkansaw and Illinois on the right. Between 6 and 7 A.M., the French and their Indian allies attacked Chickasaw cabins and a fort. The Chickasaw defended themselves from inside the cabins and fort, firing through loopholes. The French and their Indian allies took several cabins and attacked the fort, but after about fifteen minutes, a large force of Chickasaw attacked them on the flank, coming from other villages that scouts had failed to discover. The Illinois and Miami immediately fled.

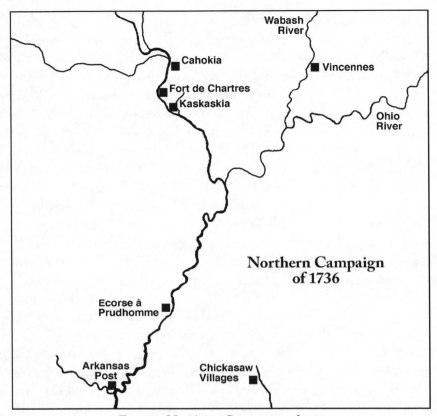

Fig. 2.2. Northern Campaign of 1736

The French subsequently interpreted the flight of the Illinois and Miami as due to cowardice or treason. People of European culture, even those born in America and long associated with the Indians, seldom understood their perspective on warfare, that it was ridiculous to attack unless one had overwhelming advantage and equally ridiculous not to retreat when faced by superior forces. The Iroquois and Arkansaw were far from their home territories and thus totally dependent on the French. They stayed and fought, winning high praise from the French survivors and retreating only when the French retreated. Both groups of Indians behaved according to rational self-interests.

Deserted by the majority of his Indian allies and attacked by a large number of Chickasaw, D'Artaguiette ordered retreat to the baggage and munitions depot. D'Artaguiette was wounded in the hand during the retreat and then shot again in the thigh. He managed to remain in command until shot again, this time in the abdomen, when he collapsed. Survivors initially thought that D'Artaguiette died at this point, but in fact he survived to be captured. The remaining officers and a few marines and militiamen rallied around their gravely wounded commander. Some were killed there, and twenty-two were overwhelmed and captured. The Chickasaw also captured ten horse loads of munitions and goods, including 450 pounds of gunpowder, 1,200 musket balls, and 30 jugs of brandy, and liberated a Chickasaw slave from the French.

Other militiamen and marines carrying their wounded managed to retreat while under continuing attack from the Chickasaw, until a thunderstorm enabled them to escape. Survivors of the retreat credited the Iroquois, Arkansaw, and a young cadet named Jacques Voisin with vital roles in preventing a general massacre (see the chapter on Jacques-Sernan Voisin). After escaping from the Chickasaw, the survivors faced an even longer retreat, during which the Iroquois and Arkansaw helped carry about twenty wounded marines and militiamen to safety. The day after the defeat, the survivors met Tisserant de Montcharvaux, the commandant of Cahokia, who was advancing with 180 Illinois, 5 soldiers, and 8 militiamen. They provided supplies and aided the withdrawal. In addition to those killed on the battlefield and on the retreat, the enraged Chickasaw burned to death nineteen of the captured French. An additional French officer and an Iroquois, captured several days later, were also burned. Three French prisoners, one captured some time previously, were spared this fate in anticipation of trading them for a Chickasaw chief held captive by the French. The three were eventually able to escape with the aid of English traders, and one, Claude Drouet de Richardville, wrote an account of the battle, his captivity, and escape.[9]

The list of those killed in D'Artaguiette's ill-fated attack on the Chickasaw or burned to death in the aftermath reads like a virtual list of the most prominent individuals and families of le Pays des Illinois. All eight of the officers were killed or captured and burned, including D'Artaguiette; the prominent and well-respected François-Marie Bissot de Vincennes, who was commandant of the Wabash Post (site of modern Vincennes, Indiana); Pierre de St. Ange; and Louis Dutisné. At least four cadets perished—one account claims six—including a cadet named Tonty, a member of the Desliettes family and perhaps the son of the former commandant. Eight soldiers also perished. Three militia officers died, all prominent men in their communities, and fifteen militia members. Prominent or humble, the total of at least thirty-eight dead was a heavy burden for the small French communities of Illinois.

There is no French record of the number of allied Indians who perished, and surely some, particularly among the Iroquois and Arkansaw, who performed heroically during the retreat. Only the captured Iroquois who was burned after stumbling into the Chickasaw camp three days after the battle is mentioned, and then only because he was with a French officer. In recent years, historians have emphasized that while the French treated native peoples as a whole better than the British, the French attitudes and behavior toward them were nevertheless exploitive and discriminatory and ought not to be romanticized and idealized. This disregard of the native casualties points in the same direction.

Reports of the number of casualties among the Chickasaw vary greatly. The main report of the battle in the French archives estimates sixty or seventy Chickasaw were killed, a number that seems an attempt to minimize the degree of the defeat. Claude Drouet de Richardville, who was taken prisoner and survived to escape, estimated twenty killed and thirty wounded. Such round numbers do not inspire confidence. William McMullin, an English trader who was in the Chickasaw village at the time of the battle, recorded probably the most accurate information, saying that eight Chickasaw were killed, including a woman and three children.[10]

Bienville, hampered by rain and high water, was not able to reach and attack the Chickasaw until May 26. The Chickasaw fought from within fortified cabins and a small fort, while the French forces advanced in the open against them. The Choctaw, appalled at the ineptitude of the French method of attack, took little part in the battle until the last phase, at least according to Bienville. The French were repulsed with heavy losses and retreated out of the conflict. Bienville would mount another grand campaign against the Chickasaw in 1740, which also failed.

Despite the defeat and death of so many prominent members of the French Illinois communities, D'Artaguiette, young, gallant, popular, and ultimately heroic, was long remembered in a local folk song that described his period of command as a golden age.

Appendix: Did Bienville Lie about His Instructions to d'Artaguiette?

Bienville's failed offensive of 1736 was a disaster in every regard. Casualties were high, the French government was humiliated, the Chickasaw were encouraged in their aggression, and the English were delighted. Bienville had conceived of the campaign and commanded it, and afterward, trying desperately to save his career, he sought to avoid personal accountability for its failure. Unwilling to accept even a modicum of responsibility, Bienville attempted to justify his every action and to fault virtually everyone else who played any role in the campaign, with the exception of the officers of the marine, who had long constituted a large portion of Bienville's chief supporters. Bienville did not extend the same immunity to the common soldiers, who died in large numbers, and he accused them of cowardice. Bienville even blamed the weather, which does not seem to have been particularly severe or unusual for the place and time of year. In this context, Bienville's report about the orders he sent to D'Artaguiette to meet him in Chickasaw territory in late March ought to be examined carefully. Bienville may have really ordered D'Artaguiette to meet him at the Chickasaw villages in early or mid-March, rather than the end of March as he later claimed.

D'Artaguiette and his forces left Fort de Chartres on February 22, 1736 (February 20 according to Parisien[11]), without waiting for the commandant at Cahokia to gather the Cahokia tribesmen and join him. If D'Artaguiette were not to meet Bienville until the end of March, he had no reason to have departed so early. The journey from Fort de Chartres to the vicinity of the Chickasaw villages could easily be accomplished in less than a month.

D'Artaguiette arrived at Ecorse à Prudhomme (site of present-day Memphis) on February 28 (February 23 according to Parisien). There he sat until March 5 (February 25 according to Parisien). He built a small fort and left twenty-five militiamen and three sick soldiers. It was not necessary for him to delay there at all. The militiamen left behind were sufficient in number to build a small fort by themselves without delaying the entire force. D'Artaguiette may have been waiting at Ecorse à Prudhomme for a message from Bienville, which suggests that the rendezvous between their forces was intended to take place well before the end of March.

At some point, Bienville did send a messenger to D'Artaguiette informing him of the substantial delay of the southern force, but Bienville, who otherwise specified relevant dates, curiously did not record when he sent the message. That information would have been critical for understanding the chronology of events.

The distance between Écorse à Prudhomme and the Chickasaw villages was about 120 miles. It took nineteen days to cover that distance (twenty-nine days according to Parisien), which seems excessive, even given rainy conditions. Four years later, a larger force covered the same ground in about the same amount of time, although it moved with extreme caution, paused frequently to hunt, and had to deal with snow and flooded rivers.[12] Still, D'Artaguiette's sluggish advance may indicate that he expected to encounter Bienville's force or at least messengers announcing Bienville's presence in the immediate vicinity well before the end of March.

By March 24, D'Artaguiette's force was almost out of provisions, and following the advice of the Iroquois, D'Artaguiette attacked the Chickasaw villages the next morning, hoping to capture provisions and a defensive position that he could hold until Bienville arrived. If D'Artaguiette did not expect to meet Bienville until the end of March, it seems odd that he was nearly out of provisions a week before that date. Bienville claimed that his original order to D'Artaguiette emphasized that he take abundant provisions. This sounds like one of many attempts by Bienville to avoid responsibility for the factor that forced D'Artaguiette's attack.

The evidence, of course, is not decisive, but Bienville's claim that he ordered D'Artaguiette to meet him at the end of March remains at least open to suspicion. The chronology of D'Artaguiette's advance to disaster is incomprehensible if he were to meet Bienville at the end of the month, but understandable if he expected to meet him in early or mid-March. Bienville's claim, as with so much of what he wrote about the campaign, may have been a frantic attempt to avoid all blame for the abysmal failure.

EIGHTH COMMANDANT:
CLAUDE-ALPHONSE DE LA BUISSONNIÈRE
(1736–40)

Claude-Alphonse de La Buissonnière was born about 1695, the grandson of a royal comptroller and son of naval *commissaire*.[1] In 1720, La Buissonnière came to Louisiana as a lieutenant of the marines. He may have owed his rank at least in part to the influence of his first cousin Mme. Alexandrine-Ernestine Gourdan, who ran the most important bordello in Paris. Her establishment was patronized by the social elite, both men and women, including aristocrats, influential government officials, and even important members of the clergy.[2]

In 1730, the governor of Louisiana, Étienne de Périer, described La Buissonnière as a "valorous and meritorious officer, who leads a well ordered life and who served well in our last expedition" against the Natchez Indians.[3] In 1731, La Buissonnière served under the Baron de Henri de Poilvilain de Cresnay, an aristocratic but inept officer, sent to Natchez with seventy officers and men to build a fort replacing Fort Rosalie after it was destroyed by the Natchez revolt. Cresnay foolishly dismissed the allied Tunica and trusted the as yet unsubdued Natchez, who claimed they wanted only peace. When the Natchez attacked the unfinished fort, the garrison found itself in a desperate fight, losing six dead. Construction was temporarily abandoned, and when resumed, La Buissonnière replaced Cresnay in command.

Meantime, in France, Mme. Gourdan's husband petitioned for La Buissonnière's promotion to captain. When, in 1732, the minister recommended the promotion, Governor Périer commented favorably, describing La Buissonnière as "attached to the service, intelligent, wise, knowledgeable about fortifications."[4] He was duly promoted.

Also about this time, La Buissonnière met Marie-Thérèse Trudeau, and they decided to marry. Officers were required to obtain the permission of the governor before marriage, but Governor Périer refused to consent. The couple married anyway. An account of their marriage and the multitude of conflicts it involved, too long for inclusion here and well deserving of separate treatment, is described in a chapter in part 3. It all led to La Buissonnière's assignment to Fort de Chartres in 1735, where he became second in command. When the commandant Pierre d'Artaguiette went off to fight the Chickasaw in 1736, La Buissonnière, as second in command, was left behind to guard the fort, a normal procedure. D'Artaguiette and almost all the other officers stationed at Fort de Chartres were killed in a single disastrous battle.

In the aftermath of the battle, Bienville wrote to the minister of the marine, Jean-Frédéric Phélypeaux, comte de Maurepas:

> The death of Mr. d'Artaguette leaves a place that is
> very difficult to fill. I intend to leave in it Mr. de La
> Buissonnière, a captain, who for the last three years
> must have acquired some knowledge of the govern-
> ment of that region, until his Majesty has provided for
> it. None of the captains who we have here unites the
> qualities necessary to lead with success there both the
> Indians and the inhabitants and the voyageurs. There is
> needed at that post an officer who is upright and of mild
> discipline because the Canadians are naturally some-
> what mutinous. They must have commandants in whom
> they have confidence.[5]

Despite this unenthusiastic endorsement, La Buissonnière proved an
active and able commandant, and there was much for him to do. His
subordinate, the young Louis de St. Ange, stationed at a post on the
Missouri River,[6] successfully persuaded the tribes in the area to reaffirm
their alliance with the French and turn against the remnants of the Fox.
Bienville then transferred St. Ange to Vincennes as commandant there,
and La Buissonnière must have been glad to have that able officer in the
post. In the mid-summer of 1736, La Buissonnière received reports that a
mixed force of Chickasaw and Cherokee in league with the English was
establishing a fortified permanent settlement on the Ohio River about
80 French leagues (180 miles) from the river's mouth, where it joins the
Mississippi. La Buissonnière informed Bienville, who wrote to minister of
the marine, "It is of extreme importance to strangle such audacious plans
at their birth. I have sent orders to Mr. De La Buissonnière to arouse
by all possible means all the nations of his department against these
newcomers and to harass them so that they will be forced to go back."[7]

In response to the crisis, Bienville ordered St. Ange to abandon the
post at Vincennes and move the garrison downstream to the junction of
the Wabash and Ohio Rivers to establish a new fort. In 1738, Bienville
dispatched La Buissonnière on a lengthy mission to the area to select a site
for the new fort, but he found that the ground was low, often flooded, and
unsuitable. Also that year, the Chickasaw and Cherokee abandoned their
settlement on the Ohio, alleviating the crisis, although English penetration of the upper Ohio valley remained unchecked. Despite Bienville's

continuing attempts to establish a major fortification on the Ohio River, nothing came of it at this time.

Meantime, in 1737, the Jesuits at Kaskaskia claimed that the Miami were forming a great pro-English conspiracy and particularly were set on undermining the loyalty of the Illinois. La Buissonnière saw matters differently: the Miami and Illinois simply wanted brandy, which the Jesuits would not supply, so they traded for rum with the British. This undoubtedly did provide the opportunity for the English to extend their influence, but the Jesuits never understood, or affected not to understand, the realpolitik of the situation and continued to oppose the sale of alcohol to Indians.

Bienville kept on pressing for the construction of a stone fort on the bluffs opposite Kaskaskia to replace the deteriorated Fort de Chartres, despite La Buissonnière's negative opinion of the site. In 1738, following orders, La Buissonnière secured stone for the fort, but the costs mounted up so quickly that in the next year the project was suspended. Moreover, war against the Chickasaw was again imminent.

Heavily criticized for the double defeat in 1736, Bienville desperately wanted a second chance to crush the Chickasaw and redeem his reputation. His mental agitation is mirrored in the turgid prose of a letter to the minister of the marine, De Maurepas, made all the more striking by its contrast to Bienville's normally clear and direct style:

> Although in the last expedition the junction of our forces
> with those of the Illinois could not be made, I think
> that if I am informed early of your Lordship's inten-
> tions, in case he orders a second campaign, I could avoid
> the misfortunes that were incurred the first time in this
> junction, whether I return by way of Mobile or by the
> Mississippi, and I could give such positive orders for the
> collecting and transportation of the provisions and troops
> that infallibly I should be in the territory of the enemy
> in the time that I should indicate. I shall have the honor
> to inform your Lordship when I shall have sounded the
> Choctaws about the route that I think the most suitable
> and least expensive. It is very much to be desired that Mr.
> Beauharnais [the governor of Canada] might be able to

send there at that time all the nations [i.e., tribes] of the
North, who are already very much disposed to it.[8]

The royal government approved the second campaign, and the preparations were immense, but Bienville's great expedition encountered problems from the beginning.[9] Initially, he intended to establish the campaign
supply depot and rendezvous point for the troops at the juncture of the
St. Francis River with the Mississippi, about seven miles north of modern
Helena, Arkansas. Bienville had Fort St. Francis constructed there and
men and materials moved to the fort, but it soon became apparent that
the site was too far from the Chickasaw villages. Bienville then designated
Ecorse à Prudhomme to the north as the new depot and ordered Fort
de L'Assomption constructed there. Men and materials sent to Fort St.
Francis now had to journey to Fort de L'Assomption, incurring expense,
delay, and losses. The saga of the oxen and horses ordered for the expedition is illustrative of the difficulties involved.[10]

Bienville purchased 160 oxen and nearly 200 horses from Illinois and
Natchitoches for the expedition. All the oxen and 80 horses came from
Illinois, and Bienville hired forty-five local French inhabitants and seventeen Indians to drive them. The oxen were dispatched in mid-March,
and the horse drive began in May. By the time the drovers reached the
first rendezvous point, Fort St. Francis, there were only 145 oxen and 50
horses; the others were lost, had strayed, or had been stolen. The drovers
turned north to the new rendezvous point, Fort de L'Assomption, finally
arriving there in December with 120 oxen and 40 horses. The animals
that did arrive were in poor condition, largely useless, and many soon
died because of insufficient fodder near Fort de L'Assomption.

In May, Bienville had decided the march against the Chickasaw villages would begin at the end of September, but at that date men and
supplies were still in transit. Finally, by December, the largest and best-
supplied army ever fielded in French Louisiana was fairly complete. From
France came fourteen cannons, two large mortars, twelve small mortars,
two thousand grenades, vast quantities of musket balls and gunpowder,
six sappers with a supply of explosive charges, and about seven hundred
troops. Convoys moved everything upriver from New Orleans. Still more
men from the garrisons of Lower Louisiana traveled up the Mississippi,

and Indians from many tribes gathered at the new fort. From Canada came an additional 230 French and about 500 Indians from northern tribes. In Illinois, La Buissonnière gathered a force of 38 marines, 48 militia, and 200 Indians and moved downriver to Ecorse à Prudhomme.[11] No exact total is possible and estimates vary, but Bienville's forces probably numbered about 1,200 French (along with a small number of Swiss) and around 1,600 Indians. In addition to the supplies continually arriving from Lower Louisiana, Illinois supplied large amounts of flour, bacon, and corn.

And then this enormous gathering of men and materials proceeded to sit, immobile. Bienville himself did not arrive until November 13, and by that time Bienville's great expedition was beginning to fall apart. The Chickasaw conducted a masterful diplomatic campaign, repeatedly sending ambassadors with peace overtures, never actually reaching an agreement but skillfully delaying the start of the French movement. Fever brought upriver with the troops from France spread among the army and the Indian allies. Men died in large numbers. Supplies began to run short, and the army continued to deteriorate. Quarrels broke out, exacerbated by inactivity, sometimes leading to violence. The winter was cold and rainy. Troops deserted. Some Indians left in disgust at the inaction. Routes to the Chickasaw villages reconnoitered in the summer proved unusable, wet, and swampy in the winter, and scouting new routes consumed time without producing good results. Bienville finally came to realize that the heavy artillery, brought from France and laboriously convoyed up the Mississippi, was impractical to move overland through the wilderness to the Chickasaw villages.

Perhaps the final blow came when Bienville's engineer, Ignace-François Broutin, estimated the amount of supplies necessary for a force from Fort de L'Assomption to attack and besiege the fortified Chickasaw villages. He calculated that for two months in the field, even a reduced force of just 800 men would require more supplies than they could possibly transport between Fort de L'Assomption and the villages in three round-trips. Two months represented the probable time required for the initial march, establishment of a base near the Chickasaw, and three round-trips to carry supplies. Three round-trips would be the feasible maximum considering available time and the capacity of men and animals. This discouraging scenario did not even take into account possible Chickasaw countermeasures.[12]

On February 2, 1740, Bienville, desperate, dispatched a force of 337 Indians and 201 French under the leadership of an able Canadian officer, Pierre-Joseph Céloron de Blainville, to move against the Chickasaw villages. Sixty Choctaw joined them on the march. The force advanced very cautiously and spent time hunting to supplement the provisions they carried, arriving in the immediate vicinity of the Chickasaw villages on February 22. Several days of skirmishing followed. The French ran short of provisions, and some of their Indian allies departed. The Chickasaw recognized the opportunity to make a favorable peace and entered into negotiations first with Céloron and then with Bienville. Negotiations dragged on for a while before Bienville concluded a peace of sorts, in which the Chickasaw promised much but delivered little. Bienville's great army dismantled Fort de L'Assomption and disbanded over the course of March. On April 1, Bienville departed for New Orleans, where, despite his attempts to present a favorable interpretation of events, it was apparent his career in Louisiana was soon to end.[13]

La Buissonnière conveyed the Illinois contingent back home. In a report of June 15, 1740, Bienville noted that La Buissonnière was "ravaged by gall stones,"[14] which may have been caused or aggravated by conditions during the campaign. In early December, La Buissonnière fell ill and died.[15] Perhaps he had succumbed to complications from gallstones, but it is also possible that the fever that spread among Bienville's army came to Illinois with the returning men and struck down La Buissonnière. The church death and burial records for the village of Chartres and the surrounding villages, which could have revealed whether there had been a significant increase in mortality at this time, have not survived, but it is suggestive that the letters that reported La Buissonnière's death also recorded the death of a Jesuit Father Boulanger and the dangerous illness of Louis-Auguste de La Loëre de Flaucourt, the *commissaire* for Illinois and a close associate of La Buissonnière's.[16]

In early 1741, Jean Jadart de Beauchamp, commandant at Mobile, wrote to the minister of the marine a fitting memorial: "M. de La Buissonnière died in the first days of December, greatly regretted by all those who knew him. This is a great loss; he was a good officer and very intelligent."[17]

NINTH AND ELEVENTH COMMANDANT:
JEAN-BAPTISTE BENOIST DE ST. CLAIR
(1740–42, 1749–51)

Jean-Baptiste Benoist de St. Clair became acting commandant of Fort de Chartres twice, but despite long service in many posts throughout Louisiana, he never became a permanent commandant in the Illinois Country.[1] His career was blighted by temerity when young and timidity when middle-aged.

Benoist was born in France about 1693 to an influential family—his uncle was the comptroller of the royal household. The young Benoist owed his appointment as an ensign in Louisiana to Antoine Crozat, the proprietary administrator of the Louisiana colony from 1712 to 1717. Benoist quickly became involved in the factionalism that constantly characterized French Louisiana but was particularly virulent during the governorship of Cadillac. Cadillac was always a difficult personality, dictatorial, pretentious, arrogant, and irritable. Moreover, he was near the end of his career. His grandiose plans in Canada had all collapsed, and he had been sent to Louisiana less because of any good qualities than to bury an embarrassment to his patron, Jean-Frédéric Phélypeaux de Maurepas, comte de Pontchartrain, the minister of the marine.

Cadillac quarreled with Antoine Crozat, the proprietor of the colony and Benoist's patron, virtually from the day he arrived in Louisiana. Cadillac also alienated the great majority of the officer corps and many civilians, who complained bitterly to France. By 1716, Cadillac had little to anticipate but a humiliating recall. At this juncture, Cadillac's son, Lieutenant La Mothe Cadillac *fils*, and Benoist fought a duel. Dueling had been outlawed in France in 1626 but remained common, especially among the officer corps. Officer duelists were seldom punished according to the law unless the duel resulted in death, but any duel resulted in official displeasure and could hold back an officer's career.[2]

Worse still were the events surrounding the duel. When at one point Benoist fell, Ensign Terrisse de Ternan, a partisan of Cadillac's, took a sword from another officer and stabbed Benoist three times. Ternan barely escaped being cashiered for his scandalous behavior. Benoist recovered from his wounds, but the entire affair left everyone involved in disrepute.[3] A duel with a superior officer, the son of the governor, had an air about it of insubordination and even sedition.

Benoist's fortunes revived to some degree when, shortly thereafter, Cadillac and his son left Louisiana. By 1720, Bienville was again governor, and he sponsored Benoist's promotion to second lieutenant. In 1725, however, Benoist again got into a tactless confrontation with a superior officer. At that time, Benoist was part of the garrison at Mobile, and there one day he was playing a game of ninepins with Major Jean de Beauchamp. The two argued about the game, and Benoist called Beauchamp a liar. Affronted, Beauchamp struck Benoist with a cane. This incident would certainly have resulted in another duel if the commandant at Mobile, Bernard Diron d'Artaguiette, had not been present. He immediately ordered both officers arrested and reported the affair to Boisbriand, interim governor of Louisiana after Bienville's most recent recall. The letter reporting this affair to the council of the Compagnie des Indes bears in the margin the notation "Recall Benoist," but that was not done. Officers, even such excitable ones such as Benoist, were in scarce supply in Louisiana.[4]

Over the next decade and a half, Benoist served at both Mobile and the small Fort Toulouse, the Alabama post attached to the Mobile command. Although he served some time as the commandant of Fort Toulouse, Benoist received no promotion. Twice, in 1730 and 1732, Governor Périer described Benoist in his evaluation of officers as "formerly involved in an incident that brought him no honor," and in 1735, Bienville, who seldom agreed with Périer about anything, recommended that Benoist be passed over for promotion because of the "stain" on his record.[5]

In 1736, Benoist returned to New Orleans because of ill health, but he evidently recovered quickly. That same year, the Chickasaw defeated Bienville's major offensive against them; there were many casualties among the French officers. To fill a vacancy, Bienville proposed to send Benoist to Illinois, noting that he was the oldest lieutenant in the colony. The transfer would gain Benoist promotion to captain, but in the interval between Bienville's recommendation and confirmation of the appointment from France, Bienville sent Benoist to command Fort Tombecbé on the river north of Mobile in Choctaw territory.[6] Here his career suffered another, very different sort of setback.

In 1737, Benoist, perhaps unnerved by the events of the previous year, overreacted to a minor raid by the Chickasaw. Diron d'Artaguiette reported in a letter to the minister of the marine, Jean-Frédéric Phélypeaux, comte de Maurepas:

In the month of June, M. Benôit, commandant at the
Tombecbé post, notified us that he had been attacked
by the Chickasaw and had driven them off with several
volleys. He asks us for reinforcements that we could, he
said, send in some little boats; that there was no time to
lose; that the garrison at New Orleans is strong enough to
send him troops, which he says are more necessary at his
post than at New Orleans, where there is nothing to fear,
while he is at the beard of the enemy and without hope of
any aid. Fortunately, my lord, the Indians have no hair at
all on their chins, for probably he would have been more
terrified. It is not imaginable how the officers fear the
Chickasaw, incapable of taking a fort guarded by fifty or
sixty men. He deserved to be relieved by M. de Bonnille
as M. de Bienville has done, and one should no longer
have enough confidence in him to give him commands.[7]

Nevertheless, in 1738, Benoist was posted to Illinois with the rank
of captain. Alphonse de La Buissonnière was commandant there, and
Benoist served as his second in command. When La Buissonnière went
to join Bienville's second expedition against the Chickasaw in 1739, he
left Benoist in command of Fort de Chartres. In 1740, La Buissonnière
died suddenly, and Benoist became the interim commandant, serving
until 1742. Governor Bienville apparently did not considered Benoist for
the permanent post, in part probably because of his previous record and
in part because of a new misstep. Overall, Benoist seems to have done
a competent job, and he was well liked by the people of Illinois, but he
again showed himself excessively apprehensive about Indians.[8] A minor
disturbance in mid-1742, little more than some ill-considered arrogant
talk by an Indian chief, alarmed Benoist, who feared a general uprising
by the Illinois. Bienville felt Benoist's response was panicky and excessive, and the disturbance came to nothing. In late 1742, Jean-Gaspard de
Bertet de La Clue replaced Benoist as commandant at Fort de Chartres,
and Benoist reassumed his old subordinate position.

Benoist, like many other officers, was a merchant in his spare time,
and this led him to collaboration with Marie-Catherine Gervais, known
generally as the Widow Gervais. Their acquaintance apparently long

antedated the beginning of their surviving correspondence in 1745. The Widow Gervais had originally lived in Illinois, but by 1745 she had moved to New Orleans and established herself as a merchant.[9] During that year, she made Benoist her agent for collecting debts and selling land she owned in Illinois. Over the next few years, the two sent goods back and forth and occasionally gossiped in their letters about current events. Their correspondence is incompletely preserved, but it nevertheless provides an interesting source concerning trade between New Orleans and Illinois.

The enterprising Widow Gervais shipped to Illinois in commercial quantities rum, brandy, coffee, sugar, and soap. Other items were for Benoist's personal consumption, with perhaps a little left over for resale: an embroidered cap (apparently a gift); a shaving cup and two cakes of soap with it; a barrel of Bordeaux wine (sent at Benoist's request); three ells of lawn (a type of cloth); a pound each of cloves, nutmeg, and cinnamon; six pounds of black pepper; twenty pounds of coffee; six pair of silk stockings; four pairs of socks; six handkerchiefs; and a dozen shirts "with trimmings." A puzzling item is a "band of starling feathers" that Benoist requested and Gervais reported she was attempting to find. Perhaps this was an item of feminine adornment wanted by some fashionable lady at Kaskaskia or one of the other towns in the Illinois Country.

Benoist sent Gervais pecans and large quantities of flour. He also mentions hams sent by a third party. Lead and skins were other items sent from Illinois to New Orleans in significant quantities during this period, but apparently Benoist did not deal with these. The Widow Gervais died suddenly in 1748, at which time Benoist reckoned that Gervais owed him 3,768 livres, 6 sols. It took until 1752 for Benoist to collect from her heirs, when court-appointed arbitrators awarded him 2,900 livres.[10]

In 1749, the commandant of Fort de Chartres, Bertet de La Clue, died, and again Benoist became the fort's interim commandant, a post he held until late 1751. In view of his many years as an officer in the colony and service as an interim commandant, Governor Vaudreuil had recommended him for the Cross of Saint Louis in 1749, which was approved the next year along with a bonus.

Benoist once again he showed himself excessively anxious about Indians. The English were penetrating ever deeper into French territory, offering often superior trade goods in greater quantities at better terms and hoping to entice tribes into their alliance. In 1751, a small band of

Piankashaw and Wea allied to the English came to Illinois, ostensibly to get munitions for a raid against the Chickasaw, but actually to promote their English alliance. Benoist, alarmed at the possibility of a great Indian conspiracy against the French, wrote to Vaudreuil, who thought his fears were exaggerated. The arrival of the new permanent commandant, Macarty, in the last days of 1751 ended Benoist's second period of command and quickly resolved the Indian problem.[11]

Benoist resumed his subordinate role at Fort de Chartres. In 1752, he commanded the autumn convoy from Illinois to New Orleans. Low water prevented the convoy from reaching New Orleans, and it had to overwinter at the Arkansas Post at great expense. Bienville lamented the expense more than blamed Benoist's management of the situation.[12] Benoist appears to have transferred from Fort de Chartres to New Orleans at this time, and there he died in 1757.

TENTH COMMANDANT:
JEAN-GASPARD DE BERTET DE LA CLUE
(1742–49)

Jean-Gaspard de Bertet de La Clue was born to a distinguished French family, one of six brothers and one sister. His elder brother Jean-François de Bertet de La Clue-Sabran eventually rose to the exalted rank of *lieutenant général des armées navales*.[1] Jean-Gaspard, who was probably born about 1700, served with distinction in the French Army from 1719 to 1732, attaining the rank of lieutenant. In 1732, Jean-François petitioned the king to promote Jean-Gaspard to captain. The petition was granted, and the minister of the marine nominated him for a captaincy in Louisiana.

Bertet commanded a company at Mobile in 1733, and he must have made an excellent impression on Bienville, who recommended him for promotion to major the following year. Paris evidently felt that the promotion was premature, and it was not approved at that time. In 1736, Bertet became the commandant at Fort Tombecbé, north of Mobile. Bienville continued to have a high opinion of Bertet, describing him in an evaluation in 1740 as wise, unselfish, capable, and devoted to his work.[2]

Bertet was finally promoted to major in 1741 and was appointed commandant in Illinois to succeed the interim commandant, Benoist de St. Clair. The next summer, Bertet commanded the convoy from New

Orleans to Illinois, and he arrived at Fort de Chartres to assume command late that year.

The Chevalier de Bertet, as he is usually called in contemporary documents, was one of the most capable commanders of the Illinois Country, but he had few opportunities to shape events during his period of command. Events beyond his control forced him into a largely reactive role. By early 1743, he was able to assure Bienville that the nervous Benoist's reports of the disaffection and potential revolt of the Illinois Indians were exaggerated,[3] but new Indian problems soon arose.

France and England were again at war from 1744 to 1748, and English naval power severely limited the flow of supplies of all sorts to French America. At one point, Bertet received no supplies from New Orleans for fifteen months, and Canada, similarly hard-pressed, issued no permits for trade in Illinois. At Fort de Chartres, the storehouse was empty of Indian trade goods, and the reserve of gunpowder had been reduced to a dangerously low level. Tribes long in contact with Europeans were dependent on European goods for survival, and the general shortage of French goods led to a split among the Miami. Some maintained their traditional French allegiance, but others led by the famous chief La Demoiselle aligned with the English, who were better supplied.[4]

La Demoiselle's pro-English faction sought to strengthen its position by cajoling other tribes, including some factions of the Illinois, to ally with them and the English. These provocateurs claimed to speak for a broad array of other tribes from the north and east, urging the Illinois to turn against the French, threatening them if they did not, and promising an abundance of English trade goods if they did. As a precaution, Bertet reduced the garrison at Fort de Chartres, once again badly deteriorated, to a small guard and moved the rest of the troops and the population from the smaller communities to Kaskaskia, where he established a defensive position. Bertet also sent appeals for aid to both New Orleans and Detroit. New Orleans was finally able to scrape together some supplies for a convoy, and Detroit sent troops. Governor Vaudreuil thought the danger was exaggerated and felt the end of the war with the English would calm the situation.[5]

In fact, La Demoiselle's machinations continued into the early 1750s. He led his followers to the Ohio Country, where he established the village of Pickawillany (modern Piqua, Ohio), and the British built a trading post and stockade there. The French Métis officer Charles-Michel de Langlade, with about 240 Ottawa and Ojibwa, eliminated this threat to French territorial claims in 1752. They attacked Pickawillany, destroyed the village, and killed, boiled, and ate La Demoiselle. The raid temporarily drove British traders and settlers out of the Ohio River valley and was one of the events that marked the drift toward the French and Indian War.

There were other Indian troubles as well. Shawnee, also influenced by the English, moved increasingly into the Ohio River valley and southeastern Illinois. In 1747, the Piankashaw and Illinois attacked the Shawnee. There was even evidence of disaffection among the normally friendly Missouri and the distant Sioux, and the Chickasaw, long enemies of the French, continued to give trouble. Despite all, Bertet was successful in maintaining stability in Illinois, and he proved skilled in dealing with Indians, establishing strong personal relationships with leaders. The Jesuit Father Alexis-Xavier de Guyenne wrote to Governor Vaudreuil:

> M. de Bertet, who knew him [Rouensa, chief of the Kaskaskia tribe] well, had succeeded by tempering kindness with force in keeping him and his village in dependence. He distributed his favors wisely. On occasion he gave the chiefs the wherewithal to maintain their prestige in the village, and with those who came to see them. He spoke always with much sang-froid and presence of mind, and was accordingly so listened to, respected, and loved that the chiefs and prominent men brought their differences to him and abode by his decisions.[6]

Early in his tenure at Fort de Chartres, Bertet supported the exploration for mines in Missouri and had Fort de La Trinité constructed on the Missouri River. Initially promising mineral finds did not prove important in the long run, and the minister in Paris ordered Bertet to encourage the inhabitants of the Illinois Country to pursue agriculture rather than prospecting, although even Paris continued to have some interest in the potential mineral wealth in Missouri throughout Bertet's time in Illinois.[7]

In 1746, the king awarded the coveted Cross of Saint Louis to Bertet, and he was given permission to wear the decoration before his ceremonial induction into the order. The actual Cross of Saint Louis did not arrive in New Orleans until 1751, after Bertet's death in early 1749. Bertet was highly regarded by the people of Illinois, and his passing was greatly regretted.

TWELFTH COMMANDANT:
JEAN-JACQUES DE MACARTY MACTIQUE
(1751–60)

Early Career

Jean-Jacques de Macarty Mactique was born in France about 1708 and raised there. There is no evidence that he ever even visited Ireland, but to the French, he was always "the Irishman." In Ireland, the Macarty family had been clients of the Lords Clare, who were supporters of the Catholic King James II. The Macartys followed the Clares to France in the wake of the Glorious Revolution of 1688 and James II's failed attempt to regain the English throne. The connection between the Lords Clare and the Macartys persisted in the new country well into the eighteenth century. Charles O'Brien de Thomond, count of Thomond and of Clare, generally referred to as Milord Clare, rose to the rank of *maréchal de France*. He was Macarty's patron and repeatedly intervened to advance Macarty's career. Macarty initially served for eight years in the Régiment de Milord Clare, and then, with Clare's backing and the rank of lieutenant, Macarty was appointed adjutant major of New Orleans.[1]

Macarty arrived in New Orleans late in 1732 or at the beginning of 1733. It was a transitional moment. Périer had been relieved as governor, and Bienville had arrived to replace him. The two men and their partisans detested each other and seldom missed any opportunity to exhibit that. Macarty, like most other military officers, aligned himself with Bienville. When Périer did not immediately vacate the governor's residence upon Bienville's arrival, Bienville sent Macarty to require Périer to do so. Macarty acted in a manner that even most sympathetically could be explained only as utterly tactless. Périer, who never ignored an opportunity to complain about Bienville or a member of Bienville's faction, wrote to the minister of the marine:

> My Lord Count de Maurepas.
> My Lord:
>
> On the second of this month I received the letter
> that your Lordship has done me the honor to write
> to me in which was that of the King to hand over the

government of Louisiana to Mr. de Bienville which I
did as soon as he set foot on land, although the day before he had the grossest message in the world sent me by
Sieur Macarty, the adjutant of New Orleans, for which
I ask your Lordship for justice since I did not wish to
obtain it for myself by having him immediately put into
prison for having come to my house drunk to tell me
that if I did not decamp immediately in keeping with
the order to do so that Mr. de Bienville had given him,
he would have my furniture thrown into the street.

He finished the harangue with several dirty words
that a drunkard usually says when he has only wine and
ignorance as his guides.[2]

Macarty did depart without throwing Périer out of the dwelling, and
Périer admitted that when he complained to Bienville about Macarty's
comportment, Bienville apologized, writing that he had not intended
Macarty "to carry a harsh message to me, but that he absolutely wished
that I should take my furniture out immediately." Périer's letter continued with a rambling denunciation of Bienville and his faction and an
expression of Périer's own indignation. Little came of it. Périer had, as
he himself admitted, a reputation for quick temper and petulance. Bienville was certainly not bothered. Soon after Périer's departure, Macarty
was promoted to captain and served as Bienville's aide major as well as
adjutant major of New Orleans. The confrontation with Périer, however,
was the beginning of Macarty's reputation as a drinker.

To some degree, the reputation may have been deserved, but it should
be remembered that this was an age in which what would be considered
heavy drinking by today's standards, particularly among officers, was the
norm. Macarty's reputation may also have been due in part to the stereo-
type of the Irish, in part to modern hostile interpretation of documents
of innocent character, and in part to the calumny of Macarty's enemies.

In 1735, Macarty married, and the couple eventually had five children,
three daughters and two sons. He established an indigo plantation north
of New Orleans.[3]

Jean-Jacques's younger brother Barthélemy-Daniel de Macarty came to
Louisiana in 1737. Since both were usually called just Macarty or Makarty

in contemporary documents, it is often difficult to distinguish which brother was mentioned. Indeed, until documents bearing Jean-Jacques's full name as commandant at Fort de Chartres became available,[4] it was generally presumed that Barthélemy-Daniel held the post, and this error still occasionally persists. Of the two, Barthélemy-Daniel seems to have been the quieter and more orderly personality. He enjoyed a respectable career in Louisiana, rising to the rank of captain. Service reports describe Barthélemy-Daniel as well behaved, precise, and dignified.[5] Jean-Jacques's temper, in contrast, led him into trouble and almost cost him his career.

In late 1737 or early 1738, Macarty fought a duel against a fellow officer, Charles Petit de Livilliers. By that date, the French monarchy had outlawed duels for over a century, although officers often continued to indulge in them. We do not know what precipitated this confrontation, but any insult or slight, real or perceived, could present one or both parties with the alternatives of fighting or being judged cowardly. Either could end a career. Officers involved in a duel could hope to escape with little more than a sharp reprimand if no one was seriously injured, but Macarty killed Petit de Livilliers with a sword thrust. Macarty's career was saved by the intervention of Milord Clare, who enlisted the aid of the minister of the marine. Before the end of 1738, Macarty had been pardoned.

Macarty visited France in 1740, perhaps to express thanks to his patron and present a more favorable impression to the ministry of the marine. If so, he apparently succeeded. In addition to his continuing role as adjutant major of New Orleans, Macarty was now appointed royal lieutenant. From 1741 to 1747, Macarty served as captain in the Louisiana garrison, kept out of trouble, traveled on inspection tours in his role as adjutant major, and favorably impressed Vaudreuil, Bienville's successor as governor.

Macarty had his first experience in the Illinois Country in 1747, when he commanded the autumn convoy up the Mississippi from New Orleans. It was not an easy journey. Unseasonable heat coupled with low water made progress slow, and men fell ill. Still, Macarty must have liked what he saw of the Illinois Country, as he began a campaign, with the support of Governor Vaudreuil in New Orleans, to be appointed commandant of Fort de Chartres. In 1749, Macarty was granted leave to travel to France, supposedly to settle urgent personal business. He traveled with Vaudreuil's recommendation for the award of the prestigious Cross of Saint Louis and a commendation to the important *maréchal* Adrian-Maurice de

Noailles. Once again, Milord Clare came to Macarty's aid. The next year, the minister of the marine appointed Macarty commandant in Illinois and the king awarded him the Cross of Saint Louis, which Macarty's old commander, the now retired Bienville, ceremoniously conferred on him.

Back in Louisiana, Macarty seems to have had momentary reservations about assuming command of the Illinois Country. He requested to be relieved of his new post and again appointed royal lieutenant in New Orleans, pleading that his family and estate needed him. It is fair to speculate that Macarty's wife had refused to follow him to Illinois with their children. The ministry of the marine was not sympathetic. Macarty went to Illinois, where he would miss his family, who remained on the plantation near New Orleans.

Illinois Commandership

Major Jean-Jacques de Macarty Mactique commanded in Illinois from late 1751 until 1760, the longest tenure of any French commander. More is known about the early part of his administration than that of any other commander because of the exceptional survival of many of his post reports written in 1752 and 1753 to Governor Vaudreuil in New Orleans. Post reports were normally not forwarded to France and did not enter the archives. Governors and *commissaires-ordonnateurs* routinely incorporated information from post letters in their communications to the minister of the marine, summarizing, editing, and reinterpreting the material according to their own interests and the version of events they wished to be accepted in France. A number of Macarty's post letters survive because they were included in a trunk of Vaudreuil's papers that he shipped to France. The English captured the ship and trunk of papers, and after many vicissitudes, the Huntington Library in San Marino, California, acquired the documents.[6] Vaudreuil had ordered Macarty to report all developments to him in full detail, and Macarty certainly did so. His reports are long and detailed but sometimes abstruse, seem arbitrary in the use of pronouns and spelling, and read much like unedited journal entries.

Macarty took command of the 1751 autumn convoy to travel to his new command. It was a large convoy, bringing four new companies to Fort de Chartres and tripling the size of the garrison, for good reason. Although France and England had officially been at peace since 1748, English traders continued to move into territory claimed by France. There they used cheap trade goods and rum to persuade Indian tribes to turn against the French and ally themselves with the English. English subterfuge spread chaos throughout the tribes of le Pays d'en Haut and the Illinois Country, even jeopardizing relations between the Illinois and the French. Macarty and the troops were sent to restore order.

The convoy left in late August 1751. Water was low, and travel was slow and difficult. The troops, newly arrived from France, were not acclimatized, and malaria, brought to the Mississippi valley with African slaves a generation earlier, was becoming endemic. About twenty men died during the journey. Near the conclusion of the trip, a bateau hit a snag in the river, resulting in considerable material loss. Along with Macarty came Lieutenant Jean-Bernard Bossu, who later wrote an often unreliable account of Louisiana, including his time at Fort de Chartres.[7] The convoy arrived in Illinois in early December 1751.

Macarty carried upriver Governor Vaudreuil's detailed orders covering sixty-one manuscript pages, bearing on virtually every aspect of military administration and civilian life—including economic, legal, and even religious matters—as well as all aspects of Indian policy. Although extensive, the orders could not have prepared Macarty for all the problems he would face, and it is no wonder that in June 1752, Macarty wrote to the minister of the marine that it was all too much for a single man and requested an administrative aide.[8]

Indian Affairs

Immediately on arriving in Illinois, Macarty found himself embroiled in an Indian scare. In October 1751, Jean-Baptiste Benoist de St. Clair, acting commandant at Fort de Chartres, wrote an alarmist report to Governor Vaudreuil: Benoist feared a general revolt of Indian tribes. A group of Piankashaw and Wea allied with the English were attempting to persuade the Illinois to join their alliance. Vaudreuil felt that the fears were exaggerated.[9] Macarty took care of the situation promptly, reporting to the minister of the marine:

> I profit by the first occasion which presents itself
> to inform you, firstly of my arrival here with four
> companies. I arrived December 8 last when a party of
> Indians of the Wabash tribes [Piankashaw and Wea]

under pretense of going to war against our enemy the
Chickasaw had scattered among the various settlements.
On the same day they [the Piankashaw and Wea] killed
a soldier and two slaves and wounded an inhabitant. The
inhabitants were warned of the attacks that had been
made. Here, one part of Indians, seeing the news arrive,
and knowing what was the matter, took to flight. They
were pursued; five were killed, four made prisoners,
among them the chief of the said Piankashaw. Several
more were wounded whom I learned were dead to the
number of eighteen before reaching their villages.

This little war was caused by some rebels in the
various tribes who put themselves under the English
flag on Great Miami River, otherwise the Falls of Ohio,
where they get help from the English, who a little while
ago established several trading houses.[10]

Macarty's account is simple and direct. Only the detail of eighteen
conspirators dead from wounds seems doubtful; it may have been a gross
exaggeration, reported to Macarty in an effort to mollify French anger
and make further retaliation less likely. Macarty clearly made light of the
"little war" and even released the Piankashaw chief after a few months'
detention. The unreliable Bossu typically gave a much longer and more
dramatic account, making himself the hero who had saved the French
by a clever stratagem and claiming the French killed twenty-two of the
enemy on the spot.[11] Macarty did not even mention Bossu in either his
short report quoted above or a longer later report. The incident did spread
distrust and apprehension between the Illinois and French. As a precaution, for a while the French carried guns when they went to mass, and
two men guarded outside the church during services.[12]

Macarty soon found himself embroiled in a much greater Indian crisis.
Continuing intertribal rivalries often led to bloody violence. Although
the Illinois from time to time raided and were raided by virtually every
neighboring tribe, the Fox were the particular enemies of both the Illinois and the French in the first half of the eighteenth century, and the
Illinois took a major part in the French-orchestrated destruction of much
of the Fox tribe in 1730. Thereafter, the French attempted to maintain

peace and alliance among the midwestern tribes in order to oppose the encroachments of the English moving from the east. Nevertheless, raids and counterraids continued to take place between the Illinois and the Fox and their allies, particularly the Sauk and Sioux. In the broad sense, the persistent hostility between the Illinois and the northern tribes may be said to have been the cause of the disaster that struck the Illinois in 1752, but a band of six or seven Fox who came down from the north in 1751 set events in motion.[13]

The Fox may have been simply a hunting party, or they may have killed an Illinois woman of the Cahokia tribe—evidence is inconclusive. The Cahokia pursued and captured them and burned all but one to death, including the son of an important Fox chief. The survivor escaped, hid in a lake, and made his way back to his tribe.[14] The French, recognizing the potential of this event to stir up broader hostilities between the Fox and their allies against the Cahokia, intervened to maintain peace.[15] The French were not successful.

The Cahokia, aware that the Fox would want vengeance, moved from their primary settlement near the French village of Cahokia and settled farther south at the village of the Michigamea, a few miles north of Fort de Chartres. There they built cabins and must have hoped that the proximity of the French fort and strength in numbers would protect them.

To the north, the Fox mustered the Sauk and Kickapoo, long associated and extensively intermarried with the Fox, and the Sioux, once enemies but in recent years allied with the Fox.[16] In May 1752, warriors from these four tribes began to move south. The sources disagree about the numbers in the war party and the date of their attack. Bossu claimed the attackers numbered one thousand and filled 180 canoes. The number is suspiciously large, particularly given Bossu's tendency to exaggerate events.[17] Macarty wrote that he learned from the Peoria commandant "M. Adanville" [Adamville], who met the force after the attack three leagues from Cahokia, that they numbered four or five hundred and had some sixty canoes, with many on foot.[18] The Fox and their allies attacked on June 1, 1752, Corpus Christi Day.[19]

Bossu provided by far the most detailed account of the attack, claiming that he witnessed it from a height overlooking the village of the Michigamea. The attack, he maintained, was carefully planned for Corpus Christi Day because many of the Cahokia and Michigamea warriors would be absent, having traveled the roughly three miles south to Fort de Chartres to witness the festivities. One wonders why Bossu would have been standing on a height in the countryside during a day of holy celebration. According to Bossu, the attackers passed by the small French fort at Cahokia and, using natural cover, approached closely to the village without detection. Then a dozen warriors, selected for their speed, launched a sudden attack, firing their guns, killing indiscriminately, and retreating quickly. The enraged Cahokia and Michigamea warriors returning from Fort de Chartres armed themselves and followed the attackers, only to fall into an ambush. The main body of the Fox and their allies lay hidden in tall grass and fired a volley into the Illinois that killed twenty-eight on the spot. Then the mass of warriors attacked the village, killing men, women, and children indiscriminately. They set fire to the village, destroying cabins, food supplies, and possessions. The attackers took a number of Illinois prisoners and led them off. At no time did the Fox and their allies display any violence toward the French.[20]

Bossu recounted that as the attackers headed back north, they fired a salvo with their flintlocks, presumably celebratory, as they again passed the fort at Cahokia, and the Fox chief flew French colors from his canoe. Macarty wrote that when Adamville encountered the raiders after the attack, they showed no hostility toward him or his party, and the attackers said that they had avoided disclosing themselves to the French for fear that the French would prevent or give notice of the attack. Both Bossu and Macarty indicated that the attackers lost only four dead. According to Bossu, one of those was a major chief of Sioux, a man who had been awarded a royal medal. Macarty wrote that the attackers had warned voyageurs to be wary that summer because the Sioux were going to send out war parties to seek vengeance for "great chiefs" who had been killed.[21]

The losses of the Illinois were much greater. Bossu related that, in addition to the destruction of the village, the attackers killed or took prisoner about eighty individuals. Macarty recounted that about seventy persons of all ages and genders were killed or captured, with ten or twelve cabins burned, and he described a horrendous scene in which the limbs of the dead were scattered about. Adamville reported that the attackers had taken thirty scalps, burned three or four captives at the stake, and held a number of captives.[22]

Immediately after the attack, the Cahokia and Michigamea abandoned their burned village and moved to Fort de Chartres. Six days
later, a Frenchman coming from Cahokia brought a false report that an
enormous force, bigger than the one that had attacked them previously,
was coming to utterly destroy the Illinois. The Frenchman's tale was
detailed and specific, and he insisted that the attack was scheduled for
the next morning. The Illinois, men, women, and children, fled at night
in the midst of a storm from Fort de Chartres to Kaskaskia, the largest
of the French villages, some sixteen miles south.[23]

The Jesuit priest de Guyenne described the Illinois arriving drenched
with rain and perishing with cold.[24] The inhabitants of Kaskaskia were
initially reluctant to provide the miserable Illinois with food and shelter.
The reason may have been more than the meanness of spirit that de
Guyenne seemed to suggest. By early June, a long time had passed since
the last harvest, and it must have been already apparent that 1752 would
be a famine year. Despite the rain on the night the Illinois fled, there
was a serious drought. The corn crop failed, and rust damaged the wheat.
Private individuals did take in some refugees, and others found shelter in
the village church. De Guyenne reported that he bought wheat to feed
them. After a few days, it became apparent that the report of an attack
was false, and the refugees returned whence they came.[25]

Bossu wrote that he addressed the survivors at Macarty's direction,
giving them corn and offering them powder, shot, and flints. Macarty also
suggested that the survivors ought to plant crops before they dispersed for
the summer hunt, leaving a few people behind to tend the crops. The Illinois
argued that they could leave no one behind, since they had no resources to
sustain them until the harvest, and, clearly terrified, they wanted to leave
the area as soon as possible. Bossu also told the Illinois that Macarty had
written to Adamville at Peoria to negotiate a peace between the Fox and
Illinois and to attempt to ransom the captive women and children.[26]

In the course of late 1752 and throughout most of 1753, Macarty and
commandants of other posts managed to ransom about ten Illinois captives. In October 1753, the governor of Canada, Michel-Ange Duquesne
de Menneville, was finally able to report to the minister that peace had
been established among the tribes.[27]

That summer, Macarty had tried to bring the Cahokia and Michigamea back to their old home, but without success. The Cahokia would

never return to their old village, and the mission chapel to the Cahokia on Monks Mound was abandoned; there was no one left to serve. The Cahokia scattered, some going to live among other tribes, including the Peoria on the Illinois River and the Miami on the Wabash. Others simply disappeared in the violence of the French and Indian War and its aftermath. The situation of the Michigamea was hardly better; many of them also dispersed. Some Michigamea did manage briefly to establish a new settlement, huddled only a quarter mile from Fort de Chartres, but it was much smaller than their earlier village, with many fewer inhabitants. It was encircled by a palisade, which had never been a feature of their earlier villages, attesting to their enduring fear.[28] The Kaskaskia and Peoria, deprived of the active alliance and support of the Cahokia and Michigamea, were badly weakened.

The Stone Fort de Chartres

Among the other matters occupying Macarty's urgent attention was the question of rebuilding Fort de Chartres. He had now about three hundred men who needed permanent housing. The wooden fort, patched together since 1732, was in the last stage of decrepitude, and most of the troops had been stationed at Kaskaskia since 1748. Vaudreuil wanted a new fort built at or near Kaskaskia, by far the largest of the Illinois settlements. Macarty and François Saucier, the chief engineer sent to Illinois to design the new fort and oversee its construction, initially were not against a Kaskaskia location, but close examination changed their mind. The Kaskaskia River was frequently too shallow for transporting materials to or from a fort near the village of Kaskaskia. Potential construction sites on the same side of the Kaskaskia River as the village were wet and subject to frequent flooding, while those on the bluffs across the river had poor access to water and were not well situated to protect Kaskaskia or the other settlements.[29]

By January 1752, Macarty and Saucier settled on a site a few hundred yards from the old wooden Fort de Chartres. Between Cahokia and Kaskaskia, it offered fairly rapid communications with both, and it was close to the smaller villages of Prairie du Rocher, Chartres, and St. Philippe. Moreover, by the early 1750s, the French were moving across the Mississippi to farm the rich soil on the west side of the river a few miles south of Fort de Chartres. Macarty had instructions to encourage agricultural production, and the establishment of a new fort near the old would help protect the nascent community of Ste. Geneviève, the Missouri town that to this day preserves much of French colonial architecture and culture.[30]

The new fort was to be much larger, formidable, and made of stone, but the government in France judged the initial estimate of 450,000 livres as much too high. The government did approve a scaled-down plan with an estimate of 270,000 livres for the project, but then in mid-1753 decided to cancel the entire project. Governor Louis Billouart de Kervaségan, chevalier de Kerlérec argued, successfully, that the work was too far advanced to realize any substantial savings by canceling it, but he did mollify Versailles by reducing costs an additional 50,000 livres by reducing the thickness of the walls to only two feet.[31] Such thin walls would not have withstood artillery, but there was virtually no possibility that anyone could move substantial artillery against Fort de Chartres in the mid-eighteenth century. The fort could still house the troops of Macarty's command and provide an effective base both for the protection of the French settlements of the Illinois Country and for the gathering and dispatch of agricultural products and other supplies to the other Illinois posts and to the Ohio River valley posts administered by Canada. By 1754, the stone Fort de Chartres was substantially complete, although some features, such as the surrounding ditch, were never finished.

Jesuits and Neyon de Villiers

In addition to Indian affairs and construction of the new fort, Macarty had to deal in Illinois with Jesuit inflexibility and a duplicitous subordinate. In 1754, Pierre-Joseph Neyon de Villiers married Kerlérec's sister-in-law, Marie-Claude-Thérèse du Bot, and Kerlérec recommended that Neyon be promoted to commandant of Illinois. France, otherwise preoccupied in the opening phase of the Seven Years' War, took no action about what must have seemed a minor matter. Kerlérec's recommendation in no way reflected dissatisfaction with Macarty. Kerlérec consistently expressed a good opinion of Macarty, describing him very positively in officer evaluation reports.[32] Moreover, Macarty himself desired to be transferred back to New Orleans to be near his family and plantation.

Neyon and the Jesuits in Illinois, however, were not willing to wait patiently for France to act, and they began a program to discredit Macarty and ensure that Neyon replaced him as soon as possible. Neyon took leave in 1754 to travel to France, where he seems to have campaigned for promotion. There he also visited the Jesuit vicar general of Canada and for the Mississippi, whose impression was less than effusive:

> M. de Neyon seems a cold man, but, so he appears to
> me, gentle and firm. . . . I beg you to consider this letter
> neither as a vote in his favor nor as a recommendation
> and even to pardon the liberty which I take of writing
> to you for M. de Neyon, but he asked me so eagerly that
> I could not refuse him.[33]

In Illinois, the Jesuits saw in Neyon the advantage of having a compliant ally as commandant. The Jesuits had long condemned the provision to the Indians of brandy and rum, which Macarty, like previous commandants, continued to supply. The liquor undoubtedly did create great social and cultural ills, of which drunkenness and alcoholism were only a part, but as in the past, the Jesuits proved better at campaigning for their position than at seeking to understand all aspects of a situation. The end of the French trade in brandy and rum would not have eliminated Indian access to alcohol. They would merely have gone, as they threatened, to the British for rum. The Jesuits ignored the importance of brandy in retaining the Indians' loyalty and preventing their defection to the British, although without Indian allies, the French, numbering no more than sixty thousand in all of North America, could not possibly maintain themselves against the English, numbering more than a million.

In 1754, in connection with Neyon's visit to France, the Jesuit superior of the Louisiana Mission wrote a vituperative, slanderous letter to the Jesuit vicar general designed to undermine Macarty's position.[34] The accusations against Macarty verged on the bizarre. He was, the Jesuit maintained, a drunkard who not only corrupted the Indians, but had made alcoholics of all the French *habitants*. The Jesuit accused Macarty of responsibility for the disastrous 1752 raid of the Fox and their allies against the Cahokia and Michigamea (see Appendix B at the end of this chapter for more discussion on whether Macarty was behind the attack on the Illinois). The letter was passed on to the minister of the marine. At the same time, the Jesuit praised Neyon in the most fulsome terms: "Neyon is pious and has led a truly Christian life in Illinois. . . .

He is feared, loved, and obeyed by the soldiers. He is gentle, tractable, and tactful, and he can do much with the Indians." He went on at great length. The letter was surely written and sent with the connivance of Neyon, even though Macarty had consistently sought to advance Neyon's career.[35] Ultimately, the campaign to discredit Macarty led nowhere. The charges against Macarty were so blatantly political that they were disregarded, and Neyon had not impressed anyone in France sufficiently for them to take action.

Deserters

Many marines discovered they did not like the military life. On February 26, 1752, twenty-one of them in Illinois deserted. Macarty put together a force of his troops and thirty militiamen to go after the deserters, but two young men among the militia persuaded the other militia members not to go, whereupon Macarty arrested the pair. The *habitants*, according to Macarty, were disaffected by the service required of them in repair of a stockade, construction of the new fort, and requisitions of pork. The arrest of the two men exacerbated the situation, but Macarty calmed it by releasing them after a short interval, while the militia agreed to pursue deserters in the future. Some of the deserters were eventually captured and sent to New Orleans for punishment.[36]

Vaudreuil suggested that Macarty act with greater tact toward the *habitants* in the future,[37] yet Macarty had only been attempting to fulfill Vaudreuil's written instruction to act vigorously in the enforcement of military discipline. Macarty repeatedly found himself involved in conflicts between abstract orders from New Orleans, Canada, and even France and real conditions in Illinois. In later years, desertion continued to be a problem, though men tended to abscond in smaller groups, usually two or three at a time, perhaps primarily disgruntled by the heavy labor and dangers of convoy duties during the French and Indian War.

Supplying the Western Pennsylvania Posts

In 1752, Duquesne became the governor general of Canada. Duquesne had four new fortified posts built in the Ohio River valley in 1753 and early 1754 as the focus of resistance against the English ambitions across the Alleghenies (fig. 2.3). Fort Duquesne, at the Forks of the Ohio (modern

Pittsburgh), where the Allegheny and Monongahela Rivers join to form the Ohio River, was the most important of these. Even in time of peace, it was difficult to supply these posts, especially since crops had failed in Canada in 1752. Duquesne ordered Macarty to furnish provisions for the posts, but Duquesne's demands were excessive. Crops had also failed in Illinois that year because of drought and were only a little better in 1753 as a result of heavy rains. In addition to what the *habitants* of Illinois consumed of their own production, Macarty had to supply his own posts and Indian allies. In poor years, little remained, and even in good years, it would strain resources to supply the Pennsylvania posts as well (fig. 2.4). It was also slow, expensive, difficult, and dangerous to ship large bateaux of food down the Mississippi and then far up the Ohio, a trip of about fourteen hundred miles, much of it against the current, and the laborious trip could be undertaken only when water levels permitted. The return trip frequently had to be made under poor conditions and could be equally taxing.[38]

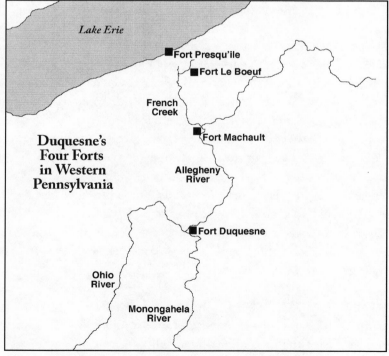

Fig. 2.3. Duquesne's four forts in western Pennsylvania

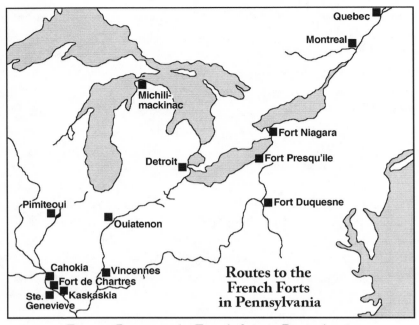

Fig. 2.4. Routes to the French forts in Pennsylvania

When Macarty was not able to supply promptly everything demanded, Duquesne, a man with a well-earned reputation for a bad temper and irritability, wrote to the minister of the marine denouncing Macarty.[39] In 1754 and 1755, the crops fared better than in the previous two years, and despite some scarcity, Macarty's system for supplying the Ohio posts from Fort de Chartres was working well. Even the irascible governor of Canada was mollified, but he thoughtlessly damaged the economy of Illinois by awarding exclusive trade rights in the Lake Erie and Ohio River valley area to select Canadian friends. Moreover, since supplies that normally would have gone from Illinois to New Orleans were diverted to the western posts, Lower Louisiana had to obtain flour from Saint-Domingue and reship some upriver to the Arkansas, Natchez, and Pointe Coupée garrisons at great expense.[40]

The French and Indian War

The formal declaration of war in 1756 was almost anticlimactic in America. There, the peace that had officially prevailed since 1748 was at best an armed truce and at worst a proxy war conducted by Indians and traders.

Duquesne was replaced as governor of Canada in mid-1755 by Vaudreuil, transferred from Louisiana. Crops failed again in 1756 and 1757, and Canada suffered severe famine during the winter of 1757–58. Despite poor harvests, the men and marines of Illinois gathered provisions and operated bateaux, carrying enormous amounts of flour and other supplies to the posts in western Pennsylvania. For example, late in 1755, Captain Jean-Daniel Dumas, the commandant of Fort Duquesne, wrote to Macarty that the English had cut his communications with Canada and made a request: "In such a delicate situation, I take it upon myself, Sir, to ask you for food. We need 120,000 pounds of flour and 40,000 of salt pork."[41] Macarty gathered all he could and sent it by convoy as early as possible in 1756. Even with the supplies from Illinois, however, the Ohio posts faced serious shortages, and garrisons had to be reduced in size.

During the war, no shot was ever fired in anger at Fort de Chartres, but in addition to supplying the French posts faithfully at tremendous labor, men from the garrison and settlements in Illinois took part in combat against the English. Two officers from Fort de Chartres, François Coulon de Villiers and Charles-Philippe Aubry, were most prominent in this role.

François Coulon de Villiers was one of six brothers.[42] Because of the practice of referring to officers in contemporary documents simply by their family names, François has often been confused with his brother Louis Coulon de Villiers and with Macarty's second in command, Pierre-Joseph Neyon de Villiers, who was no relation.

In 1754, while England and France were still at peace, another of François's brothers, Joseph Coulon de Villiers de Jumonville, led a small group of French to notify the British that they were trespassing on territory claimed by France. George Washington, commanding a detachment of Virginia militia, ambushed Jumonville's party, killing him and a number of others. This event played a major role in precipitating the French and Indian War. Louis Coulon de Villiers defeated Washington and forced his surrender at Fort Necessity that same year and captured Fort William Henry in 1757, before falling victim to smallpox.

François Coulon de Villiers served as a lieutenant in Illinois from 1746 to 1754, when he was promoted to captain. In early 1756, he headed the convoy that took supplies from Fort de Chartres to Fort Duquesne. Villiers then led a party of sixty men, half French and half Indians, to attack English communications in the area of Fort Cumberland, but he and many of his party fell ill, and the expedition had to return to the French base. After he recovered, he led a party of twenty-two French and thirty-two Illinois, Shawnee, and Delaware against Fort Granville on the Juniata River in southern Pennsylvania. Fort Granville was a substantial wooden fort with four bastions defended by a garrison of 200 men and two cannons. The French arrived at an advantageous moment, shortly after 150 men of the garrison left the fort to guard farmers at harvest some distance away. Villiers led an attack on the fort that continued all day, and during the night he had firewood collected and piled around the base of one the bastions, which he burned. By dawn, Villiers's forces had breached the fort and killed a number of the defenders, including two officers.[43] The fort surrendered, and thirty soldiers, three women, and seven children were taken prisoner. Stories soon spread in the English colonies that the French and Indians had massacred the prisoners. These stories persisted well into the nineteenth century and are still occasionally repeated.[44]

In fact, one prisoner, a sergeant, was tortured and killed by an Indian in personal revenge for a vicious beating the sergeant had inflicted on the Indian in the past. The French and Indians divided the prisoners according to custom, and Villiers brought them back to Fort de Chartres, where the French officers and civilians ransomed the prisoners held by the Indians. All the prisoners were then escorted to New Orleans, exchanged, and sent to England.[45] By the time that information reached the colonies, the capture of Fort Granville was old news, the legend of the French massacre had been well established, and apparently no one was much interested in the truth. Fort Granville was an important strongpoint, and its destruction led to the abandonment of Pennsylvania's westernmost post, Fort Shirley. In effect, Pennsylvania's defensive front was thrust back to the east, and soon raiders struck within seventy-five miles of Philadelphia.

In 1757, Villiers with two hundred Indians raided into what is now West Virginia, taking a number of prisoners. The next year, Captain Charles-Philippe Aubry led a detachment, including Villiers, from Fort de Chartres to reinforce Fort Duquesne. That year the brilliant English brigadier (acting) John Forbes moved against Fort Duquesne. One of Forbes's subordinates, Colonel Henry Bouquet, sent a column of eight hundred men under Major James Grant to seize Fort Duquesne by surprise attack, but they were detected. Aubry and the men from Fort de

Chartres were part of the force that fell upon Grant and his command, utterly routing it. The English suffered over two hundred casualties, killed or captured, including Grant himself, who was sent to Canada as a prisoner.[46] Shortly after, Aubry and his forces participated in an attack on Loyalhanna,[47] where Forbes's men were constructing Fort Ligonier. The French caused some casualties, but the English retreated to the fort, which was sufficiently advanced for defense and had artillery already emplaced. Against it, the French could make no headway.

At the same time that Forbes advanced toward Fort Duquesne, he conducted an able diplomatic offensive, persuading the Indians in the area to abandon their long-standing alliance with the French. Without Indian allies, the commandant of Fort Duquesne, Captain François-Marie Le Marchand de Lignery, had available only a hopelessly outnumbered garrison of three hundred, only a hundred of whom were fully fit. Faced with the inevitable, Lignery loaded cannons, munitions, and prisoners on the Illinois bateaux and sent them with the Illinois marines and militia back to Fort de Chartres. Lignery then demolished Fort Duquesne with fire and a tremendous explosion of gunpowder, heard by Forbes's men ten miles distant. Lignery retreated to Fort Machault, near the confluence of the Rivière aux Boeufs (French Creek) and the Allegheny River, to await developments.

In 1759, Aubry and Villiers and about three hundred marines and militiamen from Illinois moved up the lower Ohio, then up the Wabash and the Little River, from which they portaged to the Maumee River and then along the shores of Lake Ontario, eventually reaching Fort Machault, where they joined with Lignery's forces. When the English besieged Fort Niagara, the French forces rushed to its relief. Near La Belle Famille, a site about a mile south of the fort, the British built an abatis and a log breastwork manned by about 450 regulars and provincial troops. Iroquois, numbering about 450, took positions in the woods on the flanks. The Indian allies of the French deserted them just before the battle, with the exception of the small bands of Kansas and Little Osage, who had come with the men from Illinois, and a few Chippewa. About 600 French and the few Indians, a mixture of regulars, marines, and militiamen and the Kansas and Little Osage, made a brave but futile frontal attack, attempting to break through to Fort Niagara. Over half were killed or captured. Lignery was fatally wounded; Aubry and Villiers were both seriously wounded. Losses from the Illinois consisted of six officers, two cadets, two sergeants, two corporals, thirty marines, and fifty-four militiamen. With the defeat of the relief force and the walls breached by English artillery, Fort Niagara surrendered.[48]

Indians took both Aubry and Villiers captive and badly abused them. The Indians told Villiers that they were going to burn him at the stake, and the same fate probably would have awaited Aubry, but both were rescued by English officers and sent to New York as prisoners.[49]

Fort de L'Ascension/Fort Massiac

As French control of the upper Ohio River valley was increasingly contested by the English, Macarty ordered a fort built to control the lower Ohio. French officials had long realized the need to interdict both English movement down the Ohio River and raids from the south by the Chickasaw and Cherokee, allied to the English, but despite discussions, surveys, and even the drawing of plans, nothing specific was done until 1757. Then Macarty sent Captain Charles-Philippe Aubry with 150 French, 100 Indians, and three pieces of artillery to establish the fort on a low bluff on the Ohio, at the site of modern Metropolis, Illinois, close to Paducah, Kentucky.[50] The fort was initially called Fort de L'Ascension, as construction commenced on the Feast Day of the Ascension. The fort consisted of a square about 168 feet on each side with four bastions and two large internal buildings to house the garrison, which initially consisted of about 110 French marines and militia and about 50 or 60 Indians.[51]

The fort was constructed in haste with whatever timber was locally available, probably mainly cottonwood, which rots quickly. The Cherokee attacked the fort in the autumn of 1757, but the garrison repulsed them easily. In 1758, the garrison was reduced to fifty. Raids by Chickasaw and Cherokee continued in 1758 and 1759. They did not attack the fort again but wasted no opportunity to ambush members of the garrison outside the precinct. They killed seventeen during these two years, including an officer and a sergeant.[52]

The fall of Fort Duquesne and the disaster at Fort Niagara increased both the threat to Fort de L'Ascension and its defensive significance. Late in 1759 or early in 1760, Macarty ordered the fort strengthened and substantially rebuilt *pièce sur pièce*—walls solidly constructed of dressed logs laid horizontally and dovetailed at the corners—and additionally

protected by substantial earthworks and sharpened stakes. Macarty renamed the post Fort Massiac in honor of Claude-Louis d'Espinchal,
marquis de Massiac, the minister of the marine.[53] The order to reconstruct
the fort was one of Macarty's last acts as commandant of Fort de Chartres.

Later Career

In mid-1759, Macarty was commissioned as royal lieutenant and major
of New Orleans, essentially second in military command to Governor
Kerlérec. It took time for the commission to reach Illinois, and it was not
until mid-1760 that Macarty was able to assume his new post and return
to his family and home near New Orleans, as he had so long desired.
He left Neyon behind in command at Fort de Chartres, the post he had
so long desired.

Macarty had gone to the Illinois post before Kerlérec came to Louisiana. The two had never met, but they had developed respect for one another and maybe even closeness through their extensive correspondence,
despite Macarty's often peculiar prose. Kerlérec saw in Macarty a strong
aide, which he needed greatly. Kerlérec and Vincent-Gaspard-Pierre de
Rochemore, the *commissaire-ordonnateur*, were engaged in a bitter feud
that crippled government and divided Louisiana society. Canada had
fallen, and the fate of Louisiana was uncertain. Two English ships block-
aded the port of Mobile. Supplies of every sort were in short supply, and
the Indians were restive.

Shortly after Macarty's arrival, Kerlérec journeyed to Mobile for the
governor's annual month-long meetings with the allied tribes. The royal
storehouses that normally contained subsidies and gifts for the Indians
were nearly empty, and lest he go empty-handed, Kerlérec ordered the
confiscatory purchase of all trade goods in private hands, especially red
and blue Limbourg cloth, which was much prized by the Indians.[54] While
Kerlérec was at Mobile, Macarty governed at New Orleans.

Macarty played only a minor role in the Kerlérec-Rochemore feud,
but as an ally of Kerlérec, he endured petty insults from Rochemore
supporters,[55] and when he arrested Rochemore's gardener for illegal trading, the *commissaire-ordonnateur* complained that Macarty's actions were
partisan.[56] The royal government recalled Rochemore in 1761, and he
finally returned to France in 1762, but political uncertainty and internecine
quarrels continued to disrupt Louisiana. Macarty stayed in his offices

until at least December 1762,[57] and he probably retired in 1763 with the official cession of New Orleans to the Spanish.

In 1763, the royal government ordered the expulsion of the Jesuits from France and all French possessions. In accord with the royal decree, the Superior Council of Louisiana confiscated Jesuit possessions and ordered the Jesuits to report to New Orleans for deportation to Europe. In Illinois, the Jesuits had complained and conspired against Macarty, but when they arrived from Illinois with virtually nothing but their clothes and a few books, Macarty opened his home to them and extended aid until their departure.[58]

Macarty did not enjoy retirement long. He died in New Orleans on April 20, 1764. Jean-Jacques-Blaise d'Abbadie, the acting governor, recorded in his journal:

> M. de Macarty, former lieutenant of the king, is dead. For the funeral procession, I called out all the garrison's troops, about eighty men, and three cannons were fired when the body was brought out of the house. Four officers were named to carry the pall. Although these honors were not due to M. Macarty [as he was no longer in office], I ordered them in consideration of his memory and for his family.[59]

Appendix A: Sources for the Fox Attack of 1752

There are several historical sources for the events that precipitated the attack in 1752, the attack itself, and its aftermath. Each differs in some details, and each provides some material not included in the others. Some aspects remain obscure, but the sources combine to provide a reasonably accurate account. A letter from Jacques-Pierre de Taffanel de La Jonquière, governor of Canada, to Antoine-Louis Rouillé, minister of the marine, gives a brief account of events in 1751 that precipitated the carnage in 1752.[60] Bossu was an eyewitness and our fullest source for the events in 1752,[61] but he romanticized and exaggerated his personal role in affairs and larded his work on his experiences in Louisiana with details he could not have known. Official accounts by Major Macarty report the events of 1751 and 1752. Macarty was not an eyewitness, but he was in the authoritative position to receive first-person reports from the involved parties. His reports, however, are mere summaries, lacking in detail, incorporated into larger accounts of events in and around the Illinois Country.[62] La Jonquière and Vaudreuil derived their material in part from reports of Macarty and Pierre-Paul de La Marque de Marin that are no longer extant.[63] De Guyenne must have relied largely on oral reports of the attack, although he was a primary witness to later events.

The letters of de Guyenne, Macarty, and Bossu provide information about the travails of the Cahokia and Michigamea in the aftermath of the attack. De Guyenne, always concerned to show his Cahokia charges in the best light, portrayed Macarty as unsympathetic and unhelpful, while Macarty claimed he gave aid but the Illinois were fearful and uncooperative.

Appendix B: Was Macarty behind the Attack on the Illinois?

Several sources accuse or mention the accusation that Major Macarty planned the attack of the Fox and their allies on the Cahokia and Michigamea in order to punish and weaken these potentially rebellious tribes, and one modern historian, R. E. Hauser, has argued that the report is true.[64] The notion is inherently dubious. It would have required Macarty, newly arrived in Illinois, to have entered into a complex conspiracy with Marin, the commandant at Green Bay, who was the official dealing with the Fox Indians and their allies. Macarty was part of the Louisiana command, while Marin was part of the Canadian command, and there is no indication that Macarty and Marin had ever met. It seems highly unlikely that either man would have endangered his career by entering into a complex conspiracy with a stranger, contrary to all policies of their respective commands.

In addition to the inherent improbability of the conspiracy, the bases for the accusation are slender and lack credibility. First, there were mere rumors among the Illinois. These fears and suspicions were due to the Illinois' guilty conscience over their role in the conspiracy against the French in late 1751. Macarty himself reported such rumors and clearly felt they required no answer, nor did his superiors make any inquiry into the rumors or do anything else indicating they took them seriously.[65] If Macarty's superiors had been part of a plot to attack the Illinois, it would have been discussed without fear in their correspondence, to which the Indians had no access. If they suspected Macarty had been acting without orders, they would have, at a minimum, instituted an inquiry, demanding full details and explanations from all parties concerned in the matter.

Second, a Sauk chief secretly told the prisoners whom he released to the Peoria that "the French were the cause of the attack," and the Wabash tribes also claimed "the French" were responsible.[66] The Sauk and Wabash tribes obviously sought to mitigate their own role in the attack, deflect retribution, and drive a wedge between the French and Illinois. Even Hauser, who argued for Macarty's guilt, recognized that the northern tribes' reports "might be discounted because of the conflicting interests that would have seen them quite satisfied with any Illinois alienation from the French."[67] Again, Macarty reported these accusations and felt no need to defend himself, and his superiors made no inquiries. In contrast to these rumors, de Guyenne, a Jesuit missionary to the Cahokia, reported that a prisoner who had been taken by the Fox and later released convinced the Cahokia that the French had known nothing of the attack.[68]

For Hauser, the strongest evidence is a letter by the Jesuit superior of the Louisiana Mission, Michel Baudouin.[69] The missive, discussed above, is a masterpiece of character assassination and gross exaggeration, a scurrilous attempt to blacken Macarty behind his back and have him replaced with a favorite of the Jesuits, Neyon de Villiers. Even in this letter he provides no direct evidence against Macarty and relies heavily on the unsubstantiated reports from the northern Indians. Again, Macarty's superiors paid no attention to the accusations.

In short, Macarty's involvement is inherently unlikely and rests on no solid evidence whatsoever.

THIRTEENTH COMMANDANT:
PIERRE-JOSEPH NEYON DE VILLIERS
(1760–63)

Early Career

Pierre-Joseph Neyon de Villiers was born in France about 1718 to a poor noble family. He was commissioned ensign in the French Army in 1735 and rose to captain in 1747. The end of war in 1748 brought the specter of demobilization, which he avoided by attaining appointment as captain in the marines in Louisiana in 1751 through the influence of the Duc de Luxembourg. As one of his last acts before departing Illinois in 1752, Vaudreuil proposed Jean-Jacques de Macarty Mactigue as commandant of the Illinois Country and Neyon de Villiers as second in command.

In Louisiana, Kerlérec became governor in 1753, and Neyon de Villiers married Kerlérec's sister-in-law, Marie-Claude-Thérèse du Bot, the following year. Kerlérec recommended to the minister of the marine that Neyon succeed Macarty as commandant of Illinois. Kerlérec consistently gave Macarty good evaluations and was not dissatisfied with his performance in Illinois, but Macarty desired to be transferred back to New Orleans to be near his family and plantation, and this was an obvious opportunity to advance Neyon's career. By 1754, however, the royal government was engaged in the Seven Years' War, and sorting out assignments in distant Louisiana was not a high priority.

Meanwhile, the Jesuits in Illinois opposed the policy, supported by Macarty, of providing alcohol to the Indians, ignoring that it was necessary to retain their loyalty. The Jesuits saw in the sanctimonious Neyon someone who would agree to abolish the trade in brandy and rum. Realizing it might be years before the royal government would act on Neyon's promotion unless prodded into action, Neyon and the Jesuits formed an alliance to discredit Macarty and hasten Neyon's appointment.[1] Their efforts failed, and Neyon had to wait until 1760 to become commandant of Fort de Chartres and the entire Illinois Country.

The years must have seemed to pass slowly for Neyon. Documents contain relatively little about his activities between 1754 and 1760. He seems to have spent almost all the time at Fort de Chartres serving as Macarty's administrative assistant. He conducted no raids against the English like Charles-Philippe Aubry and François Coulon de Villiers, although writers, deceived by the similarity of names, have sometimes attributed Coulon de Villiers's activities to Neyon de Villiers.[2] We know he broke his leg in 1758, but the details of how he received the injury are lacking.

Also in 1758, Kerlérec, frustrated that his recommendation that Neyon be promoted to major commandant of Illinois had not been approved, repeated the recommendation and also nominated Neyon for the Cross of Saint Louis. Both were finally granted in 1759, and Neyon became commandant early in 1760, when Macarty was reassigned as royal lieutenant and major of New Orleans.

Pierre-Joseph Neyon de Villiers had waited to become commandant of Fort de Chartres for six years, and he held the post for almost exactly three years. During that period, he faced such problems that he must have wondered if the long-sought promotion were a curse rather than a blessing.

Political Feuding in Louisiana and Illinois

As the brother-in-law of Governor Kerlérec, Neyon was inevitably made a party to conflicts involving the governor, the most virulent and destructive of which was the feud between Kerlérec and the *commissaire-ordonnateur* Vincent-Gaspard-Pierre de Rochemore, who came to Louisiana in 1758. The feud became so bitter that Rochemore lashed out at anyone allied to Kerlérec, and Kerlérec behaved similarly. When in 1760 Kerlérec, in response to a slight toward a member of his faction, nullified the appointment of Rochemore's brother-in-law, de Normand, as *commissaire* for Illinois, Rochemore refused to redeem any letters of exchange from Illinois.

Letters of exchange were written pledges to settle debts by making payments at specific future dates. In this case, the *commissaire* in Illinois would normally draw letters of exchange to pay expenses incurred by the Illinois command, and the letters of exchange would eventually be redeemed by the *commissaire-ordonnateur* in New Orleans. Letters of exchange were legitimate negotiable instruments that could be transferred to third and even subsequent parties. By refusing to redeem letters of exchange from Illinois, Rochemore not only crippled Neyon's ability to purchase necessities for his command but also reduced to chaos financial relations in the Illinois Country in general, where the letters of exchange frequently passed from hand to hand, functioning rather like currency.[3] The controversy was put to rest and letters of exchange from Illinois were again accepted when de Normand's nomination was apparently withdrawn and he was given the post of royal scrivener in New Orleans.

Antoine-Simon Griffon d'Anneville, who had been the *garde-magasin* (storehouse keeper) at Fort de Chartres since 1759, then exercised the additional position of local *commissaire*. According to Kerlérec, Anneville, who was an appointee of Rochemore's, opposed Neyon in Illinois much as Rochemore opposed Kerlérec in New Orleans.[4]

In 1762, Rochemore was recalled to France, but he did not leave the colony until 1763. As a parting shot, late in 1762, Rochemore appointed Antoine Fazende as *commissaire* for Illinois.[5] Fazende had become an ensign in 1754 and never rose above that rank, although he served until 1766, the last few years in the caretaker garrison waiting for the Spanish takeover. In 1758, Kerlérec described him as "an unpretentious officer, narrow-minded, lacking any talent, but having a good attitude toward the service."[6] When Fazende and an assistant, Lefèvre d'Inglebert, departed New Orleans for Illinois, they brought so much baggage that the convoy had to add a bateau, at royal expense. The pair never reached Illinois. Falling ill at the Arkansas Post, they returned to New Orleans, and Rochemore's replacement appointed others.[7]

The La Chapelle Affair

While the recall of Rochemore lessened Neyon's annoyance from that quarter, his troubles multiplied from other sources. Québec fell to the British in the autumn of 1759, and the French attempt to recapture the city failed in 1760 when the English fleet arrived with reinforcements. With the fall of Montréal, substantial French resistance ended in Canada. Louisiana and particularly Illinois, previously a backwater of the war, now became central concerns. Indians and French escaping from the advancing British moved from the north into the Illinois Country. The Illinois tribes, although grown weak in numbers and military prowess, resented the intrusion of other tribes into the area. There was only relatively minor intertribal violence, but an already tense and unsettled situation was made more so.

At Detroit, a young French captain, Pierre Passerat de La Chapelle, obtained leave from his commanding officer to attempt an almost impossible feat, as outlined in the following letter given him by his commanding officer[8]:

> I approve entirely, sir, your determination to lead the
> detachment which I entrusted to your command, to
> New Orleans, in order not to be forced to deliver it up to
> the English and to preserve this troop for His Majesty's
> service. You are undertaking a difficult task full of peril
> and danger. I know that you are brave, hardy, energetic,
> and resourceful in adversity; you know how to com-
> mand and how to secure obedience. But the leading of a
> detachment of 200 men towards so distant a destination
> across an inhospitable country and one unknown to you,
> without a guide or a second officer is not an easy task.
> You will have to surmount many difficulties; winter ap-
> proaches. My best wishes accompany you; in spite of the

miseries that you will have to endure your lot is happier
than mine. For I shall have the shame of turning over
my garrisons to the English and becoming their prisoner. Sad end to a career! Pity me; be of good courage
and the grace of God go with you.

Bellestre[9]

La Chapelle would indeed face great difficulties, none greater than Neyon
de Villiers!

La Chapelle's command swelled to an even greater number. The
commandant at Detroit had disbanded the Ottawa militia, 110 men,
both Canadian French and Métis (of mixed French and Indian par-
entage), who also wished to avoid English captivity and were moving
toward Louisiana. He proposed to take them along with his troops,
which they accepted. La Chapelle and his command then moved west
from Detroit to Lake Michigan, suffering attacks from hostile Indians
on the way. They moved south along the shore, then across country to
the southwest, reaching the Illinois River near the old Fort St. Louis
(modern Starved Rock), which La Salle had established long before.
Discovering that Fort St. Louis had long been destroyed, La Chapelle
and his men built a fort and snug winter cabins on Buffalo Rock, on
the north side of the river a few miles to the east of the ruins of Fort
St. Louis. La Chapelle named the camp Fort Ottawa in honor of the
ex-militiamen who had aided the troops so much in fighting off Indian
attacks, hunting, and building the fort.[10] Through trade with the Illinois
Indians in the area, the hunting skills of the former militia members,
and conservation of the provisions brought from Detroit, La Chapelle's
men were comfortably situated for the winter. Canada had surrendered,
but hope endured that France would remain in control of Louisiana,
including the Illinois Country. The ex-militiamen elected to stay at Fort
Ottawa in the spring, when La Chapelle intended to continue with his
troops to New Orleans.

Shortly before the fall of Montréal, Governor Vaudreuil ordered Captain Louis-Joseph Liénard de Beaujeu de Villemonde, commandant at
Michilimackinac (now Mackinaw City, Michigan), to evacuate his troops
to Illinois rather than surrender to the English.[11] Beaujeu departed in
October with four officers and 128 enlisted men. Beaujeu and his men

established winter camp on the Rock River to the west of Fort Ottawa, but they fared poorly, with little shelter and few provisions, and were ravaged by illness. Men died; others deserted.

In December, an officer of Beaujeu's command came to Fort Ottawa seeking aid. La Chapelle immediately prepared a relief convoy, which he accompanied to Beaujeu's camp. Beaujeu peremptorily ordered La Chapelle to carry a letter personally to Fort de Chartres. When La Chapelle explained he was needed at Fort Ottawa because there was no other officer to assume command, Beaujeu threatened to arrest La Chapelle and send him to Fort de Chartres bound. La Chapelle reluctantly set out for the fort on foot, a long and miserable trip in the midst of winter. On his arrival, Neyon de Villiers accused La Chapelle of desertion from Detroit and ordered him to return to Beaujeu carrying a sealed letter and some small amount of provisions.

On the journey back, La Chapelle injured his foot. When he encountered one of Beaujeu's officers, he entrusted the letter and provisions to him, and then La Chapelle returned to his men at Fort Ottawa. There he discovered that no sooner had he departed for Fort de Chartres than Beaujeu sent one of his officers to take command of Fort Ottawa, along with the troops, ex-militia (lawfully discharged at Detroit), cabins, and provisions. The former militia members, however, refused to yield the fort to Beaujeu's man, and by the time La Chapelle was finally able to return to Fort Ottawa, most of his troops were willing to desert and join the ex-militia. La Chapelle calmed the situation and decided not to yield to either Neyon or Beaujeu, but rather to follow the commission he had received in Detroit to take his troops to New Orleans.

The ex-militiamen and local Indians helped La Chapelle and his men prepare for the trek. For thirty days, La Chapelle and the men, guided by Indians, dragged heavy sledges through deep snow. Avoiding Fort de Chartres and Neyon de Villiers, La Chapelle and his party reached the Mississippi south of the fort. There they built barges and canoes, obtained still more canoes from Indians in the area, and set out for New Orleans by water. La Chapelle and his entire command, intact and in good health, arrived on April 20, 1761, completing an epic journey of well over twelve hundred miles.

Rather than receiving congratulations and appreciation of his achievement, however, La Chapelle found that his troubles were far from over. Neyon had written an accusatory report to his brother-in-law, Governor Kerlérec, who ordered La Chapelle back to Fort de Chartres. Neyon immediately had La Chapelle incarcerated in the Fort de Chartres prison.

Beaujeu and Neyon then made cardinal errors. Beaujeu, furious that La Chapelle had refused to surrender his command to him, accused La Chapelle of criminal acts of insubordination, misappropriation of authority, and misuse of royal funds. By accusing La Chapelle of military crimes, Beaujeu had, without realizing it, effectively removed the case against La Chapelle from Neyon's disciplinary authority, which extended only to minor offenses. Such accusations could be judged only by a court-martial, a much higher authority, which would be held in France.

Neyon now, realizing Beaujeu's mistake, attempted to intimidate La Chapelle into silence. He continued to imprison La Chapelle, stopped La Chapelle's letters addressed to Governor Kerlérec, alternately cajoled and threatened La Chapelle to desist from insisting on a court-martial, searched La Chapelle's possessions illegally, attempted to confiscate his copies of important documents that would facilitate his defense, seized writing materials, and tried to substitute rewritten documents for originals.[12] La Chapelle remained unmoved and managed to thwart Neyon's plans at every turn. Growing desperate, Neyon pled that Beaujeu was a Canadian, less than perfectly fluent in French, and had merely expressed himself poorly. This was clearly false; Beaujeu was an experienced, mature officer from a distinguished Canadian military family.[13]

Finally, Neyon and Beaujeu attempted to rewrite the charges against La Chapelle, reducing them to insignificance, and appealing to the fraternal brotherhood of officers, Neyon sought to persuade La Chapelle to simply let the whole matter pass away quietly. La Chapelle, however, remained unmoved: the accusations had been made public and thus had challenged his honor as a gentleman and an officer. He demanded the court-martial.

Neyon eventually had no alternative but to release La Chapelle, who did get his court-martial in France. He was completely exonerated and even rewarded with a pension in recognition of his remarkable retreat. Both Governor Kerlérec and Neyon de Villiers received letters of reprimand for their behavior in regard to La Chapelle.[14]

Kerlérec's Indian Strategy and Pontiac's War

Neyon had still bigger problems to face. Rumors reached him that the British were assembling enormous forces to march on Illinois, and there was little he could do about it. Neyon did increase the garrison at Fort Massiac, first sending Philippe-François de Rastel de Rocheblave as commandant with fifty men,[15] and then further supplementing the garrison with the troops that Beaujeu had brought to Fort de Chartres. These measures might have proved a hindrance to raids into the Illinois Country by English-allied tribes south of the Ohio River, but if the British sent a major force down the Ohio River, Fort Massiac could hardly be expected to provide more than a slight delay. If the British moved from Detroit or Michilimackinac, Neyon could offer even less resistance. He had no significant strongpoints between the British in the north and Fort de Chartres itself, and the fort, designed only to overawe and perhaps repulse an Indian attack, could not resist artillery.

Governor Kerlérec had anticipated that a time might come when Louisiana would have to defend itself. He thought that the allied tribes, guided and supplied by the French, could be united into an effective force against the British. Working with little support, perpetually short of goods and munitions to supply the Indians, Kerlérec managed to counter British attempts to win over the Choctaw and masterfully established an alliance with the Cherokee (figs. 2.5 and 2.6). Although Lower Louisiana was critically short of gunpowder to supply the allied southern tribes and for local defense, Kerlérec shipped several thousand pounds of the precious substance to Fort de Chartres so that Neyon could distribute it to the Cherokee and other tribes. In the summer of 1760, the Cherokee put that gunpowder to use, destroying Fort Loudoun (in what is now western Tennessee) and killing or capturing the entire garrison and resident civilians. In early 1762, France had not yet decided definitely to divest itself of Louisiana and the Illinois Country, and the government finally decided to embrace Kerlérec's plan to rally the Indian allies. That year, a French convoy loaded with troops and supplies arrived in Louisiana. Kerlérec encouraged the southern tribes to organize an offensive against the British and sent orders to Neyon to do the same with the Illinois and other northern tribes, coordinating their effort with the southern tribes.

Fig. 2.5. Governor Kerlérec's commission of the Cherokee chief Okana-Stoté, February 27, 1761. U.S. National Archives.

Kerlérec's plan ultimately failed. British naval dominance limited the flow of resources from France, the feud between Kerlérec and the *ordonnateur* Rochemore crippled government in Louisiana, the government in France supported the effort too little and too late, and the corrupt contractor responsible for the 1762 convoy sent only a fraction of the supplies that were supposed to be on the ships, and those were of poor quality. Finally, the pusillanimous French regime ceded Louisiana to Spain.[16] Nevertheless, Kerlérec's planning provided organization and inspiration for Pontiac's uprising, which involved, with few exceptions, those northern tribes long allied with the French whom Kerlérec and Neyon had encouraged to unite against the British. This analysis contrasts with the earlier conventional interpretation, based almost entirely on British sources, that the hostilities were due primarily to Indian frustration with British policies and behavior.[17]

On November 3, 1762, France ceded by secret treaty New Orleans and French holdings west of the Mississippi to Spain. On February 10, the final treaty ending the Seven Years' War was signed by representatives

Fig. 2.6. Vignette of Governor Kerlérec and
Cherokee chief Okana-Stoté, February 27, 1761.
Detail of the commission. U.S. National Archives.

of France, Britain, and Spain. On April 7, news of the end of hostilities
reached New Orleans. The cession to Britain of the French territories
east of the Mississippi, with the exception of New Orleans and the land
immediately surrounding it, was quickly made public, but the cession of
New Orleans and the French territories west of the Mississippi to Spain
was not announced officially until September,[18] although rumors had
circulated throughout the summer.

In the north, Pontiac and his allies struck in May 1763. Over the next
few months, they captured or destroyed eight British-held forts and besieged Forts Detroit, Pitt, and Duquesne. The Indians expected that the
French would support their offensive with munitions and supplies, and
these expectations focused most particularly on Neyon, who, at Fort de
Chartres, was vitally situated to provide such aid. In October, however,
Jean-Jacques-Blaise d'Abbadie, who had succeeded Kerlérec as governor,
wrote to Neyon informing him that peace had been established between

France and Britain and ordering Neyon to end the Indian offensive and reconcile the tribes to British rule. Neyon dispatched officers to tell the tribes to cease their war and repeatedly refused to supply Pontiac and other Indians engaged against the British. Some fighting continued into 1764, but the French refusal to supply the Indians essentially put an end to the war.

Leaving Illinois

By the time Neyon de Villiers received official notice that the French and Indian War was over, his plans to leave Fort de Chartres and Louisiana for France were already far advanced. On October 28, 1763, in New Orleans, Madame Marie-Claude-Thérèse du Bot, acting in her own name and for her husband, Neyon de Villiers, conveyed to Kerlérec "the sum of 80,463 livres, 17 sols, and 1 denier in colonial currency . . . for the purpose of converting the said notes into drafts to be drawn . . . in Paris."[19] Neyon and his wife, in short, had cashed out their holding in Louisiana and were sending the money back to France with Kerlérec, who departed for France on November 17.

Over the next months, Neyon cooperated with British representatives who reached Illinois well in advance of any appreciable body of troops and prepared in haste to leave Illinois. On December 1, 1763, he wrote to Kerlérec that it seemed necessary to evacuate Fort de Chartres as the only way to stop Indian resistance to the English.[20] Neyon intended to do so in early March 1764, when the river would be best for navigation. He also indicated that he was already well advanced in moving artillery from Fort Massiac to Ste. Geneviève on the western side of the Mississippi, lest it fall into English hands. Those cannons he did not move, he had disabled.[21] By that date, he had also reduced the Fort Massiac garrison to just fifteen men and one officer. D'Abbadie recorded in his journal that on January 30, 1764, he sent a boat to Illinois with orders for Neyon to evacuate the posts he commanded. The winter of 1763–64 was unusually severe, with spring late in coming, so Neyon was not able to leave de Chartres until June 15, but by July 2, he was already in New Orleans, and within two weeks, he was on his way to France.[22]

Neyon's departure was curious in several regards. He had orders to evacuate the posts under his command, but apparently he had no formal order, certainly none from France, relieving him of his command of the

Illinois Country, where much remained to be done in turning over the area to the British. Neyon took with him from Fort de Chartres just seventy officers and soldiers and a number of inhabitants, apparently motivated at least in part by Neyon's eagerness to abandon Illinois. They were transported in an enormous convoy of twenty-one bateaux and seven pirogues, probably the largest convoy ever on the Mississippi. Auguste Chouteau criticized Neyon for having persuaded a large number of civilians to abandon Illinois. The size of the convoy indicates the criticism was true.[23] Neyon left behind forty men under Louis Groston de St. Ange de Bellerive, who remained to complete the sad duty that Neyon de Villiers had abandoned, turning Fort de Chartres over to the British.[24]

In France, Neyon aided Kerlérec in his continuing feud with Rochemore, which dragged on even beyond the death of the principals, and then in 1772, Neyon was appointed colonel in Guadeloupe. In 1775, he was promoted to brigadier general, and two years later, he became commandant of Marie-Galante, a small island south of Guadeloupe. He fell ill there and departed for France in 1779, where he hoped to recover, but his ship was captured by the English, and he died at sea.

FOURTEENTH AND LAST FRENCH COMMANDANT: LOUIS GROSTON DE ST. ANGE DE BELLERIVE (1764–65)

Louis Groston de St. Ange de Bellerive was born in Montréal in 1702, the youngest son of a sergeant of the marines, Robert Groston de St. Ange. In 1720, Robert served at the small Fort St. Joseph in what is now southern Michigan, and there Louis joined his father. He subsequently followed his father to Illinois, where his father became an officer. In 1724, Louis, along with his mother, joined his father and his older brother, Pierre, at Fort d'Orléans on the Missouri River, founded the previous year by Étienne de Véniard de Bourgmont with the aid of Robert Groston de St. Ange. Louis accompanied Bourgmont on his first unsuccessful attempt to reach the Padouca (Plains Apache).[1] Late in 1724, Bourgmont left Fort d'Orléans to return to France, where he remained. Robert was left in charge of Fort d'Orléans, aided by his two sons.

In 1727, Robert transferred to Fort de Chartres, where he served as second in command until he became commandant of Fort de Chartres and the Illinois Country in 1730.[2] Pierre also served at Fort de Chartres along with his father, while Louis remained at Fort d'Orléans with the rank of ensign. There is little evidence of his activities there, which indicates that his administration was successful. Problems created correspondence. Most importantly, his diplomacy and personal influence retained the alliance of the Missouri tribes with the French despite concerted efforts of the Fox to disrupt the alliance. Louis Groston was the commandant of a small fort in the Missouri valley as late as 1736.[3]

During 1736, Louis's father retired and the Chickasaw killed his older brother, Pierre, along with almost all the other officers of Fort de Chartres and François-Marie Bissot de Vincennes, commandant of the post on the Wabash River.[4] Louis de St. Ange was the natural choice for the new commandant at the Wabash Post. The former commandant of Fort de Chartres, Pierre d'Artaguiette, praised Louis highly as a brave young man of great merit, and the new commandant, La Buissonnière, reported that he was well known and well liked among the Indians. Robert Groston de St. Ange petitioned Governor Bienville to appoint Louis, his sole surviving son, to the post, and Bienville was glad to do so, noting the service of Louis's father and brother. Bienville also described Louis as vigorous and active, praised his command of Indian languages, and noted that the Indians at the Wabash requested Louis's appointment as commandant.[5]

Louis de St. Ange was appointed in 1736 and promoted to half-pay lieutenant, and two years later he was promoted again, to half-pay captain.[6] The garrison was too small to permit full-pay status. The settlement on the Wabash seems not to have had an official name, and it was called variously the Wabash Post (Poste au Ouabache); Post of the Piankashaw (Poste des Pianguichats), after the neighboring tribe; Vincennes (Poste Vincennes, spelled variously), after François-Marie Bissot de Vincennes, who had founded the post in 1732; and St. Ange (Poste St. Ange), after the new commandant, who would serve there almost thirty years. St. Ange seems to have promoted the founder's name for the settlement rather than his own, and the name survives in modern Vincennes, Indiana.

St. Ange served as commandant of Vincennes from 1736 to 1764. Few documents from his long tenure survive. He sent some reports to the commandant of Fort de Chartres and others directly to the governor in New Orleans, but the survival of the reports of any post commander, whether from Vincennes or Fort de Chartres, is exceptional, since the material in those reports was normally redacted into the reports of the governor to the minister of the marine. Moreover, later the English noted that the records of the village had been destroyed by "rain, rats and insects."[7]

On becoming commandant, St. Ange faced an immediate crisis. In the aftermath of the French defeat in 1736, the Chickasaw and Cherokee had moved in force to the Ohio River, where they seemed to be establishing a permanent village, and most of the Piankashaw left their village near Vincennes to move higher up the Wabash. The French at Vincennes had relied on the friendly Piankashaw for protection against both the English and the English-allied Chickasaw and Cherokee. Without them, the settlement was dangerously exposed and could no longer serve as a check on English movements in the area. Also, much of the economy of Vincennes relied on furs and hides traded from the Piankashaw and sent to New Orleans in exchange for vital imports. In view of these developments, Governor Bienville ordered the garrison of Vincennes to abandon the settlement and establish a new fort at the confluence of the Wabash and Ohio, but the Chickasaw and Cherokee left the Ohio, relieving the crisis.

Bienville continued to be interested in establishing some sort of fort on the Ohio and transferring either the garrison of Vincennes or that of Fort de Chartres there, but nothing was done. It proved difficult to find a favorable situation for such a fort, the estimates of costs were great, and the Piankashaw refused to move to the area. With the withdrawal of the Chickasaw and Cherokee, the Piankashaw began to return to the vicinity of Vincennes, and regular life resumed in the settlement.

The garrison and civilian populations varied in size during the years of St. Ange's administration. In 1758, the garrison was apparently at its largest, forty men. Over the years, St. Ange granted about seventy parcels of land to settlers at Vincennes, and the grants were confirmed by the governors of Louisiana, but in 1758, the governor of Louisiana, Kerlérec, estimated there were only eighteen to twenty *habitants* at Vincennes. By *habitant*, Kerlérec may have meant to indicate only substantial farmers, while a rather larger population may have lived there as subsistence farmers and Indian traders. Still, Vincennes remained a small village, with a population of probably no more than several hundred at the most, although the population increased substantially, if only temporarily, with the addition of a variety of displaced persons in the years immediately after the cession to the English.[8]

Throughout St. Ange's long tenure at Vincennes, his reputation remained untarnished. In 1758, Governor Kerlérec wrote that he was "an excellent officer for this country, and particularly for the Indians, whom he leads . . . as he pleases. A man of great probity, a zealous servant of the king, having always considered it beneath his dignity to engage in commerce. He is thus impoverished."[9]

It must have been with heavy heart that St. Ange received the order to leave Vincennes, his home for nearly three decades, to become the commandant of Fort de Chartres. It was in no way a desirable promotion. Neyon de Villiers, the commandant since 1760, exhibited unseemly eagerness to abrogate his responsibilities and leave behind not only Illinois but all of Louisiana, and St. Ange was left to the sad task of handing over the fort and all the Illinois Country east of the Mississippi to the English.

Jean-Jacques Blaise d'Abbadie succeeded Kerlérec as governor of Louisiana in October 1763, and on September 15, St. Ange was officially discharged from his old commission and immediately reinstated by Governor d'Abbadie as commandant of Illinois with the rank of half-pay captain. Information moved slowly upriver to Illinois. On December 1, Neyon still did not know about the change of administration in New Orleans and addressed a letter to Kerlérec as governor, indicating that he wished to leave Fort de Chartres in March. On January 30, 1764, d'Abbadie sent orders to Neyon to evacuate the Illinois posts. That was a poor time to send a message up the Mississippi, especially because the winter of 1764 was unusually severe, and one wonders if the message had even reached Illinois by Neyon's proposed date of departure. In any event, the winter was so harsh that Neyon was not able to leave until June 15, 1764.[10]

St. Ange's role at Fort de Chartres was much more than just a melancholy wait for the English to arrive. There was a great need to maintain order in this critical period. He reported on Pontiac's continued hostility to the English and met with chiefs of the Illinois, Osage, and Missouri to explain the cession of the eastern side of the Mississippi to the English and urge peace and quiet. The peace established by Macarty between the Illinois and the Sauk and Fox had broken down, and St. Ange was now able to reestablish it. Many French inhabitants had left Illinois for New Orleans and France along with Neyon de Villiers, and still more were selling their lands on the east bank or simply abandoning them and moving to the west bank, some to Ste. Geneviève and vicinity, others to the newly founded St. Louis. Individual English officers reached Fort de Chartres, and St. Ange cooperated with them, but British troops only arrived, after several failed attempts, to take control of Fort de Chartres and the Illinois Country on October 9, 1765. On that date, Captain Thomas Stirling arrived with a detachment of the 42nd Regiment, the famous Black Watch. The next day, Fort de Chartres was formally handed over to the British. Stirling noted that St. Ange declared he would never lower the French flag, so that task had to be done entirely by the British. Lieutenant James Eddington, a British officer, described the dismal scene as the last French flag in North America was brought down:

> When we came in sight of Fort Chartres, which is on the E. side, the Fort being built of stone and plastered with Lime, appears very white. With the Village and plain it makes a very agreeable prospect. We cross'd over to the E. side about a mile below the Fort. Upon rowing up along the bank, a French Sergeant from the Fort with a party came and challeng'd us as to who we were; which, having answer'd he went off. We arriv'd about 3 o'clock at the Fort, and for that night encamp'd in the plain just by it. We were receiv'd very politely at the landing by Monsr. St. Ange, a very Gentlemanly looking old man, and the rest of the French Officers, and we sup'd in the Fort that night with them.

> Days run .... 15 miles
> Distance from Fort Pitt (to) Fort de Chartres ...... 1081 miles

> The men being all properly dress'd, we got under Arms about 10 o'clock and march'd to the Fort with our Drums beating. Before we came to the Gate an Officer with a party came out of the Fort and planted himself on the Road some distance from our Front. Our Detachment immediately halted and an officer with a party went forward to him. The French Officer challeng'd "Who's there," "What Regiment" and what we were marching for, all which being matter of form. We having hanswer'd to each challange he call'd to us we might advance. We accordingly resum'd our March and found an Officer Guard drawn up at the inside of the Gate, with

rested Arms and a Drum beating a March as we passed on to
the Square.

There were about Forty French Soldiers in the Colony,—I
was sent with the Officer at the Gate, with the same number
of Men to relieve him. His Guard was compos'd of old Men
looking like Invalids without any sort of uniform. Most of
them had on Jackets of different colours and slouch'd Hats,
and their Arms seem'd to be old and in very indifferent order. When the Sentries were relieved and the Guard just
ready to march off, The French colours were pull'd down.
Upon sight of this those Honest Old Veterans were greatly
Chagrind. They could not help venting their indignation, by
shrugging their shoulders and declaring when they fought
under the Marshals Berwick Saxe and Lowendale, no such
dishonour was then ever seen. In fact, all Europe trembled
at the French name.[11]

The process was completed with the signing of a formal document
acknowledging the transfer and containing a detailed description of the
fort, its buildings, and contents.

St. Ange spent several days arranging accommodations for his men
across the Mississippi and then moved to the new town of St. Louis,
where he assumed personal command—or rather, continued in command,
since he had been commandant of the entire Illinois Country on both
sides of the Mississippi since June 1764. St. Ange transported more than
just his forty troops to St. Louis. He also took the essential elements of
the civil government of Illinois: Joseph-François Lefebvre Desruisseau,
the *procureur général* (chief civil magistrate) and *garde-magasin*; Charles-
Joseph Labuxière, notary; and Pierre Pery, *greffier* (court clerk). Lefebvre
fell ill in August 1766 and died in 1767, and Labuxière assumed his duties,
serving simultaneously as notary, assistant *procureur général*, *commissaire*,
garde-magasin, judge, and militia lieutenant. He must have been a very
busy man. In addition, St. Ange also took with him the interpreter of
Indian languages and the gunsmith, both of whom were vital to the
maintenance of good relations with the Indians.

St. Ange faced numerous problems in the five years he controlled St.
Louis. Despite polite early relations with the British, tensions developed

between the two sides of the Mississippi. English traders operated illegally in the Missouri River valley, to the chagrin of St. Louis merchants and traders. Many of the French inhabitants of the eastern side of the Mississippi did not find the British occupation congenial and moved to the western side. The British made some ineffective attempts to prevent their departure or at least thwart the departing residents from disassembling their homes and taking them with them. The British lieutenant Alexander Fraser naively wrote that St. Ange enticed French *habitants* to St. Louis "for the Advantages of Enjoying their Ancient Privileges and Laws,"[12] rather than considering that the *habitants*, faced with the loss of those traditional privileges and laws if they remained in British territory, needed no enticement to move to the western bank. The English were generally suspicious of St. Ange. For example, they believed, wrongly, that St. Ange tried to fix the blame on them for the murder of Pontiac by a Peoria Indian.

St. Louis was a boisterous town in these years, filled with unruly voyageurs, fur traders, English deserters, vagabonds, adventurers, displaced persons, and Indians, all frequently drunk. St. Ange had to maintain order, but not so strictly as to drive the trade on which St. Louis lived to the English side of the river. The defeat of the French in the Seven Years' War had led to great disturbances among the Indian tribes, of which Pontiac's uprising was only a part. Indians of many tribes and bands from both sides of the Mississippi came to St. Louis, expecting customary gifts, but New Orleans could provide little in the way of trade goods, and St. Ange frequently had to rely primarily on his personal status among the Indians and his diplomatic skills. St. Ange was also called on to deal with Indian problems beyond St. Louis, as violence increased between tribes and against traders from far up the Arkansas River in the south to the Minnesota River in the north, but his garrison was far too small and ill equipped to take direct action, and there was little he could do about these distant conflicts.

In New Orleans, the Spanish finally arrived in March 1766 in the person of Antonio de Ulloa y de la Torre-Girault,[13] who arrived with a few subordinates and only ninety soldiers. Ulloa did not wish to take official possession of the colony until sufficient Spanish forces arrived, so a strange dual administration emerged of Ulloa and Aubry, the French transitional governor. Ulloa soon dispatched a small convoy to St. Louis, commanded by Captain Francisco Ríu y Morales. Neither Ulloa nor Ríu was the right man for his task.

Ulloa was an intellectual and probably a genius, one of the bright lights of the Enlightenment, but personally ill suited to his new role. The inhabitants of New Orleans wished to remain French and resented the coming of Spanish rule, but a more diplomatic individual better supplied with resources might have been able to achieve a peaceful transfer of power. Events in New Orleans led people subsequently to describe Ulloa in unflattering terms, but it is at least apparent from near contemporary accounts that he was honest, honorable, and upright, yet at the same time remote, pedantic, and tactless, not a man to confer with others or take advice. Moreover, he arrived with insufficient forces to overawe the elite of New Orleans.

Ulloa lacked authority and resources to resolve many of the problems he faced in Louisiana, such as economic chaos caused by old French paper money and bills of exchange circulating at constantly depreciating rates and the new, harshly restrictive Spanish trade regulations. He seems to have had limited understanding of the needs and concerns of the colony, failed to represent those concerns effectively to Spain, and lacked the social skills to convince the New Orleans elite of his good intentions. Protests led to disorders, which were used by a relatively small group of the Creole elite to force Ulloa out of the country. He set sail from New Orleans on November 1, 1768, and departed from La Balize at the mouth of the Mississippi as soon as he could get a favorable wind. Aubry did not approve of the revolt that drove Ulloa out of the colony, but there was nothing he could do to prevent it.

Meanwhile, Ríu's convoy had a slow, troubled journey to St. Louis, and by the time it arrived in September 1767, Ríu had lost control of his men, some of whom deserted, while those remaining were sullen and insubordinate. He had been instructed to build a fort at the juncture of the Missouri and Mississippi Rivers, but the area was unsuitable, low, swampy, and frequently flooded. Ríu constructed a small fort with a grandiose name, Fort Don Carlos el Señor Príncipe de Asturias, somewhat upstream on the southern bank of the Missouri, and a tiny blockhouse on the opposite bank, but the area was also low and subject to flooding. Fort and blockhouse quickly decayed and served no real purpose. In April 1769, a year and a half after he had arrived, Ríu returned to New

Orleans, having accomplished nothing of value. St. Ange remained in command at St. Louis.

Effective Spanish control came to Louisiana on August 18, 1769, when General Alejandro O'Reilly landed at New Orleans with three thousand troops. He executed five principal instigators of the rebellion, a sixth was killed in an incident in prison, and he sent others to prison in Havana. It has become traditional in Louisiana to hail six as martyrs and condemn "Bloody" O'Reilly, but he came as a needed tonic to New Orleans. The chronic factionalism that had plagued the city from its founding disappeared, and a period of unprecedented growth and prosperity followed.

Within a week of arriving, O'Reilly wrote to St. Ange, who answered promptly with a long appraisal of the state of Spanish Upper Louisiana. St. Ange also presided over an oath of allegiance to the Spanish king sworn to by the citizens of St. Louis, and the inhabitants of Ste. Geneviève took the same oath. O'Reilly offered to let St. Ange continue as commandant of Upper Louisiana, but St. Ange, aged and ill, replied that he was not sure he was able to fulfill the duties and was content to retire.

Direct Spanish rule came to St. Louis in the person of Pedro José Piernas, who arrived with a convoy in May 1770 to replace St. Ange and assume the office of lieutenant governor. Before his dispatch to St. Louis, Piernas had expressed the opinion to O'Reilly that St. Ange was useless, but O'Reilly knew otherwise. O'Reilly's instructions to Piernas explicitly ordered:

> The lieutenant governor shall preserve the best of relations with Monsieur de St. Ange, whose practical knowledge of the Indians will be very useful to him. He shall do whatever he can to gain his friendship and confidence, shall listen to his opinion attentively on all matters, and shall defer to him so far as possible without prejudice to the service.[14]

Piernas came to appreciate the wisdom of O'Reilly's instructions, and it appears that St. Ange continued to aid and advise the Spanish governor even after his retirement. In 1774, St. Ange died in St. Louis at the house of Madame Marie-Thérèse Bourgeois Chouteau, where he had been residing. Among the few personal papers in his possession at the time of his death was his appointment in 1736 as commandant of Vincennes.[15]

PART THREE

People of
Fort de Chartres

DURING THE YEARS between the construction of the first Fort de Chartres (1719–20) and the surrender of the fourth Fort de Chartres to the British (1765), thousands of people passed through the post: soldiers, settlers, Indians, missionaries, voyageurs, travelers, and many others. Most left no or only slight traces in the scattered and incomplete documents surviving from the eighteenth century. In only a relatively few cases is there enough evidence for even a short biography. The ten presented here from among that small group represent a cross section of humanity, selected for the variety of their experiences, ranging from an ill-fated chicken thief to an aristocrat who served three different national monarchs. Their stories are individually thought-provoking, and collectively they represent a vivid picture of the vital and varied community that was French Illinois.

Women are underrepresented in these ten essays, appearing mainly in association with the men in their lives. This reflects both the legal reality of French colonial life for most women and the state of the sources. Indians are even more poorly represented, and Africans and African Creoles almost entirely absent. This is regrettable, but again, it reflects the state of the sources.

MARIE ROUENSA-8CATE8A:
THE MOTHER OF FRENCH ILLINOIS

Marie Rouensa-8cate8a was born in a Kaskaskia Indian village on the Illinois River about 1677.[1] The village was located on the Illinois River across from Le Rocher (Starved Rock), where René-Robert Cavelier de La Salle and his second in command, Henri de Tonty, were to build Fort St. Louis in 1682–83. The village was brutally ravaged by the Iroquois in 1680, and the infant 8cate8a, not yet named Marie, and her parents were lucky to escape with their lives. Faced with the continuing threat of Iroquois raids, the hostility of the Fox to the north, and the depletion of resources in the vicinity of their old village, the Kaskaskia moved southward along the Illinois River to Pimeteoui (modern Peoria), where they camped with the Peoria Indians. There, in or about 1694, the Jesuit Father Jacques Gravier converted 8cate8a to Christianity, giving her the Christian name Marie. Henceforth, Christianity became the major focus of her life.

Even before the conversion of Marie, Jesuit missionaries had made converts among the Kaskaskia. Father Gravier counted 206 baptisms between the end of March and the end of November 1693.[2] Relatively few males in the prime of life turned to the new religion; converts were much more commonly people in extremis, infants or elderly, and young women, for whom Christianity offered, in addition to religious fervor, potential improvement in their social position and treatment. Marie was distinguished from other young women converts, according to Father Gravier, in two regards: the depth of her devotion to her new religion, and her position in the tribe as the daughter of Rouensa, the highest chief among the Kaskaskia.[3]

While Marie wished to remain unmarried and devote her life to Christ, her father wished her to marry a French voyageur and trader, Michel Accault.[4] In 1694, Accault was forty-eight years old and had already lived a colorful, even gaudy, life. He had been with La Salle and Henri de Tonty in 1680 and then explored the upper Mississippi with the Récollet Father Louis Hennepin, who exaggerated his achievements and played down Accault's role. By 1694, Accault was famous, or perhaps notorious, for his debaucheries, which must have been monumental to distinguish him from other voyageurs, who were generally known for their wild and wicked ways—at least, according to the missionaries. Missionary denunciations, while vivid, often lacked specifics and in this case may have been exaggerated for effect.

Rouensa undoubtedly wished his daughter to marry Accault to strengthen relations with the important trader and ensure his and his tribe's privileged access to sought-after and increasingly vital European goods. Accault undoubtedly wished to marry Rouensa's daughter to strength relations with an important Kaskaskia chief and ensure his privileged access to the tribes' furs and skins, in addition to whatever charms Marie possessed. For Marie, marriage to Accault, a trader old enough to be her father, must have seemed a horrible alternative to an idealized virginal life in the service of Christ, but both her culture and her new religion taught that a dutiful daughter honored and obeyed her parents.

Marie repeatedly refused to marry Accault and, in doing so, infuriated her father, who thought that Father Gravier had encouraged her to disobey—a charge that Gravier emphatically denied. Outraged, Rouensa went to extremes, as Gravier reported:

> As I went through the village calling the savages to prayers, the father stopped me when I passed before his cabin, and told me that, inasmuch as I was preventing his daughter from obeying him, he would also prevent her from going to the chapel. . . . He had just driven his daughter out of the house after depriving her of her upper garment, her stockings, her shoes, and her pretty ornaments, without a single word of remonstrance or a single tear from her. But, when he wished to take away what covered her, she said: "Ah! My father, what are you trying to do? Leave me; that is enough, I will not give you the rest; you may take my life rather than deprive me of it." Her father stopped short and, without saying a word, drove her from his house. Not wishing to be seen in that plight, she hid herself in the grass on the water's edge, where an old catechumen who was going to the chapel found her, and threw her his jerkin. She covered herself with it, and at once came to the chapel, where she responded to all the prayers and chants with the others, as if nothing had happened to her.[5]

In subsequent days, Rouensa both entreated and menaced his daughter and continued to attempt to prevent tribesmen from attending Gravier's chapel, even threatening to go to war. Finally, Marie announced that she would be willing to marry the French trader under the conditions that Accault reform in manners and morals, her parents convert to Christianity, and Gravier's mission be allowed to proceed without hindrance. After the marriage was duly consummated, Gravier reported that Accault "is now quite changed, and he has admitted to me that he no longer recognizes himself," and Rouensa now supported Christianity and encouraged Gravier's mission.[6]

In 1695, Marie gave birth to a son, Pierre Accault, at Pimeteoui. The Kaskaskia continued to move to the south, settling in 1700 on the west bank of the Mississippi by the mouth of the small Des Peres River, south of the Missouri River and near the site of modern St. Louis. Here in 1702, Marie gave birth to a second son, Michel Accault *fils*. Her husband, Michel Accault, seems to have died about this time, though no specific record of his death survives. Marie, like most women of the time, did not remain a widow long, marrying Michel Philippe, a French trader, probably shortly before the Kaskaskia moved once again in 1703.

This time the Kaskaskia moved to their final destination, the southern end of the American Bottom, along with the Jesuit missionaries and a number of French traders, some married to Kaskaskia women. The settlement took its name from the tribe, Kaskaskia; it developed into the largest town in French Illinois and eventually became the first capital of the state of Illinois. There Michel Philippe and Marie Rouensa-8cate8a settled down with her two sons. In 1704, Marie bore a daughter, Agnès-Philippe, followed by two more daughters and three more sons. All eight children lived into adulthood. During this time, Michel Philippe became a leading citizen of Kaskaskia, a successful farmer, a major landowner, and an officer in the local militia. Judging from the honor paid Marie after her death—the only woman to be accorded burial within the church—she remained closely committed to the Jesuit mission and proselytizing among the Kaskaskia.

In 1717, the royal government transferred Illinois from the control of Canada to Louisiana, administered by the Compagnie des Indes. In 1719, Pierre-Sidrac Dugué de Boisbriand came upriver from New Orleans to become the first commandant of the Illinois Country. When Boisbriand removed the Kaskaskia to a separate village, several miles away from what henceforth was French Kaskaskia, Marie remained in French Kaskaskia, where she had become an integral part of the community.

In 1725, Marie fell ill and dictated her will, directing the distribution of her substantial estate.[7] It seems a very French document. Marie was at pains to ensure the will would be processed according to prevalent French law, the Coutume de Paris, specifying, as the law required, that her estate be divided, one half going to her husband, the other half to be divided equally among her children by both husbands—with one exception: her second son, Michel Accault *fils*, was to be "disinherited because of his disobedience, as well as the bad conduct he has exhibited towards me and the entire family . . . as much for his disobedience as for the marriage that he has contracted despite his mother and his relatives." Apparently Michel had married an Indian woman who had not converted to Christianity, wedding her *à la façon du pays*, "according to the fashion of the country," in the Indian manner and without the sanction of the church. The Kaskaskia parish register exists for this period, and there is no record of the marriage.

A week later, Marie dictated a codicil to the will that reveals additional detail and somewhat mollifies her disinheritance of her son:

> I have pity for my son Michel Aco, who has chagrined me with his folly and his flight, and I no longer wished to deprive him absolutely and forever of his claim to my possessions. Should he return and repent, my wish is that he should have the right to his possessions. If, however, he is unfortunate enough to persist in his folly, never to repent, and to remain among the savage nations, I wish to transfer his possessions to his brothers and sisters.[8]

In essence, Marie had come so far from her Indian origin that she was willing to disinherit a son for abandoning French culture to live as an Indian.[9]

In one regard, Marie's will at first seems to depart from its general French character—language. When Marie Rouensa made her will, she was attended by the Jesuit Father Jean-Baptiste Le Boullenger, the royal notary Du Vernay, the interpreter for Indian language Jacques Lalande, and an additional witness. After conferring with Marie, Father Le Boullenger dictated the will in French to Du Vernay, and then Lalande read it to Marie twice in the Illinois language. When Marie added the codicil, an interpreter also was among those present.

Marie's reliance on the Illinois language nearly thirty years after her conversion to Christianity, marriage to two French men, and residence in an increasingly French community may seem at first strange and unreflective of her apparent adoption of the life of a French woman. It may, however, simply reflect that Marie's religious life, the center of her personality, was dominated by the Jesuits, who had converted her and who constituted the mission to Kaskaskia.

At the end of the seventeenth and beginning of the eighteenth centuries, the Jesuits were in conflict with both the other religious order active in Illinois, the Seminary of Foreign Missions, and the French government.[10] The issue less concerned jurisdiction, at least initially, than conflicting visions of missionary ideals.[11] The Jesuits sought to enter into the culture of the Indians and there to establish Christianity within the Indians' own society and customs. This was particularly reflected in the Jesuit emphasis on learning and using the Indians' own language. In contrast, the Seminary of Foreign Missions priests, who established themselves at Cahokia in 1698, disparaged Indian culture and followed the government-approved policy to *franciser*, or "Frenchify," the Indians, to deracinate them and convert them into French men and women in language, culture, and religion. This too was reflected in language. The seminary priests persistently neglected to become proficient in the Illinois language and as a result were persistently ineffective in communicating with most of the people they hoped to convert. They were still relying on translators at the end of the French regime.

As French voyageurs, traders, and settlers entered Illinois in greater numbers, it became increasingly difficult for the Jesuits to implement their somewhat romantic vision of an enduring Christianized native culture. The Illinois were becoming Frenchified less through the ineffective efforts of the seminary priests than through daily association with traders and *habitants*. The Jesuits recognized this, faced reality, and modified their position to something approximating that of the seminary priests,[12] but some of the old Jesuit attitudes persisted. They retained their commitment to native languages and sought to protect the Illinois against the corrupting influences of the voyageurs and French *habitants* in general. The separation of the Kaskaskia Indian village from the French town of Kaskaskia and Marie Rouensa's continued reliance on the Illinois language also seem to reflect manifestations of Jesuit ideals.

A few days after adding the codicil to her will, Marie Rouensa died. She received the singular honor of burial under the floor of the parish church of Kaskaskia. Burial within the church, described just two years earlier as the finest in the colony, was a rare distinction reserved for the most respected members of the parish. Marie Rouensa was the only woman ever to be so honored.

Marie Rouensa died just five years after the establishment of Fort de Chartres. She lived, quite comfortably, at Kaskaskia about sixteen miles to the south and may not have ever seen the new installation. Yet her relation to Fort de Chartres was twofold. Her conversion to Christianity played a major role in the Christianization of the Kaskaskia and other Illinois tribes and in the mixing of French and Indian that created the town of Kaskaskia. The development of French settlements in the Illinois Country, Kaskaskia by far the largest of them, led to the establishment of official government presence, Fort de Chartres.

On a more personal level, Marie's family was intimately connected to the officer corps of Fort de Chartres. Marie's daughter, Agnès-Philippe, married Nicolas-Michel Chassin, the civilian warehouse keeper (*garde-magasin*) of the Compagnie des Indes at Fort de Chartres and councilor of the Provincial Council of Illinois, the highest civilian authority in le Pays des Illinois. After Chassin's death, Agnès-Philippe married René Roy, surgeon major at Fort de Chartres. Another daughter, Elizabeth, married Alexandre de Celle Duclos, an ensign at Fort de Chartres. The connection continued into the next generation: the daughters of Agnès-Philippe and Elizabeth both married officers of the marine, and Elizabeth's son married an officer's widow. By the third generation, Marie Rouensa's descendants were part of the elite of both Upper and Lower Louisiana, entry to which had come through marriages with Fort de Chartres officers.

ÉTIENNE DE VÉNIARD DE BOURGMONT AND IGNON OUACONISEN (FRANÇOISE MISSOURI): AN EXPLORER AND AN INDIAN IN PARIS

About the time that Marie Rouensa lay dying in Kaskaskia, another Indian woman was touring Paris. Her Indian name, Ignon Ouaconisen, is recorded in a French source unfamiliar with Native Americans in general and Indian nomenclature in particular.[1] The French generally knew her by her baptismal name, Françoise Missouri, often called the Missouri Princess.

There is no record of the birth of Ignon Ouaconisen. Some have suggested a date as early as 1700, but that date is an assumption based on still other assumptions ultimately derived from unsubstantiated rumor, as discussed below. It is more likely that she was born around 1710. She was a Missouri Indian, daughter of the most important chief of the tribe. In her youth, the Missouri were settled near the juncture of the Grand and Missouri Rivers in what is now central Missouri. They spoke a language of the Siouan family and were closely related to the Oto and Iowa tribes. In their own language, they called themselves Niútachi, meaning "People of the River Mouth." The name Missouri is a French derivation from an Illinois word meaning something like "People with Dugout Canoes."

The first French to meet the Missouri were *coureurs des bois*, unlicensed traders who moved from the Mississippi up the Missouri River to trade for furs and hides. These were followed by French explorers with more or less official credentials, prominent among them Étienne de Véniard de Bourgmont, a man to whom Ignon Ouaconisen would be closely tied.[2]

Bourgmont was a colorful, adventurous, talented, at times criminal, and at times idealistic character. Born in France in 1679, he was the son of a respected surgeon, and his great-uncle was the grand vicar of the bishop of Québec. His family seems to have included less reputable elements as well; in 1698, the nineteen-year-old Bourgmont was apprehended along with his stepfather and uncle poaching on the lands of a monastery. He seems to have left for Canada about this time without paying the fine he incurred.

In 1702, Charles Juchereau de St. Denys, with a detachment of the *troupes de la marine*, established a short-lived tannery near the mouth of the Ohio River. Charles is not to be confused with the more famous Louis Juchereau de St. Denys. Bourgmont was part of St. Denys's command, perhaps serving as a cadet. For a year and a half, Bourgmont traded for furs and hides among the Mascouten, probably for the tannery.

In 1705, Bourgmont held the rank of ensign at Fort Pontchartrain (Detroit), commanded by Antoine Laumet de La Mothe Cadillac. In early 1706, Cadillac traveled to France and left behind Bourgmont to serve as interim commandant of the garrison and deal with a simmering feud between the Ottawa and Miami. Bourgmont was just thirty years old and had no experience in Indian diplomacy. He was unable to contain the situation. Increasingly violent confrontations over two months culminated in an Ottawa attack on a group of Miami, killing a number of them. The Miami along with some Huron fled to the French fort. The Ottawa attacked the fort, and the French, Miami, and Huron fired on them from the fort. About thirty Ottawa were killed, and in the midst of the clash, the missionary priest and a French sergeant were also killed. Cadillac's report of the incident led the marquis de Vaudreuil, the governor general of Canada, to criticize Bourgmont harshly for failure to maintain control of the Indians and mediate the situation before violence broke out.[3] Before the end of 1706, Bourgmont deserted.

It is not apparent whether Bourgmont deserted because of resentment of Vaudreuil's criticism or because of a woman. Certainly, when he decamped he took away with him a woman widowed in the attack on the fort, who, according to Cadillac, already had an unsavory reputation.[4] This woman, known by several names but most commonly Madame Montour, became famous, respected, and influential in her own right, despite Cadillac's defamatory remarks. The alliance between Bourgmont and Montour did not endure long. Bourgmont seems to have had no trouble attracting women, but his attachments tended to be short-lived.

For over six years, Bourgmont lived as a fugitive, adventurer, and apparently a *coureur de bois*, yet there were odd aspects of his outlaw life. Despite his long absence, he was never struck off the books as an officer of the marine, and there was little attempt to apprehend him. Rumors persisted that he was acting on Cadillac's behalf, trading illegally with the English. Cadillac was certainly capable of such behavior, but substantial evidence is lacking. It is even possible that Bourgmont had not deserted at all, but rather was functioning as a secret agent, reporting on conditions first around the Great Lakes and later in the Illinois Country and Missouri. It has also been suggested that he was protected by his social status as an officer and a gentleman, the authorities seeking to avoid the scandal of an officer behaving badly. In many other instances, however, there was no hesitancy to expose and punish scandalous behavior by officers of much higher status and superior family connections.

In 1712, Missouri, Osage, and Illinois, along with other tribes, journeyed to Detroit to take part in a campaign against the Fox. It was probably at this time that Bourgmont entered into a native marriage with a Missouri woman, who would bear him a child. The following year, Bourgmont traveled to Illinois, where he lived openly, along with his Missouri wife and two other French traders, who also had alliances with Missouri women. Jesuits at Kaskaskia complained about his licentiousness, which probably meant no more than that he was cohabiting with an unconverted Indian woman and ignoring their authority. The complaints reached the governor of Canada and the Jesuit confessor of Louis XIV. The minister of the marine ordered Bourgmont's arrest, but Bourgmont remained free and even made a trip to Mobile, then the administrative center of Louisiana. There is no evidence of what Bourgmont did at Mobile, but Cadillac was then governor, and it is possible that the two conferred.

Bourgmont returned to the Missouri Indian village. In 1714, it became apparent that he still was a wanted man. The governor of Canada ordered his arrest but lamented that it was virtually impossible to achieve in remote Missouri. The king ordered Cadillac to arrest Bourgmont when he came to Mobile, but by the time the order arrived, Bourgmont had long since departed. Bourgmont, however, was about to use his pen to change the course of his life. In a short time, he wrote two surviving reports. The first, "The Route to Be Taken to Ascend the Missouri River," is a laconic journal, or perhaps a summary of a journal, presenting geographic information, distances, compass headings, and landmarks, tracing the course of the Missouri River from its mouth to its juncture with the Platte River in eastern Nebraska, some 635 miles by river. The report enabled the cartographer Guillaume Delisle to produce the first good map of the lower Missouri.

The second work, "Exact Description of Louisiana, of Its Harbors, Lands and Rivers, and Names of the Indian Tribes That Occupy It, and the Commerce and Advantages to Be Derived Therefrom for the Establishment of a Colony," is substantially longer.[5] The parts of the work that describe the area around Mobile and the settlements and tribes along the Mississippi contain little new, but the work also provides a detailed account of the Missouri River and its major tributaries and the Indian tribes living there as far north as the Platte River and a less thorough account beyond that into the area of modern South Dakota.

Bourgmont's reports rehabilitated him in the eyes of the Compagnie des Indes and the French Crown. Although Bourgmont virtually disappeared from written records between 1714 and 1718, he was no longer pursued as a wanted outlaw. Rather, he seems to have acted as the French

representative on the Missouri. In 1718, he took a delegation of chiefs
from Illinois and Missouri to Dauphin Island, near Mobile, to solidify
alliances among the tribes and with the French, but disease killed all
but one of the Indians. Bourgmont conducted that Indian back to his
tribe along with presents to compensate for the deaths. Also in 1718,
Bienville, who was once again governor, recommended that Bourgmont
be awarded the Cross of Saint Louis, the most prestigious royal decoration for service to France.

Many important events occurred in 1720. During that year, Boisbriand
completed the first Fort de Chartres. France and Spain were at war, and
the Spanish Villasur expedition met with grief at the hands of Indians in
south-central Nebraska, igniting French fears of Spanish penetration into
the Missouri watershed and beyond. It was also the year of the height of
the Mississippi Bubble, the wild enthusiasm for the stock of John Law's
Banque Royale, which controlled the Compagnie des Indes. Bourgmont
returned to southern Louisiana early in 1720 and then embarked for
France, accompanied by a son he had had with a Missouri woman.

Bourgmont arrived in France at the height of the Mississippi Bubble
fervor, when not merely all of France, but all of Europe, seemed to believe
that Louisiana and especially the Illinois Country contained wealth beyond
measure. The royal government granted Bourgmont the rank of captain of
the marines, awarded him the coveted Cross of Saint Louis, and named
him commandant of the Missouri River, a position and status parallel to
the commandant of the Illinois Country at Fort de Chartres. While in
France, he also married a French widow, who brought a substantial dowry.

Before 1720 had finished, the Mississippi Bubble burst, the stock collapsed, and John Law fled from France, but the Crown and the Compagnie
des Indes retained interest in the potential of Missouri. Bourgmont was
able to turn that interest into a contract in which he endeavored to make
peace among all the Indian tribes between Louisiana and Mexico, open
trade with the Spanish, establish a post on the Missouri to block potential
Spanish expansion into that area, and convey a delegation of Indians from
the principal tribes to visit France. The Crown promised it would grant
letters of nobility if he succeeded.

In early 1722, Bourgmont sailed for Louisiana, accompanied by his
son, but leaving behind the French wife he had married the previous year.
In Louisiana, he found all in disarray. The colony had received scanty

support since the collapse of John Law's scheme, and a hurricane had destroyed much of what was there. New Orleans was short of supplies and had been able to send little to Illinois, where scarcity also prevailed. Neither Bienville in New Orleans nor Boisbriand in Illinois thought Bourgmont was likely to succeed, and neither was enthusiastic about wasting scarce resources on a doomed effort. Still, a royal order could not be ignored, and they reluctantly provided what they could. Bourgmont faced formidable challenges with minimal resources.

Bourgmont's effort was bolstered by the Missouri Indians who had heard of his arrival and traveled three hundred miles from their village on the Missouri River to greet him and his son. The expedition nevertheless proved difficult. In addition to the shortage of men and supplies, two officers who had been assigned to the mission at Fort de Chartres turned out to be insubordinate and dishonest, and they even attempted to undermine Bourgmont's status with the Indians. Boisbriand recalled them. A third officer, Robert Groston de St. Ange, and his two sons provided vital assistance to Bourgmont in establishing his post on the Missouri, Fort d'Orléans. A first attempt to reach the Padouca (Plains Apache) from Fort d'Orléans failed when Bourgmont fell ill. A second expedition traveled from the Missouri River to the plains of central Kansas, where Bourgmont negotiated a peace between the Padouca and the Missouri and other tribes allied with the French.[6]

Late in 1724, Bourgmont gathered a group to go to France, consisting of four chiefs of the Missouri and one woman, Ignon Ouaconisen, daughter of the paramount Missouri chief; four chiefs of the Osage; one chief of the Oto; and perhaps a number of interpreters and others.[7] The group traveled to Fort de Chartres, where it had been intended that the commandant, Boisbriand, would join the group along with five Illinois chiefs. Boisbriand, however, was called to New Orleans to become interim governor in place of Bienville, who had been recalled to France. In his place, Father Nicolas-Ignace de Beaubois, head of the Jesuits in Illinois, was to escort the Illinois. The situation must have been awkward. Bourgmont had been the object of the Jesuits' ire only a few years earlier, and Beaubois was self-righteous, tactless, and almost habitually critical of military officers. While Beaubois and the Illinois would travel with Bourgmont and the larger group, Beaubois would seek at the same time to disassociate himself and the Illinois from Bourgmont.

When the delegation reached New Orleans, the Superior Council initially planned to send all to France and even discussed adding several chiefs of southern tribes to the party, but they soon realized the expense of hosting such a large gathering and dismissed all but a small group of five chiefs and Ignon Ouaconisen. Also traveling with Bourgmont was Father Beaubois, an Indian slave named Pilate, and Sergeant Dubois, who had accompanied Bourgmont on his expeditions from Fort d'Orléans.

The party left New Orleans on the ship *La Bellone*, which rammed several floating logs and was damaged when it ran aground before it put in at Dauphin Island. While at anchor there, it suddenly sank.[8] Bourgmont and his party survived, but the Indians were distressed that they lost all the presents they had brought for the king and the officers of the Compagnie des Indes. The group set sail on a new ship and arrived in France in late September 1725. One chief died during the voyage.

In France, Bourgmont and the three chiefs from Missouri met with the officers of the Compagnie des Indes, and then Beaubois and the Illinois chief met with them separately. Then all four met together again with representatives of the Compagnie. The Indians made speeches, translated into French by Bourgmont or Beaubois, before the officers of the Compagnie and later before the king. One wonders how much editing and rephrasing went into the translations. The Indians were given tours of the palaces at Versailles and Marly and sites throughout Paris intended to impress and amaze. They were presented with elaborate French court clothing. The dress selected for Ignon Ouaconisen is described as "the color of fire with flowers of gold." Louis XV, then fifteen years old, received them at the Château de Fontainebleau, and the Indians hunted deer in the royal forest for the amusement of the court.

Much speculation and gossip surrounded Ignon Ouaconisen, whose very presence was curious by French standards. People ignored the obvious explanation that she had been sent out of respect by her father, the paramount chief, who did not feel that circumstances allowed him to make the trip. The Missouri were allied with the French, and both were engaged in a bitter war with the Fox. Rumor suggested without evidence that Ignon was Bourgmont's mistress, and modern writers have built on the rumor, claiming equally without evidence that she was the mother of Bourgmont's son, born about 1714. To accommodate this idea, modern writers suggest, again without evidence, that Ignon was about twenty-five years old in 1725, born about 1700. Each dubious supposition has been built on a previous dubious supposition. It would have been virtually unthinkable for a Missouri woman to remain unmarried at twenty-five. She was probably about fourteen or fifteen years old, still unmarried but of marriageable age by both Indian and Illinois French norms. Bourgmont's son did not accompany his father to France. Presumably, he remained behind with his Missouri mother.

In Paris, Ignon Ouaconisen was baptized in Notre Dame Cathedral as Françoise Missouri, and then she married Sergeant Dubois, who was given a promotion. This has led to much romantic exaggeration, such as claims that Dubois was made a captain and given command of Illinois. In fact, all he got was an "expectancy of ensign," assurance that he would be promoted to ensign when a vacancy arose.

Louis XV awarded Bourgmont his coveted letter of nobility, granting him the rank of *écuyer* (squire). Rather than return to America, Bourgmont retired to his family estate, where he died in 1734. Sergeant Dubois conducted the Indians back to Missouri. He received his promised promotion and may have become the commandant of the tiny garrison at Fort d'Orléans.[9] The chiefs, loaded with presents from the king, rejoined their tribes. Françoise Missouri, however, through her conversion and marriage, had virtually become a French woman and lived as such for the rest of her life. She bore two children to Dubois.

Less than three full years after returning to America, in 1728, Sergeant Dubois was killed by Indians. No specifics are known about the event, but the Fox Wars were then at their height. Generally, women did not remain widows long, and Françoise Missouri soon married Louis Marin, captain of militia in New Chartres.[10] This was Louis-Hector Marin de La Malgue, probably a member of the Marin family prominent at the Baie des Puants (modern Green Bay). Two members of the family, father and son, were commandants there and had reputedly grown wealthy controlling the fur trade. Louis did not enter the marines, but rather became a trader and at times served as a translator. The couple had three children together before Françoise Missouri's death in early 1739.[11] Death at an early age was frequent in the eighteenth century.

Françoise Missouri remained a fascinating figure, and fictions grew up about her. The earliest was the baseless journalistic supposition that she was Bourgmont's mistress. The further claim that she was the mother of his son grew out of that early gossip. A derogatory story appeared in the first edition of Jean-François-Benjamin Dumont de Montigny's account of his years in Louisiana. Montigny, who resided in Louisiana from 1719 to 1738, actually did not did not mention Françoise Missouri or Dubois in the manuscript of his work, but l'Abbé Jean-Baptiste Le Mascrier edited and substantially rewrote the text before it appeared in print as *Mémoires historiques sur la Louisiane* in 1753.[12] Le Mascrier was opposed to marriages between French and Indians, and to illustrate the dangers of such unions, he interpolated a fantastic and false tale.[13] According to the abbé, upon returning to America, the pair settled at an unnamed fort, where Dubois became commandant. Françoise, however, was not happy in her new role and conspired with Indians, who overwhelmed the fort and killed Dubois along with the rest of the garrison, and then Françoise Missouri returned to live with her tribe. Actually, Françoise had nothing to do with her husband's death, after being widowed married a prominent and prosperous Frenchman, and continued to live within the French community for the rest of her life.

In 1753, Jean-Bernard Bossu, officer at Fort de Chartres and travel writer, gave a brief account of Françoise Missouri's life. Modern authors have often stated that Bossu met Françoise Missouri at that time, but Bossu did not write that. He merely stated that her daughter was at that time still living.[14]

There are yet living descendants of Françoise Missouri, the Missouri princess, the adventurous Indian woman who saw Paris and, like Marie Rouensa and others, mastered life across cultural boundaries, both Indian and French.[15]

TERRISSE DE TERNAN:
A RESTLESS AND WORRISOME PERSONALITY

Terrisse de Ternan was troublesome throughout his life. Although he was from an upper-class family, his early choice of profession was privateer, often in the eighteenth century little more than a pirate. His family resorted to a common solution to the embarrassment caused by the young man. A relative was a *fermier général*, a lessee of the right to collect royal taxes, and the *fermiers généraux* were famous for their wealth and influence. In 1714, through their influential relative, the family procured a commission for Ternan as an ensign and shipped him off to Louisiana, then governed as a proprietary concession by Antoine Crozat, another *fermier général*.[1]

There Terrisse de Ternan quickly showed his contrarian nature. He was one of the few military officers who sided with the unpopular governor Cadillac, and Cadillac chose him to arrest another officer, Vitrac de La Tour, who had quarreled with the irascible governor. Although La Tour threatened homicide and broke his sword over his thigh rather than surrender it, Ternan managed to make the arrest. The event may have endeared him to Cadillac, but it did nothing to further his popularity with his fellow officers.[2]

In 1716, Ternan was present as a supporter when Cadillac's son La Mothe Cadillac *fils* fought a duel against Benoist de St. Clair on Dauphin Island. La Mothe Cadillac *fils* managed to wound Benoist three times, and when Benoist fell, Ternan, using another officer's sword, assaulted Benoist, stabbing him three times more. Amazingly, Benoist recovered, probably saving Ternan from a murder charge, but Ternan's disgraceful behavior led the colonial proprietor Crozat to recommend that he be stripped of rank and recalled to France.[3]

Events in Louisiana not of Ternan's making spared him of even that fate. After two years of constant conflict with Cadillac and complaints from the colony, Crozat stripped Cadillac of his office and recalled him to France. Disappointed at the costs of the colonial venture, Crozat surrendered control of the colony to a new proprietor, the Compagnie d'Occident. Amid these changes, the Council of the Marine transferred Ternan to the small and remote Yazoo Post.[4]

In 1718, the War of the Quadruple Alliance broke out, pitting France, Austria, Britain, and the Dutch Republic against Spain. The weak French colony of Louisiana duly attacked the weak Spanish colony at Pensacola. The confrontation between the two colonies was a minor affair in a minor war, but not bereft of exhilarating and gallant events. The French captured Pensacola; the Spanish recaptured it and attacked the French at Dauphin Island unsuccessfully. The French then captured Pensacola for a second time, only to see it revert to Spain in 1722, about two years after the end of the war. The records do not mention Ternan's role in these events, but at Dauphin Island, the Council of Commerce appointed Ternan second lieutenant in 1720, and he seems to have commanded a few soldiers and Indians at Pensacola before its return to Spain.[5]

By 1727, Ternan was an ensign again, described as a former second lieutenant. Either Paris had not confirmed Ternan's promotion to second lieutenant or he had been demoted in the interval. Étienne de Périer, the governor of Louisiana, and Jacques de La Chaise, the *commissaire-ordonnateur* of the colony, sent Ternan to Illinois that year. Surprisingly, they described him to the directors of the Compagnie des Indes as very well behaved and prudent, but they also admitted that the greatest reason they chose him was his audacity,[6] a characteristic needed in Illinois. The Fox Indians and their native allies threatened Illinois from the north; the Chickasaw, allied to the English, were a constant problem and soon became a greater danger when they gave refuge to the Natchez after they massacred the French colonists at the Natchez settlement.

From 1727 until 1733, Ternan resided in Illinois. There he became a second lieutenant again and served simultaneously as the *garde-magasin* at Fort de Chartres or, to give him his more formal title, *agent des affaires de la Compagnie au poste des Illinois.*[7] This was a bureaucratic office of importance, in charge of the storehouse of supplies, munitions, and trade goods.

Ternan could be both cruel and compassionate. He hated the commandant Claude-Charles Dutisné and seemed to take malicious glee in the commandant's slow decline to death from a mistreated bullet wound in the cheek. Ternan was the case officer when a black slave, Jean Baxé, engaged in a scuffle with a French man, François Bastien. Although the Code Noir de La Louisiane of 1724 prescribed death for a slave who assaulted a free man, Ternan wrote that the case did not seem so serious as to merit that sentence. Although Ternan delivered this judgment in the name of the officers of Fort de Chartres acting in the name of the Compagnie des Indes, it is apparent that he was principally responsible for saving the slave's life. Baxé was sentenced to make an apology to Bastien on bended knee, to be whipped on three different days, and to bow to Bastien whenever he encountered him.[8] By eighteenth-century standards, this was lenient treatment indeed.

Despite his responsibilities, Ternan found time and energy to continue his troublesome ways. He fell out with Governor Périer, who changed his evaluation, now describing Ternan as "a restless and worrisome personality" and a "drunkard" with a "malicious tongue."[9] In addition to his abhorrence of the commandant Claude-Charles Dutisné, Ternan alienated and annoyed the Jesuit missionaries so much that they tried to have him recalled. Ternan wrote to a friend about the quarrel:

> The complaint sent against the Jesuits created a great stir. They say that it will be denied and that they have their powers from the Pope. They threaten me because they say it is I who wrote, and do not doubt that they will use their best efforts to have me recalled, having striven for that purpose for two years, but come what may, I shall always give warning of what seems to me against the people's rights and the interests of the *Compagnie*, which charge I assumed with pleasure.[10]

In 1729, when this was written, the Jesuits were in the midst of a controversy over the church of Ste. Anne at Chartres, the village that had grown up by Fort de Chartres. When the church was built in the late 1720s, the inhabitants requested a priest, but the Jesuits had no one available and could only promise to supply one sometime in the indefinite future. Unwilling to wait, the inhabitants of Chartres and Prairie du Rocher petitioned the Seminary of Foreign Missions at Cahokia, which provided a priest. The Jesuits protested and ultimately obtained confirmation from France that the villagers did not have the authority to choose the priest for their church, but by the time the Jesuits found someone for the post, the seminary priest was thoroughly established in the position and refused to withdraw. No one was willing to expel him, and although the controversy continued for years, the Jesuits never obtained control of the church and parish.[11]

The Jesuits apparently accused Ternan of having written the petition requesting the seminary priest, and even writing to a friend, Ternan did not quite explicitly admit or deny that he was the author, although it seems overwhelmingly likely that he was. Ternan had no personal stake in this controversy. His motivation may have been as he claimed, the people's rights and the interests of the Compagnie, but it is quite possible he consented to write for the villagers because of a previous clash with the Jesuits or even merely from fondness of controversy and tumult. Modern investigators of the affair have not noticed Ternan's role.[12]

Yet there was another, more attractive side to Terrisse de Ternan. He wrote letters from Fort de Chartres and Kaskaskia to Michel Rossard, the chief clerk of the Superior Council in New Orleans, both a close

friend and sometimes a business partner.[13] The letters provide us with
our most vivid source for life in early Illinois, and Ternan's observations
about contemporary gossip and news are spiced with mordant Gallic wit:

> I received with pleasure your long and pleasant letter
> of the 15th of last June, in which you detail the news
> of your capital, which consists mostly of murders, as-
> sassinations, and marriages, which caused such tragic
> bloodshed in your streets. I expect that it must now be
> somewhat calm, considering that these sorts of virgini-
> ties must be resolved and have taken the ordinary course
> of nature. It appears that your convent has been put to
> rout, since, notwithstanding the vows made by your
> brothers, one of them has married, without public scan-
> dal however, and to whom I wish much contentment
> which he has every reason to expect, having married a
> very virtuous lady. You should induce our friend Massy
> to make a finish, as it is dangerous for so gallant a man
> to remain so long in celibacy.[14]

Ternan complimented Rossard's wife, sent greetings through him to
other friends, and reminisced with nostalgia about dining and drinking
with Rossard. Ternan liked his wine. He wrote with a fine sense of self-
mockery about his attempt to make wine from the native Illinois grapes
and his inability to wait until it was fully ready before drinking it.

In addition to his position as an officer of the marines, Ternan was
a small-scale trader. Officers often carried on trade to supplement their
somewhat meager salaries, as did some enlisted men and many civilians.
Ternan's letters reveal that he sent a variety of products downriver to
New Orleans: onions, hams, beaver pelts, tobacco, and flour.[15] In turn, he
desired a variety of goods, most for trade, some for his own consumption:
knives of all kinds, brass kettles, vermilion, gunpowder, lead, several types
of cloth, brandy, sugar, coffee, stockings, women's shoes, ribbons, English
crockery, and even billiard balls. Clearly, Ternan was trading with both
Indians and French. He even did a little farming, growing his own onions.

Despite his sometimes charming letters, by 1733, Terrisse de Ternan was
at the end of his career in the Illinois Country and the rest of Louisiana.
In that year, he left the colony by ship, ostensibly on a leave of absence.

Bienville, who had returned as governor the previous year, had no more use for Ternan than had Périer, the previous governor. In a letter to the minister of the marine in Paris, Bienville wrote, "I was assured that he [Ternan] was not expecting to return. I hope so. I have known him for a long time, and I can say with certainty that he will not be missed."[16]

Ternan's life after he left Louisiana is obscure. The sole clue is a pamphlet published in Grenoble in 1759 by a lawyer named Léon, containing a précis of a legal dispute between heirs to the estate of Terrisse de Ternan. It is not certain that this was the man who served at Fort de Chartres; he may have been a near relative. It is possible the former officer returned to France to settle down peacefully at the family estate near Grenoble for the rest of his life, but that seems out of character for Terrisse de Ternan and a fate he would have loathed to accept.[17]

CLAUDE CHETIVAU:
THE MAN WHO WANTED TO GO TO CANADA

In 1725, the commandant of Fort de Chartres was Claude-Charles Dutisné, and he had a problem. Claude Chetivau was fifty-five years old, born in Soissons, France, in 1670. He was about five feet, four inches tall by French measure (five feet, eight inches by English measure), with gray curly hair and a gray beard, gray eyes, and an aquiline nose, and like most people of his class, he was illiterate.

Chetivau came to Louisiana in 1719. From the beginning of the Compagnie des Indes' administration of Louisiana in 1717 until the bursting of John Law's Mississippi Bubble in 1720, the Compagnie attempted to increase the population of the colony by sending people exiled from France: tobacco smugglers, army deserters, vagabonds, libertines, prostitutes, illicit salt dealers, and other petty criminals. Claude Chetivau was one of these, an illicit salt dealer. Salt was highly taxed in France, and penalties for evading the salt tax were severe, so he may have initially felt himself lucky only to be exiled. The Compagnie des Indes, however, made no adequate provision to support the exiles in Louisiana, and few had any skills to cope with a new life in a primitive and unfamiliar environment. They died by the hundreds.[1]

Chetivau was lucky. He survived, probably because the Compagnie sent him to Illinois, where food was more abundant and the climate healthier. Still, he was unhappy. On March 2, 1725, Chetivau found himself in the Fort de Chartres jail, charged with attempted desertion.

We do not know much about how Chetivau lived in Illinois. He had been sentenced to bondage for the Compagnie des Indes for ten years, and the Compagnie may have put him to any number of tasks or even rented him out to work in the lead mines on the west side of the Mississippi or to work for farmers during the planting and harvesting seasons. From the notes about his trial, we learn he was a cook by trade, but that specialty must have been in little demand in Illinois, although it is possible he was employed as such in the fort. He certainly traded with the Indians, probably on his own behalf, but indications are that he was no more than a petty trader. It was not a rich living; Claude Chetivau was unhappy and thought he could do better in Canada.

Chetivau approached François Cecire, nicknamed "Bontemps" (Good Time), the king's interpreter for Indian languages, asking that Cecire find an Indian to take him to the Miami, the Indian tribe living at that time primarily in Indiana but also in Wisconsin and Ohio. From Miami territory, Chetivau would have found it relatively simple to get to Canada. Chetivau indicated he would give the Indian a gun, a small kettle, a hat, and a pouch for guiding him. Cecire asked if Chetivau had permission to go, and Chetivau equivocated, saying that he did not think the gentlemen, by whom he meant the officers, would prevent him from going, and that he had already told Monsieur Dutisné that he wanted to go to Canada. Cecire held a responsible and well-paid position, and he was not about to risk his post over this very dubious proposition. He reported to Commandant Dutisné, adding that he had heard a rumor that Chetivau wanted others to go away with him. Dutisné, in turn, informed Marc-Antoine de La Loëre des Ursins and Nicolas-Michel Chassin, important officials of the Compagnie in Illinois and members of the Provincial Council.

So Chetivau found himself in jail, and the council launched a preliminary investigation. Pierre Melique, a lieutenant of the garrison, was summoned but indicated that he knew nothing. He may have heard Chetivau speak about going to Canada but paid no attention to it. Jean Huber, a local inhabitant, testified that he knew Chetivau, but not well, and now knew only that Chetivau said that Monsieur Dutisné had arrested him because he wanted to go to Canada. So far, the testimony did no harm to Chetivau, but now François Cecire testified to what he had earlier reported to Dutisné.

After the depositions of the witnesses were read to the council and it had affirmed their accuracy, the council turned its attention to Chetivau. Chetivau's testimony was disorganized and in places self-contradictory. He claimed he no idea why he had been imprisoned, that he had not tried to get an Indian to guide him to the Miami. He had, he maintained, only asked Cecire to interpret to an Indian to whom he wished to sell a gun. He continued, saying that several months earlier he had had a conversation with Cecire, who told him he would do better in Canada than here in Illinois, to which Chetivau replied that he would try to get permission to go to Canada. Cecire said he would try to find an Indian guide, should he get permission. Later, Chetivau claimed, Cecire told him the trip would have to wait until autumn.

After Chetivau was confronted with what the witnesses had said, he was further interrogated. He now admitted that he had brought a gun and a kettle to the Indian so that the Indian would guide him to the Miami if he got permission to leave Illinois. He denied that he had been condemned to ten years' servitude in Illinois, although that was contradicted by a letter from a man whose name is not fully legible in the court record.[2] Chetivau also told an unlikely tale that he had encountered the Commandant Dutisné on the main road by Fort de Chartres, where Dutisné said he did not care whether Chetivau went to Canada. This was a foolish move, for it pitted Chetivau's word against that of Dutisné, who was not only commandant in Illinois, but a member of the council that was trying Chetivau.

Under oath, Dutisné told a much different story. He testified that he had heard Chetivau had a featherbed for sale, but when he went to inquire about it, Chetivau tried to present it to him as a gift, which he refused in the presence of witnesses. Chetivau told him that he was miserable in Illinois and would be better off in Canada, and Dutisné recognized the proffered gift as an attempted bribe to ignore Chetivau's escape.

After discussion, the members of the council decided that Chetivau would be forbidden to leave the precincts of Fort de Chartres without permission of the council, on pain of six weeks in prison, and that his belongings, which had been confiscated when he was arrested, would be released to him only to the degree that he needed them to live. This was quite a light punishment, especially since his testimony was directly contradicted by that of the commandant, who was also his chief judge. Perhaps the council was lenient because Chetivau, at the worst, wished to desert and may have planned to do so, but did not actually desert, and the mild remedy they imposed prevented that in the future.

Chetivau's goods seem to have been soon released to him. On October 27, 1725, he was able to give six trade guns and a note for seven pots and a pint of brandy in exchange for a small two-room house at the village of Chartres by the fort.[3] At the end of the next January, he traded the house at an apparent loss, for seven and a half pots of brandy and one pound of vermilion, to a lieutenant of the garrison.[4] In any event, Chetivau remained in Illinois and in trouble.

By April 1726, Pierre-Charles Desliette was commandant at Fort de Chartres, and now he had to deal with Claude Chetivau. In addition to his other achievements, Chetivau was a gambler. There was no prohibition against gambling in early Illinois, but there was against cheating. On April 14, Jacques Brochard filed a petition with the commandant accusing Chetivau of having cheated him five days earlier of 600 livres' worth of goods in a card game of *brelan*,[5] an early ancestor of poker. This was a considerable sum. A large house could be purchased or a laborer hired for two or three years for that amount.

Brochard's petition explained that after losing to Chetivau, he had carefully examined the cards, which proved to be marked. The face cards, aces, and tens had been carefully shaved to be slightly shorter than the other cards, which had also been shaved to be narrower than the high-value cards. Brochard at some point showed the cards to witnesses and demanded that Chetivau return his goods, but Chetivau refused, and Brochard filed his petition with the commandant.

Desliette ordered a hearing for May 19, 1726. Chetivau's answer to the charges was in part rambling and irrelevant, and in part clever and shrewd. First, Chetivau complained that Brochard had not revealed that six days before his 600-livre loss, Brochard had won 195 livres from Chetivau and then two days later another 95 livres. Moreover, Brochard had paid off his 600-livre debt with merchandise that even he had valued at only 530 livres and that Chetivau had been able to sell for only 250 livres, which he used to pay off debts incurred by his earlier losses. This did not address the question of cheating, but Chetivau went on to make stronger arguments.

Brochard had voluntarily paid his gambling debt and only later had alleged cheating. The deck of cards had remained in Brochard's possession and could have been altered at any time subsequent to the game. If Brochard's petition were to be allowed, he would have an unfair advantage in that whenever he won, he would be satisfied, but whenever he lost, he could invent a complaint of cheating to avoid payment. If Brochard had made a complaint at the time of the game in the presence of other players, before the payment for the loss had been settled, and had shown the cards to have been marked, he could reasonably have demanded satisfaction, but not after the game was over, the loss paid, and the matter settled. Chetivau also offered to produce the testimony of La Vignes and La Fatigue, *habitants* of Kaskaskia, who were present at the game, saw no marked cards, and heard no complaint at the time from Brochard.

Finally, Chetivau claimed that Brochard's complaint was really the work of La Rigueur, a partner of Brochard's who financed his gambling in anticipation of a share of the winnings. Chetivau concluded by stating that Brochard had no grounds for his complaint and should be condemned to pay all expenses involved in the case.

We do not know whether Chetivau or Brochard won this case. Witness testimonies, responses to the initial arguments, and most importantly, the final decision do not survive among the archive of documents from the village of Chartres. Nor does Chetivau appear in other surviving documents later than this case. That does not mean that the man who had been sentenced in New Orleans to ten years' indentured servitude in the Illinois Country, had wanted to sneak away to Canada, and had been involved in a dubious high-stakes card game suddenly went straight. Relatively few documents survive from the early days of Fort de Chartres, a small fraction of what must have originally existed. Given Claude Chetivau's history of encounters with the law, it seems likely that he continued to be a troublesome individual, and one can only wonder about his ultimate fate.

(FRANÇOIS-)PIERRE BOUCHER DE BOUCHERVILLE: ESCAPE TO FORT DE CHARTRES

Pierre Boucher de Boucherville (1622–1717) rose from a soldier-interpreter of Indian languages to governor of Trois-Rivières, respected author, and lord of his own seigneurial parish, ennobled by Louis XIV. He also fathered fifteen children, one of whom, born in 1689, was baptized François-Pierre. The son, however, always went by the first name of Pierre, invoking the name of his famous father. Pierre the son joined the marines in 1702 as a cadet and served at Detroit under Cadillac. As a cadet, he was entrusted with more responsibilities than customary because of his knowledge of Indian languages. By 1721, he was an ensign and commandant of a small post.[1]

In 1727, René Boucher de La Perrière, Pierre's uncle, established a post near the Sioux on the Mississippi River in the vicinity of modern Frontenac, Minnesota. Pierre went as second in command. Fort Beauharnois, named for the governor of Canada, was a small establishment consisting of a square log stockade about thirty-one yards on a side, with two bastions at opposite corners. This small space held a chapel, officer's residence, soldiers' barracks, storehouse, traders' quarters, guardhouse, and powder magazine. In addition to Ensign Boucherville, residents were the Jesuit Father Michel Guignas and sixteen soldiers and traders. This tiny establishment was not meant to project military might, but rather to serve as a center for French traders and as a source of intelligence and diplomacy among the tribes of the area, primarily the Sioux, Fox, Mascouten, and Kickapoo. In 1728, Pierre Boucher de Boucherville found himself commandant of the post when his uncle fell ill and returned to Montréal. Events soon led Boucherville to abandon the post and flee with his men toward Fort de Chartres.

The escape of Pierre Boucher de Boucherville and his small command is recorded in a single manuscript written by Boucherville and signed by him and others of his command testifying to its truthfulness, supplemented by several contemporary letters. The manuscript presents a vivid account of the dangers faced by the French who in the early eighteenth century penetrated into le Pays d'en Haut, the "Upper Country," the Great Lakes territory north of Illinois.[2]

Fort Beauharnois was too small to withstand any concerted attack. The post relied primarily on its utility as a source of trade goods to the tribes of the area to keep it safe. The traders intended to deal primarily with the Sioux, but their chief fear was the Fox, who had long been hostile to the French, and in the autumn of 1728, the danger to the little post was particularly acute. A major French campaign against the Fox, commanded by Constant Le Marchand de Lignery, had miscarried. The

French and their allies managed only to burn the Fox's crops and villages and increased the tribe's hostility. When Lignery sent a party of French traders and Menominee Indians to inform the men at Fort Beauharnois of the Fox danger, Boucherville had several traders and Menominee go to the nearby Sioux, asking them to protect the fort from the Fox. The Sioux were noncommittal, and the Menominee advised that the Sioux were not to be trusted.

At this point, Boucherville prudently decided that the men should evacuate the fort, citing an insufficient stock of provisions for winter. Two courses lay open to them: toward Canada or toward Fort de Chartres. Boucherville and Fort Beauharnois were part of the Canadian command, and relations between Canada and the Illinois Country had been tense during the 1720s. Canada resented the detachment of Illinois from Canada and its assignment to Louisiana in 1717. The Canadian administration lost no opportunity to complain about Louisiana's management of Illinois, and Louisiana complained to France that the Canadians did little or nothing to discourage northern Indian raids into Illinois.[3] Yet Illinois was closer, and despite the disagreement between administrations, Boucherville and his companions could be sure of a cordial reception at Fort de Chartres—if they could get there, six hundred miles downriver (fig. 3.1).

On October 3, 1728, canoes loaded with trade goods and supplies, Boucherville and his company were ready to depart, but about half a dozen of the traders decided to remain at the fort. They argued that the Fox threat was exaggerated and that they would not be able to trade their goods if they left. If they remained, they would also have a virtually trade monopoly in the area and be able to deal with both the Sioux and the Fox, who, despite their hostility toward the French, sought French trade goods.

Boucherville, the priest Guignas, and ten men in three canoes began their long trip down the Mississippi. Past the mouth of the Wisconsin River, they found the ashes of Fox campfires, and by the mouth of the Wapsipinicon River, they saw the canoes that a Fox hunting party had beached on the shore. The French decided it was safer to lie concealed during the day and travel by night. Doing so, they successfully passed a major Fox village by the mouth of the Rock River, but approaching the Skunk River, they encounter a group of Kickapoo and Mascouten, who forced Boucherville and his party ashore and took them captive.[4]

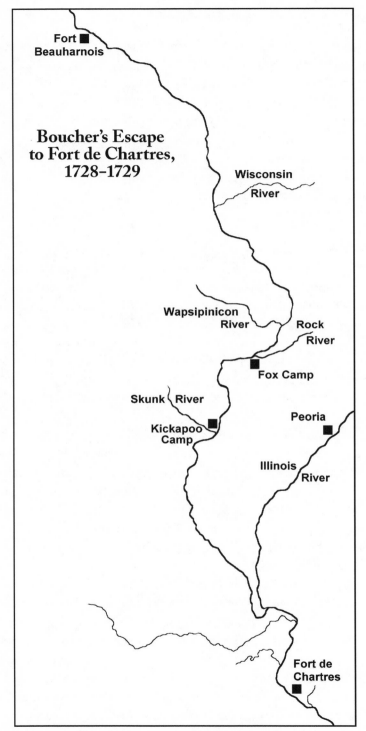

Fig. 3.1. Boucher's escape to Fort de Chartres, 1728–29

The Kickapoo and Mascouten were traditional allies of the Fox and seldom cooperated with the French. The Mascouten had originally lived in Michigan, but war with the French-allied Potawatomi had almost wiped out the tribe and driven the survivors to the area of the modern border between Wisconsin and Illinois. There they settled among the Fox and Kickapoo. The Kickapoo were noted for their fierce independence and tenacious cultural integrity.

Brought to the village of the Kickapoo and Mascouten, the best that Boucherville and his party could hope for was that they would be looted of their goods, but it soon appeared that they were destined for a worse fate. The Indians placed them in the lodge of a chief named Ouiskouba to await his return from a hunting trip, and they could anticipate no good welcome. During the summer, Desliette, the commandant of Fort de Chartres, led a combined force of French and allied Indians that attacked a hunting camp of Kickapoo and Fox near Chicago, killing among others Ouiskouba's family.

As they awaited Ouiskouba's return, tribal elders urged that the captives be put to death, but the younger warriors argued that the decision was Ouiskouba's. One can only imagine the trepidation of the French captives. Ouiskouba, however, proved to be in a forgiving mood. He still mourned his family, but he said "his heart was good,"[5] and he did not blame Boucherville or his companions. Moreover, he had visited Montréal two years previously and wished friendship with the French. He gave Boucherville his word that no harm would come to him or his companions.

In the following weeks, Boucherville met with the chief men in the Kickapoo camp, presenting gifts to them and attempting to win release. Boucherville argued that should any Fox appear, there would be trouble. The Kickapoo replied that they feared the French and the tribes allied to the French and would retain Boucherville's group as hostages, advising them, "Prepare yourselves to spend the winter with us and begin to build your cabins."[6]

Boucherville's party built cabins and settled down on good terms with the Kickapoo, but they must have had little confidence in their situation. The Kickapoo had promised not to surrender them should the Fox appear, but no one outside the village knew they were being held captive there. If the Fox applied enough pressure, the Kickapoo could surrender them without fear of repercussions. As far as the French would know, Boucherville and his men would simply have vanished in the wilderness, as so many others had.

In early November, ten Fox warriors came to the village. They offered the Kickapoo a calumet pipe and wampum belts, symbols of alliance, and other presents, attempting to get the Kickapoo to surrender the French to them. The Kickapoo refused, and Boucherville sought to buy off the Fox by giving them presents, nominally as recompense for Fox killed in the recent hostilities.[7]

At this point in Boucherville's narrative, two pages are missing, but the missing material is supplied by three letters reporting the events to France.[8] The Fox accepted the gifts and departed, but Boucherville had no confidence that they would leave his party in peace. Then three of the French, the two brothers Montbrun, cousins of Boucherville, and a soldier, escaped from the Kickapoo camp. This placed the Kickapoo in a dangerous position. Boucherville assured them that his cousins would report that the party had been treated well, but the Kickapoo appreciated that once the French learned that they held Boucherville and his men, the Kickapoo would be held responsible for their safety.

Boucherville's narrative resumes: Deciding their camp was too exposed, the Kickapoo moved to an island in the river, but an island could not protect against subversion. A Kickapoo chief married to a Fox intended to assassinate Father Guignas, but when he sought to enlist two young men in his plans, they betrayed his confidence to chiefs who favored the French. Again, Boucherville was able to calm the situation with gifts, and he recorded that henceforth the Kickapoo guarded the cabins inhabited by the French night and day to protect them.

The party of ten Fox who had visited the Kickapoo camp encountered a much larger group of Fox a few days after their departure and now returned with a group of thirty. Again, they demanded the surrender of the French, doing so in a manner contrary to custom and regarded as arrogant by the Kickapoo and Mascouten. Again, the Kickapoo refused to surrender the French, and the Fox departed, threatening vengeance.

Several days later, the group of thirty Fox encountered a Kickapoo and a Mascouten who were hunting. They slaughtered them and carried their scalps back to the Fox village, where the chiefs were appalled at their actions, realizing that this would mark a definitive break between the tribes. When the Kickapoo learned of the death of the hunters, they realized the same thing. Some tried to blame the rupture on Boucherville, who replied that he had warned them that if they did not send his party on their way to Illinois, there was likely to be trouble. The Kickapoo admitted he was right but asked, "What are we to do in the present predicament? We are between two fires; the Renard [Fox] has killed us, the Illinois has killed us, the Frenchman is angry at us."[9]

Boucherville assured the Kickapoo and Mascouten that if they would send him to Illinois with two escorts, he could make peace with the Illinois and French. They accepted his plan and chose two men, a Kickapoo and a Mascouten, each born of an Illinois mother, and together with Boucherville they departed for Illinois on December 27, 1728, in the middle of one of the most severe winters ever recorded. After an arduous trip, the three arrived at the village of the Peoria, at the site of the modern city of the same name, where they were cordially received and feasted.

Suffering from frostbite, Boucherville could go no farther, so he wrote a letter to Desliette, the commandant of Fort de Chartres, which he sent by messenger along with a letter from Father Guignas, the calumet and wampum belts with which the Fox had sought to bribe the Kickapoo, and a plea from the Kickapoo and Mascouten asking for peace with the French and Illinois and help against the Fox.

Desliette promptly answered that peace would be established with the Illinois and French as soon as Boucherville's group arrived safely at Fort de Chartres along with a delegation of the Kickapoo. Then they all could move against the Fox to avenge the wrongs they had suffered. Desliette also sent along some trade goods to distribute to the Kickapoo and Mascouten and promised more as soon as the next convoy arrived. Although the Illinois were ready to attack the Fox immediately, Desliette counseled them to wait until spring.

Boucherville was soon ready to return to rescue his men, but he was delayed eleven days by a Jesuit who wished to consult about Father Guignas. Finally on their way, thirty Kickapoo met Boucherville along with his original escorts and a single Illinois and escorted them back to their village, which greeted news of the new alliance with great enthusiasm. The Kickapoo sent out two war bands against the Fox. The first returned without doing anything, but the second secured by deceit two important Fox chiefs, whom they killed and scalped. Thirty Illinois soon arrived, returning Kickapoo captives, a woman and two children, further strengthening the new pact between the tribes.

On March 1, 1729, the Mississippi was finally free of ice, and the French could leave for Illinois. Father Guignas preceded the main party with an escort of two Mascouten chiefs. Boucherville and the rest of the French departed a few days later, escorted by seven pirogues of Kickapoo. The Illinois feasted with the entire party on their arrival, and then a detachment of twenty French escorted them to Fort de Chartres.

Boucherville and his entire party had escaped a host of dangers to arrive safely at the fort, but ironically, the half dozen traders who had remained behind at Fort Beauharnois not only had survived but also had faced much less danger. The Fox, not wishing to antagonize the Sioux who traded at Fort Beauharnois, also traded peacefully there and even prevented a group of Winnebago from stealing traps and other property from the traders. One of the traders visited a Fox village in central Wisconsin for several weeks and accompanied Fox leaders who visited Fort St. Joseph in southern Michigan in a fruitless quest to make peace with the French.[10]

After his adventurous escape, Boucherville continued to serve in the marines in Canada, rising to the rank of captain and holding a number of responsible posts. He retired in 1758 after fifty-six years' service and received the Cross of Saint Louis. He died in 1767.

CLAUDE-ALPHONSE DE LA BUISSONNIÈRE AND MARIE-THÉRÈSE TRUDEAU: MARRIAGE WOES

The course of true love never did run smooth, according to Shakespeare, and that was certainly the case with Alphonse de La Buissonnière and Marie-Thérèse Trudeau.[1] Modern writers have regarded the events surrounding their marriage as little more than an amusing tale, but the background of the people involved reveals a more complex story of deep divisions in the society of French Louisiana.

We do not know how the couple first became acquainted, but they probably met in the early 1730s. In 1730, La Buissonnière was thirty-five years old and unmarried.[2] He was a man of some social standing, the grandson of a royal comptroller and son of naval *commissaire*, but not wealthy, even by the standards of provincial Louisiana.[3] He had come to Louisiana as a lieutenant of the marines in 1720. In 1730, the governor of Louisiana, Étienne de Périer, described him as a "valorous and meritorious officer, who leads a well ordered life and who served well in our last expedition," against the Natchez Indians.[4] When, in 1732, the Ministry of the Marine recommended La Buissonnière's promotion to captain, Governor Périer commented favorably, describing him as "attached to the service, intelligent, wise, knowledgeable about fortifications," and La Buissonnière was duly promoted.[5]

Périer's favorable opinion was soon to change, as a result of La Buissonnière's desire to marry Marie-Thérèse Trudeau, the daughter of François Trudeau, an early settler of Louisiana. She was born about 1718,[6] and thus was about fourteen years old when she first met Alphonse de La Buissonnière, not an unusual age for courtship and marriage in French Louisiana.[7] The conflict about their relationship would take years to resolve and involve events in New Orleans, Natchez, Mobile, Pensacola, Illinois, and France.

The story of the marital woes of Alphonse and Marie-Thérèse is contained in three letters from Jean-Baptiste Le Moyne de Bienville and Edmé Gatien de Salmon to the minister of the marine, Jean-Frédéric Phélypeaux, comte de Maurepas. Bienville both preceded and succeeded Périer as governor of Louisiana, and Salmon was the *commissaire-ordonnateur* of Louisiana and first councilor of the Superior Council, the second most important officer in the colony.

Bienville and Salmon wrote the first letter about the marriage on September 22, 1733,[8] shortly after Bienville had returned to Louisiana as governor for the third time. According to the letter, about two years earlier, La Buissonnière had become enamored of Marie-Thérèse, the daughter of a very respectable early settler. Governor Périer opposed the marriage, as both were poor. La Buissonnière went to the garrison at Natchez but continued to court the girl, despite the efforts of Périer and Bienville to discourage the union. Périer argued that La Buissonnière would face ruin with a wife and a flock of children he could not support. La Buissonnière initially seemed to listen to these arguments but soon said that he could not call matters off without dishonoring Marie-Thérèse.

At this point, Périer, about to depart for France, send a letter to Father Raphaël Destrehan de Luxembourg, superior and vicar general of the

Capuchins in Louisiana, claiming that La Buissonnière was already married in France. Sieur de Pence, ensign on the supply ship plying between France and Louisiana, *La Gironde*, also wrote to Father Raphaël in similar terms.

When La Buissonnière applied to Father Raphaël to have the marriage bands announced, the priest showed him the letters and indicated that nothing could be done until these claims were resolved. The ship *La Gironde*, bearing Périer and Pence, had in the meantime departed New Orleans and was pausing at La Belize, the fort by the mouth of the Mississippi River at Southeast Pass. La Buissonnière, maintaining that the claims were calumny that dishonored him, obtained permission from Bienville to go to La Belize, from which he brought back a letter from Pence declaring that he had written to Father Raphaël only with the design of preventing the marriage and that in fact La Buissonnière was not married in France. La Buissonnière did not talk to Périer, who had gone ashore at the fort, but he believed he had enough to disprove the accusations, also showing Father Raphaël letters from his relatives in France that clearly indicated that he was not married, for they exhorted him to marry there in Louisiana. The priest, however, replied that Périer's letter was sufficient itself to prevent the marriage from going forward.

Although La Buissonnière and Marie-Thérèse's parents begged Father Raphaël, Bienville wrote, he would not permit the marriage, and Bienville felt it best to send La Buissonnière to the garrison at Mobile. There, however, Marie-Thérèse's father and a sister contrived to help the pair elope to Spanish Pensacola, where they paid a Franciscan to marry them.[9]

Bienville assured in his letter that he remonstrated angrily with La Buissonnière because of his behavior and said that he would have had him arrested, but instead ordered him to depart in a week for garrison duty in Illinois. Word spread in New Orleans that La Buissonnière intended to take his bride, whose status was still in dispute, with him. At this point, said Bienville, he realized it was not for him to make judgments of an ecclesiastical nature, but the vicar general of the Jesuits in Louisiana, Father Nicolas-Ignace de Beaubois, pointed out that the affair was likely to cause trouble in Illinois between the officers and the missionaries. The officers would support their comrade if the missionaries opposed the disputed marriage, and this would lead to complaints to Father Raphaël. So Father Beaubois requested that Bienville prevent Marie-Thérèse from traveling to Illinois and constrained La Buissonnière to resolve all opposition to his marriage.

Bienville agreed this was a wise precaution, and he requested that the Superior Council demand that Father Raphaël explain his reasons for continuing to oppose the marriage. Raphaël did not appear before the council but sent a request to the *procureur général* to have him enforce Périer's decision that the marriage was null and void.

At the same time, Father Raphaël communicated to La Buissonnière a declaration that the marriage was clandestine, sacrilegious, and null, prohibiting the couple from living together under pain of major excommunication and ordering fasting and penance. Despite Bienville's earlier statement that he knew not to interfere with ecclesiastical matters, he could now not resist indicating weaknesses in Raphaël's approach, noting that Raphaël was here acting as a judge but without the formality of a hearing and failed to indicate in what capacity he was acting, whether as grand vicar, officiant, or *curé*. Moreover, he criticized Raphaël's logic, pointing out that if the marriage was clandestine, it was null; and if it was null, there was no sacrament; and if there was no sacrament, there was no sacrilege—a very Jesuitical argument!

Bienville continued that La Buissonnière had now departed for Illinois, where his stay would be long, since the garrisons in that distant region did not change regularly as did those near New Orleans. The Superior Council, Bienville reported, declared that opposition to the marriage was invalid and that the Jesuits would not nullify the marriage. Bienville, rather than allow the situation to remain unresolved, allowed the pair to depart for Illinois but had Sieur Pierre d'Artaguiette, the commander of the convoy, embark them separately. Bienville concluded that it had always appeared that Périer's opposition was insufficient to impede the marriage.

Throughout the letter, Bienville endeavored to portray himself as judicious and balanced in attempting to solve the problems presented by the romance. He claimed to have supported his predecessor, Périer, in opposition to the marriage but ultimately concluded that once the marriage had taken place, there was inadequate reason to condemn it. He attempted to show deferment to ecclesiastical authority, agreeing with the Jesuit but portraying the Capuchin as less than reasonable.

Périer's opposition to the marriage of Alphonse de La Buissonnière and Marie-Thérèse Trudeau, if taken at face value, might seem initially no more than inept paternalistic concern that grew to anger over La Buissonnière's disobedience of orders.[10] The background of factional disputes in Louisiana, however, reveals Périer's opposition to have been an attack on Bienville and his supporters at the expense of the couple, and Bienville's letter is anything but candid, filled with omissions that hide and disguise the actual dynamics of the situation surrounding the couple and their marriage.

Disagreements, common in any society, easily flared to enduring feuds in early Louisiana, and rivalries tended to align themselves in support of or opposition to the most powerful figure in the colony, the governor. Before Périer became governor, Bienville had been removed in large part because of factionalism, and those who had opposed him had happily supported Périer, but now Périer was gone and Bienville was back in charge.

A basic division existed in the government of Louisiana itself. The governor and the second-ranking official, the *commissaire-ordonnateur*, were nominally independent of one another, but in reality their powers were ill defined and overlapping, and *commissaires* repeatedly became the center of opposition to governors. Bienville's personality also contributed to problems with a succession of *commissaires*. He was an able administrator but also authoritarian, easily offended, and implacable toward opposition, and the *commissaires* generally were no more accommodating.

Among Bienville's supporters were personal allies, many of those who had supported his brothers in the past, and many military officers—the *gens d'épée*. Along with the *commissaire*, lesser bureaucrats—the *gens de plume*—formed much of the opposition to Bienville, particularly the officials of the Compagnie des Indes, which had returned the colony to royal control in 1731 but continued to exercise trade concessions.[11]

Bienville's supporters among the *gens d'épée*, secure in their status, associated confidently and cordially with the Creoles and Canadians who had migrated to Louisiana. The lesser officials of the *gens de plume*, often with something of the air of *arriviste* about them, tended to look down on these groups and frequently failed to understand that colonial life both diminished class differences and permitted much greater social mobility than in France. The Creoles and Canadians naturally resented such attitudes and tended to support Bienville, who was himself a Canadian and had been an important figure in Louisiana from the earliest colonization.

Disputes between the Capuchins and Jesuits flared in the 1720s and carried over into the 1730s and even later, further dividing society.[12] The Capuchins provided the parish ministry for New Orleans, Mobile, and other settled area in southern Louisiana, while the Jesuits were in charge of missionary activity elsewhere.[13] This apparently clear division of power and responsibility broke down in actual practice when the Jesuits established their administrative center in New Orleans, the only practical location. The Jesuits, aided by Bienville, developed there a large plantation, storehouse, and chapel. They also assumed ecclesiastical oversight of the Ursuline convent in New Orleans and conducted services in the chapel of the hospital administered by the Ursulines, replacing the Capuchins. The Capuchins felt the Jesuits, favored by Bienville, infringed on their rights and regretted the departure of Périer, who had particularly benefited them. The personalities of the leaders of the orders further exacerbated tensions. The Jesuit Beaubois was intelligent, dynamic, and tactless; the Capuchin Raphaël was quick to take offense, quick to assume the worst motivations of Beaubois, and quick to complain to France. Raphaël also had a long history of hostility toward military officers and a preoccupation with perceived sexual improprieties.

In his letter, Bienville claimed that Périer objected to the marriage because both parties were poor, and if married, their family would be a burden on the colony; nowhere in the letter did Bienville disagree with this characterization. La Buissonnière may have had little beyond his modest salary as a captain of the marines, though others with no more than he supported families in Louisiana. Périer did not raise this or any other objection to the marriage of one of Marie-Thérèse's sisters to another officer, a lieutenant, in 1726.[14] Whatever the state of La Buissonnière's finances, François Trudeau, Marie-Thérèse's father, was far from poor and quite willing to support his daughter in her marriage.[15] Bienville barely mentioned Marie-Thérèse's father in the letter, describing him only as a very respectable early settler. François Trudeau was much more, and an examination of the man reveals both Bienville's deceptive reticence and the effect of factions in the daily life of Louisiana.

Bienville omitted to mention in the letter that his family had been connected to that of Trudeau since before the birth of either man, and that he was very much Trudeau's patron. François's father, Étienne Truteau, arrived in Montréal in 1659, where he married François's mother, Adrienne Barbier, in 1667. Étienne was a master carpenter and participated in the fur trade, and in Montréal, he became acquainted with Charles Le Moyne, sieur de Longueuil et de Châteauguay, father of Bienville. In 1675, Le Moyne formally deeded by notarial contract to Étienne a portion of his seigneurie, Longueuil, near Montréal, which Étienne occupied since at least 1671. This became the Truteau (later Trudeau) family home.

François, born in 1673, was the third of fourteen children of Étienne and Adrienne Truteau and a childhood friend of the Le Moyne children, including Pierre Le Moyne d'Iberville, the founder of Louisiana, born in 1661, and Jean-Baptiste Le Moyne de Bienville, born in 1680. In addition to their childhood friendship, they shared a Canadian culture that was already substantially different from that of France. In 1697, François, at the time engaged in the fur trade, signed his name to a contract.[16] Just as his father had, François became a master carpenter, for which literacy was a necessity.

The connection with Bienville shaped François Trudeau's life and his daughter's marital fortunes. François came to Louisiana when Bienville founded "old" Mobile in 1702. There François married Jeanne-Louise Burel, whose father Étienne Burel, along with his wife and three daughters, came to Mobile aboard the ship *Pelican* in 1704 as chaperones of the *filles du roi*, orphaned girls of good families sent to marry the colonists. When accusations were leveled at Bienville's administration of the colony in 1708, François Trudeau was one of half a dozen prominent citizens who testified for the governor; his father-in-law was another.[17]

François was much in demand as a master carpenter in the early days of the Mobile colony. With Bienville's permission, he even worked for the Spanish in Pensacola when Spain and France were at peace, and when they went to war in 1719, François fought to defend the French colony. In one incident, he along with just one other Canadian and six Indians repulsed an attempt of about a hundred Spanish to land on the west side of Mobile Harbor to replenish their water supplies.[18] Throughout his time at Mobile, Bienville relied heavily on the Canadian contingent among the settlers, including Trudeau. When Bienville sent La Buissonnière to Mobile, he placed him where François had friends and influence and where it would be easy for the couple to elope to Spanish Pensacola. It is hard to imagine this was entirely accidental.

By the time Marie-Thérèse met Alphonse de La Buissonnière, François possessed a fine, large plantation near New Orleans and was perhaps the wealthiest man in New Orleans. The census of 1721 shows him, his wife, and seven children enjoying the services of two French servants, and he owned one Indian and thirty-one African slaves, one more slave than Governor Bienville and more than three times as many as anyone else in the vicinity of New Orleans. Of the seven horses the census recorded in New Orleans, Trudeau owned four, and he had nine head of cattle, enough to provide several teams of oxen. Between 1724 and 1727, he was by far the greatest contributor to the building of the church that would become the first cathedral in New Orleans, exceeding even Bienville.[19] In 1731, he owned thirty slaves and twenty-three slave children, and in addition to his plantation, his family also enjoyed a succession of town houses in New Orleans.[20]

François Trudeau also played a public role in New Orleans. He was the commanding officer, the captain, of the New Orleans militia, a position of importance, and he would soon become a member of the Superior Council, the chief legal authority in Louisiana, which worked closely with the governor. His career is a prime example of financial success and social mobility possible in the colony.[21]

Yet Périer depicted the Trudeau family as poor, presuming that Bienville's report is accurate. Most likely Bienville did not object because he realized that debating the issue would not strength his case materially and would undermine his carefully constructed facade of impartiality, exposing him to charges of factionalism. Bienville had been ousted as governor in the past largely because of such charges.

Enthusiastic supporters of Bienville, the Trudeaus had clashed with the Capuchins and the anti-Bienville faction in general a decade before the marriage scandal. A letter of October 1723 written by the fiscal auditor Jacques de La Chaise to the directors of the Compagnie des Indes recounts the quarrel.[22] That year, the Capuchins were holding services in a room of a house that had been left to them while a new church was being erected. Lay church trustees (*marguilliers*), undoubtedly with the advice and consent of Father Raphaël, purchased and installed pews, which were rented to favorites.

Madame Jeanne Burel Trudeau, the wife of François, complained to Paul Perry, the councilman vested with oversight of church matters, that the pews ought not to have been installed and rented without the permission of the Superior Council, with the implication that the choice pews had been unfairly distributed. Perry took up Madame Trudeau's cause and told Father Raphaël that he did not blame the friars, but rather faulted François Duval, the head of the church trustees and a close ally of La Chaise. Raphaël defended Duval, attacked Perry for poor church attendance, and threatened to resign if not allowed to control his church. La Chaise was so outraged by the affair that he too threatened to resign if not supported in the affair.

La Chaise's letter includes mocking references to Madame Trudeau as "the wife of a carpenter, mother-in-law of the cashier" and to the Superior Council as "these little gentlemen who, seeing themselves invested with the character of councilors, wish to impose upon persons who know more about it than they do." To La Chaise, the Capuchins, and the anti-Bienville faction in general, the Trudeaus were social-climbing inferiors, partisans of the pro-Bienville bloc. François Trudeau's ostentatious donations to the building of the future cathedral of New Orleans between 1724 and the completion of the building in 1727 were perhaps in reaction to this denigration of his family rather than out of simple piety. The situation was defused by the recall of Bienville as governor at this juncture and the completion of the much larger church with many pews.

The rest of the story of the marriage appears in two subsequent letters, the first written on April 1, 1734.[23] By that time, Périer had long departed from Louisiana, never to return; the Jesuit Father Beaubois was soon to be recalled to France; and the Capuchin Father Raphaël was two weeks in his grave. None of these circumstances are mentioned in Bienville's letter. Bienville wrote that the convoy carrying La Buissonnière and Trudeau departed for Illinois, but at Natchez, Marie-Thérèse came down with smallpox. She returned to her father's house in New Orleans to recuperate, where she remained at the time the letter was written. Moreover, the Superior Council and *procureur*, having considered the statements of Périer, Raphaël, and La Buissonnière, had decided that the marriage was valid. Bienville did concede that the marriage was a rash and thoughtless act but sought to excuse it.

Bienville interwove this account with reasons the marriage should be validated by the authorities in France. If it were not recognized as legitimate, Marie-Thérèse would be dishonored, which she did not deserve, having always acted prudently and under the guidance of her parents. Her father, Bienville assured, had lived in the colony for more than thirty years and was an honorable and prudent man, loved and esteemed throughout the community. Moreover, he was the son of a captain of the militia in Canada, was himself the captain of the New Orleans militia, and had been proposed to be a member of the Superior Council. The father was inconsolable about what his daughter's situation would be if the marriage were not validated and still more so because of the disgrace it would bring to his other children and grandchildren, including two daughters already married, one who had first married a lieutenant of the marine infantry and was now in a second marriage to the *commissionaire* of the treasury of the marines, and the other married to one of the principal men in Louisiana. Bienville also argued that La Buissonnière was a very good officer, and it would be very bad to lose him. Bienville concluded the letter with the hope that the minister would be moved to have mercy. In effect, Bienville presented the minister in Paris with these alternatives: forgive the offense and validate the marriage, or create significant social disruption throughout the colony.

Bienville wrote to the minister of the marines again on April 14, 1735.[24] Only the first paragraph of this letter refers to the marriage. Bienville reported that, in accord with previous communication from the minister, he had informed La Buissonnière that approval of his marriage to Miss Trudeau had been obtained by the minister's good grace, and that since La Buissonnière's departure, she had constantly resided in her father's house, where she had conducted herself very wisely. In the margin of the paragraph is the note "*approuvé.*" The marriage had finally ceased to be the subject of factional dispute, though such disputes would continue to characterize French Louisiana and carry on beyond the end of the French administration.

Marie-Thérèse did not travel immediately to Illinois. The Chickasaw War had virtually closed the Mississippi to travel in 1734–35. On November 22, 1735, Marie-Thérèse was in Mobile, where she signed her name as "Trudeau La Buissonnière, wife of Alphonse La Buissonnière" as witness to the posting of marriage bands. Another witness was Pierre Juzan, the aide major at Mobile, who earlier that year had married Marie-Thérèse's sister Marie-Françoise, who had probably assisted Marie-Thérèse and Alphonse in eloping to Pensacola.[25] The year 1735 was a busy one in Louisiana. Bienville was preparing for a major campaign against the Chickasaw. Marie-Thérèse's aging father, François, stepped down as captain of the New Orleans militia that year, presumably to make way for a more vigorous commander during the campaign, and he was quickly appointed to the Superior Council. On August 15, 1736, François hired a free black man named Scipion "to go to the Illinois as rower in Madam La Buissonnière's boat."[26] Marie-Thérèse finally joined her husband when the convoy reached Illinois in the late autumn.

Bienville's campaign against the Chickasaw went terribly wrong. Contingents from Louisiana and the north failed to make juncture and were badly defeated individually. Almost the entire command structure of the Illinois garrison was wiped out, but La Buissonnière, the second-ranking officer in Illinois, had been left behind in command of Fort de Chartres. Now Bienville appointed him commandant of the Illinois Country.

La Buissonnière proved an active and able commandant, but the couple had only a short time together. La Buissonnière died suddenly in early December 1740. On August 6, 1741, Marie-Thérèse married Louis Robineau de Portneuf, a well-regarded twenty-three-year-old ensign at Fort de Chartres. A daughter, Félicité, was born to the couple on September 25, 1745, but Marie-Thérèse did not live to raise her. On April 2, 1749, an inventory was made of the property of Louis Portneuf and Thérèse Trudeau. In Illinois, such inventories were made within a day or two of the death of one of the marriage partners. Louis did remarry, but not until a decade later.[27]

JACQUES-SERNAN VOISIN:
A HERO OF THE CHICKASAW WARS?

In 1736, Bienville, the governor of Louisiana, launched a major campaign against the Chickasaw. His plans miscarried badly, and the campaign was a disaster.[1] Southern and northern forces failed to rendezvous and were defeated individually. After a hard fight on March 25, the Chickasaw routed the northern force, led by Pierre d'Artaguiette, the commandant of Fort de Chartres, and killed or captured all the marine officers, including D'Artaguiette himself. The Chickasaw burned most of those captured. The surviving French and Indian allies fled, closely pursued by the Chickasaw. Reports circulated that a sixteen-year-old named Voisin took charge of the chaotic situation, conducted a fighting retreat, and saved the day. The reports became a matter of controversy before the end of 1736 and remain so today.

On October 26, 1736, Maurepas, the minister of the marine, wrote from Paris to Bienville in Louisiana, criticizing his conduct of the failed campaign and making recommendations for promotions and replacements for the officers who had been killed.[2] Maurepas's letter contains what is evidently the earliest surviving mention of Voisin's heroics and the recommendation that Voisin be promoted from cadet to ensign. Maurepas wrote that Voisin, only sixteen years old, conducted reconnoiters and took charge of the retreat, conducting it very well. Maurepas also noted that in April, Bienville had recommended Voisin's promotion, although in that letter Bienville apparently had not mention Voisin's role in the retreat.[3]

There is no mention of Voisin in the surviving correspondence sent from Louisiana to the minister between d'Artaguiette's defeat and Maurepas's letter. From whom, then, did Maurepas hear an account of Voisin's actions? An obvious possibility is the thirty-eight Christian Iroquois who fought alongside the men from Illinois during the retreat and then returned to Canada,[4] although it is also possible that private correspondence or ecclesiastical officials' reports spread the account.[5]

On February 15, 1737, Bienville answered Maurepas's letter. Bienville's letter is defensive, the bulk of it devoted to self-justification and attempts to lay the blame for the disaster on others. Bienville argued that the French soldiers in both the southern and northern expeditions were cowards. It is in this regard that he wrote about Voisin:

> The report of the Arkansas and the declaration of a part of the Frenchmen who returned from M. D'Artaguette's expedition confirm the belief that he was hardly better served by his troop than I was by mine. In this connection I can assure my lord that the story that he was told about Sieur Voisin, the younger, is a pure fable and that I have heard nothing of the sort from any of those who have returned from that defeat although I questioned them all at that time.
>
> The order of the King being precise I shall have him examined when he returns from Mobile where he

has gone on the King's boat in the position of a pilot's
apprentice at fifteen or twenty livres per month. His
promotion has caused general surprise among the staff
of the officers, and if I had charge of the matter, I
should postpone his admission because I know that my
lord was surprised, and I can add that Sieur Voisin is
not capable of such a fine feat of courage and presence
of mind.[6]

Bienville's letter cannot be taken at face value. In the face of severe
criticism from the minister and royal displeasure, Bienville maintained
that the defeat was not his fault, but rather due to the cowardice of his
soldiers. The tale of Voisin's well-conducted withdrawal and fighting
spirit contradicted Bienville's contention. Bienville even treated Voisin's
promotion as something surprising and distasteful, ignoring the fact
that he had recommended that promotion in April, about a month after
the battle and shortly after the accounts of the battle had reached him.
Finally, Bienville's statement that Voisin was incapable of heroics is at
best subjective and dubious.

Despite Bienville's claim that the account of Voisin's heroics was false,
the story survived and grew, chiefly because of Father Pierre-François-
Xavier de Charlevoix's classic *Histoire et description générale de la Nouvelle
France*, published in 1744:

All the world knows the loss sustained by the colony in 1736,
in the persons of the brave Chevalier d'Artaguette and a
great number of officers of merit, and the noble actions of the
Jesuit Father Senat, who preferred to expose himself to the
certain peril of being taken and burned by the Chickasaws,
as he really was, rather than not assist to their last breath the
wounded who could not retreat or be transported by those
who did. This retreat, which was the work of a young man of
sixteen, named Voisin, may be regarded as a masterpiece in
point of skill and bravery. Pursued for twenty-five leagues,
he lost, indeed, many men, but it cost the enemy dearly,
and he besides marched forty-five leagues without food, his
men carrying in their arms the wounded who were able to
bear transportation.[7]

Charlevoix's rhetorical account serves a specific role within his larger work. He could hardly avoid mention of the Chickasaw defeat of French arms; it was the most recent notable event in French America. Yet to end his work with a bare account of a severe defeat would undermine his work's positive emphasis on French achievements in America. Charlevoix avoided this by omitting the specifics of the defeat while emphasizing the heroics of the fallen commandant d'Artaguiette, the martyred Father Senat, and the young Voisin.

Modern accounts of the Chickasaw Wars that include the story of Voisin's actions usually do so without citation of any source, and the story appears often to have been merely copied from one work to another. All seem ultimately dependent on Charlevoix's account. Many accounts of the wars omit any mention of the incident. Presumably, their authors either do not know Charlevoix's account or accept without discussion Bienville's dismissal of the story.

Voisin's subsequent life casts but little light on the question of his actions on the Chickasaw retreat. Jacques-Sernan Voisin, sometimes called Voisin *le jeune* (Voisin the Younger), was the son of Pierre Voisin, who emigrated from Brittany with his family. Pierre prospered in Louisiana, becoming a successful large-scale merchant in New Orleans. He was also an officer in the New Orleans militia and for a time an acting member of the Superior Council of Louisiana. While not a member of the nobility in any sense, he was a man of substance whose son could reasonably aspire to a career as an officer of the marine in Louisiana.[8]

Jacques Voisin was also born in Brittany. According to Charlevoix, he was sixteen years old in 1736, which would place his birth in 1720, but a list of officers serving under Bienville, dated June 15, 1740, gives Voisin's age as twenty-three, which would place his birth in 1717 and indicate he was nineteen at the time of the retreat.[9] Voisin first appears in the records in 1734,[10] when he joined the Illinois garrison as a cadet, a soldier serving in the ranks and aspiring to become an officer. It is not apparent when Voisin was first enlisted in the marines. Aristocratic cadets were sometimes enlisted as mere children, but Voisin, son of a provincial merchant, would not have enjoyed that early advantage. There appears to be no record of his service anywhere before going to Illinois in 1734, and it is likely he first entered the marines in that year. Voisin's name appears among the Kaskaskia manuscripts in documents of 1735 and 1736, chiefly in regard to slaves that his father had sent with him to be sold in Illinois.[11]

In 1736, Voisin went with the Illinois soldiers, militia, and Indians on the Chickasaw campaign, which ended so disastrously for them in late March. In April, Bienville recommended him for promotion to second ensign. A cadet would often serve for six to ten years before promotion to second ensign, but Voisin had probably served only about three years. There is no direct evidence of Bienville's motivation. He may have recommended Voisin's promotion because of the vacancies resulting from the Chickasaw defeat, or he may have done so at least in part because of Voisin's behavior during the retreat, although Bienville did not mention it specifically and later found it expedient to feign ignorance of it. Bienville's reports to the minister were always self-serving and far from scrupulously truthful, especially when defending himself against serious charges from France.

Bienville did recommended a number of officers and cadets for promotion, many to fill the posts in Illinois of those killed in the Chickasaw campaign, but at this same time, Bienville removed Voisin from Illinois and sent him to an obscure posting as an apprentice pilot operating out of Mobile, far from the surviving militia members who had personal knowledge of the retreat.[12]

Voisin's subsequent military career was respectable but hardly distinguished. He remained in southern Louisiana and never returned to Illinois. He was promoted to second ensign in 1738, and the following year, Bienville elected to take him on his second Chickasaw campaign in the place of another ensign who had been involved in a scandal.[13] Voisin married in 1745 and in later years raised a family and developed a substantial plantation.[14] He was promoted to full ensign in 1746 and lieutenant in 1752. He was commissioned as captain in 1759, but his letter of appointment was lost at sea, so his promotion was not formally recognized until 1762. In the last years of the French regime in Louisiana, he was commandant of the small Fort Ste. Marie at English Turn on the Mississippi, a little downriver from New Orleans.[15] He initially remained an officer of the Louisiana garrison under the Spanish administration, then retired, and died in early 1777.[16] During his career, he was described in service evaluations as well behaved, attentive to duties, useful, diligent, and punctual, all respectable virtues though not necessarily those that leap to mind in describing a military hero.[17] In short, he had a reputable military career, fairly typical of an officer in Louisiana, during more than three decades after the Chickasaw campaign of 1736, nothing during it tending to credit or discredit the report of his early heroics.

Evidence is simply not adequate to allow any firm conclusion about Voisin's actions during the retreat in 1736, but a few factors are suggestive. During the initial stages of the battle, the Chickasaw managed to kill or capture virtually all the officers of the Illinois garrison and militia on the scene. Voisin, a cadet, served in the ranks with the common soldiers, yet as a cadet, he had a status above that of a common soldier. A cadet was a member of a higher social class than a common soldier, almost certainly better educated, and would in the normal course of affairs become an officer. As a cadet, Voisin was one of few survivors with anything like a claim to leadership. He survived the chaotic fighting retreat and perhaps provided a measure of leadership and inspiration.

There is a tendency among survivors to seek something redeeming in even the worst defeat, and stories tend to grow with repetition. A positive account of Voisin's actions may have traveled to Canada and hence to France. There is no indication that Voisin spread the account of his actions or sought to exaggerate it. Both Bienville's and Charlevoix's accounts are clearly biased, and the truth is probably unrecoverable. The real importance of this affair may not be the question of Voisin's actions, but rather that it serves as a reminder of an obvious precept: we can never simply accept any historical document at face value, no matter who the author may have been, whether governor, highly regarded church historian, or anyone else.

JEAN DUCOUTRAY:
THE CHICKEN THIEF OF KASKASKIA

By modern standards, eighteenth-century European attitudes toward theft were harsh, but legal processes were observed with a punctiliousness that would suit any contemporary court, as the sad tale of the chicken thief of Kaskaskia reveals.[1]

Jean Ducoutray was born in 1724 in Paris. He arrived in New Orleans in July 1751, and by the next year, he was a member of the detachment from Fort de Chartres stationed at Kaskaskia. A legal document describes him as five feet, two inches by French measurement (the equivalent of five feet, six inches by the English standard), probably about average size for the soldiers in Illinois. He had brown hair, gray eyes, a small nose but large mouth, and a thin and tanned face. He was illiterate, a condition common to most of the soldiers and inhabitants of both France and Illinois at the time.

Ducoutray first ran afoul of the law, as far as we know, in the jurisdiction of the city of Beauvais in the Picardy region of France. There he stole six francs from a fellow cobbler. The authorities apprehended and convicted him, then branded him on the shoulder with the letter *V* for *voleur*, thief. The sources do not mention it specifically, but it is probable that the court also sentenced Ducoutray to deportation to Louisiana and enlistment in the French marines, where he was assigned to Fort de Chartres and the garrison at Kaskaskia.

Like many of the common soldiers and inhabitants of French Illinois, Ducoutray had a nickname, in his case either ironically prophetic or perhaps revealing a long-standing proclivity. He was known as "Poulailler" (Hen House). On July 13, 1752, Jean Ducoutray was on guard duty, but at about 2 A.M. he proceeded to the property of Joseph Brazeau and his wife, Françoise Dizier. There he entered the poultry yard through the surrounding picket fence and approached the hen house. The hen house was *poteaux-en-terre* (posts in ground) style, like many other buildings in the Illinois Country, with roof-bearing posts set vertically in a trench and joined by a horizontal beam at the top, to which a roof was attached. The spaces between the vertical posts were filled with *bousillage*, a mixture of clay and grass or some other fibrous material. The whole structure would usually be whitewashed. Archaeology has revealed the appearance of such a hen house. Typically, it would have been a narrow building about four feet wide, perhaps two or three times as long, and four and a half to five and a half feet in height.[2]

Ducoutray dug through the *bousillage* and pulled out a vertical post, leaving a hole four and a half feet high and a foot and a half wide. He seized nine hens, which he quickly beheaded. Françoise Dizier heard some disturbance among the chickens before dawn but did not suspect that any mischief was afoot. At dawn, she went to the chicken house and there found nine chicken heads and one headless chicken. Apparently, Ducoutray could carry only eight at one time. Françoise immediately suspected that a soldier had taken the poultry, and she requested a sergeant, George-Joseph Jacquemet, nicknamed "Versaille," to seek the thief.

In the meantime, Ducoutray had taken the chickens to the river, where he plucked them, then returned to his post and started to stew the chickens. His sergeant, Jean-François Bedaque, called "Ste. Jean," awoke to the scene and promptly inquired whether Ducoutray had bought the chickens. Ducoutray did not answer but rather left quickly. Bedaque dressed, followed, and, joined by Jacquemet and a third sergeant named Moreau, questioned Ducoutray, who quickly broke down and confessed. Bedaque led the hapless chicken thief to jail and informed the adjutant of Kaskaskia. At this point, the legal processes began.

On that same day, July 13, 1752, de Mazellières,[3] captain of the marine company garrisoned at Kaskaskia, wrote to Jean-Jacques de Macarty Mactique, knight of the Military Order of Saint Louis, major commanding for the king in Illinois, informing him that Ducoutray had been arrested and requesting that an inquiry into the matter be commenced. On the same day, Sieur Rousselet de Boisroger, adjutant of Kaskaskia and lieutenant of marines, acting as *procureur* of the king, and assisted by Jean-Baptiste Berlot Barrois, clerk of the court, instituted a court-martial. Witnesses were called: Françoise Dizier, the three sergeants, and Jacques Dégagné, a settler whose pig someone had attempted to steal the same night. After the witnesses were initially examined, they were reexamined in the light of one another's testimony.

On July 14, Ducoutray was questioned about the chicken thievery and his earlier conviction for theft in France and was confronted with the testimony of the witnesses. He denied nothing in regard to the chickens. The following day, a council of war assembled before Commandant Macarty and considered the testimony, finding Ducoutray guilty and ordering him to be expelled from the marines and turned over to civilian justice for a new trial and punishment if found guilty there. Ducoutray and the records of the court-martial were promptly passed over to the civilian authorities at Kaskaskia, where he was locked in the local jail. Now the entire process began anew.

On July 17, Joseph Buchet, who resounded in the titles of chief secretary of the marine, subdelegate of the *commissaire-ordonnateur* of Louisiana, and judge of Illinois, accompanied by Barrois, clerk of the court, examined the ravaged hen house and questioned anew the witnesses Françoise Dizier and the three sergeants. Each swore to tell the truth, and that he or she was not a relative, connection, servant, or domestic of the accused. The testimony given on July 13 was then read, and each testified to its truth.

The next day, July 18, Ducoutray was questioned and admitted the crime fully. Buchet seemed to struggle to understand why Ducoutray had committed the crime, so easily detected. Ducoutray declared that no one had induced him to commit the theft, that he had done it of his own will. He admitted that he had adequate rations and had received his pay, which was paid in advance every five days. He indicated that he had intended to share the chickens with his fellow soldiers, but that they were in no way involved in the theft. He said that he knew stealing was against the law and that thieves were punished. The only explanation he made of the crime was that he had acted through weakness. He admitted his previous theft and punishment in France but denied that he had attempted to steal Jacques Dégagné's hog. Ducoutray's testimony was then read back to him, and he affirmed its truth and appended his usual mark. Yet this was not the trial, but rather only the preliminary civil inquiry.

That same day, the actual trial began. André Chevalier, *procureur* for the king in Illinois, acted as prosecutor before Joseph Buchet, chief secretary of the marine, subdelegate of the *commissaire-ordonnateur* in Louisiana, and judge in Illinois. Again the witnesses were called: Françoise Dizier and the sergeants Jean Bedaque, George Jacquemet, and Jean Moreau. Again the testimonies were read, and each witness swore it was the truth and there was nothing to add or retract. The next day, Ducoutray was confronted by each witness, whose testimony was read and again sworn to be truthful. Then on July 20, André Chevalier called for Ducoutray's conviction "of theft with burglary, for the second time, as he has previously been convicted and branded, in reparation of which let him be condemned and led to the king's galleys, there to serve as a galley slave in perpetuity, his goods to be confiscated to the king, if there be any." This was duly ordered, with the added provision that fifty livres and interest from Ducoutray's assets be paid to Joseph Brazeau, husband of Françoise Dizier, in damages and that Ducoutray also pay the cost of the suit, the remainder of Ducoutray's assets to go to the king.

Ducoutray was then sent to New Orleans, where on October 31:

> Sieur Raguet, acting as procureur general, shows that
> one Ducoutray, called Poulailler, was imprisoned and
> tried in Illinois by court martial before Lieutenant
> Rousselet de Boisroger, convicted and condemned; the
> case was then turned over to the civil jurisdiction; after
> testimony, reexamination, confrontation and second
> interrogation of the accused, he was again convicted
> and condemned. It was found that he had already been
> tried in France and branded for theft. His case was tried
> according to the rigor of the ordinances, and as it is to
> the interest of the public that crime remain not unpun-
> ished, the present petition, in the form of a complaint,
> was presented by the procureur general at New Orleans,
> that Ducoutray be interrogated and heard again on the
> salient facts in the suit instituted in Illinois, the whole
> procedure to be gone over anew, following order of M.
> Raguet, acting Procureur General in said place. Signed:
> Raguet[4]

Ducoutray was committed to the prison, and on November 3, the third trial began with his interrogation. Again he admitted to the theft. His account differed from his earlier confessions in only a few minor elements; for instance, he now said the theft had taken place between midnight and 1 A.M., whereas earlier he had said 2 A.M. On November 10, the *procureur général* asked for a different punishment than galley slavery suggested in Illinois. He wanted to hang Ducoutray, but the next day, the court, which consisted of the governor of Louisiana, the *commissionaire-ordonnateur* of Louisiana, the major of marine, the *commissionaire* of marine and second councilor, and the councilor assessor, passed final judgment: Ducoutray was to be branded with a fleur-de-lis on his left shoulder and whipped, have his goods confiscated, and then be sent to France, there condemned to the galleys.

The final document in this sad story is a letter dated August 24, 1753, from the minister of the marine to the *intendant* of Rochefort, informing him that the prisoner "Ducourtrait called Poulailler" was sentenced by a Louisiana military tribunal to life in the galleys at Brest.[5] After that, silence.

By modern standards, Ducoutray's offense, stealing eight chickens, seems minor but his punishment incredibly harsh. During the eighteenth century, legal punishments were generally severe, but if the chicken theft had been his first offense, he might have escaped with a fine, a short imprisonment, and perhaps a lashing. Minor offenses seem to have been often treated in Illinois with less than the full rigor of French law. Eighteenth-century law, however, was not indulgent to repeat offenders. Ducoutray had been previously convicted for theft and could expect no mercy, a fact he must have known, which makes his crime all the more difficult to understand. Although his fate was hard, Ducoutray would have had to admit that he had received due process of law, including repeated opportunities to explain his actions and any mitigating circumstances.

JEAN-BERNARD BOSSU:
OFFICER AND TRAVEL WRITER

Jean-Bernard Bossu was a minor officer who served briefly in Louisiana and at Fort de Chartres late in the French regime. He became a popular author whose works are significant sources for some aspects of French Louisiana and Illinois but have often been accorded too much credibility (see the appendix on Bossu's books at the end of this chapter).

Bossu was born in France in 1720. He served in the War of the Austrian Succession, during which he was severely wounded and earned a commission as a second lieutenant. When the war concluded in 1748, the government demobilized the army, and many officers faced unemployment. Bossu pursued an alternative, entering the colonial service. On the recommendation of the *brigadier des armées* Chevalier de Grossolles, he received a commission as lieutenant and arrived in Louisiana in 1751. Bossu later published two accounts of his years in America, written in the form of letters. This was a common literary form during the eighteenth century. Bossu claimed to have started writing these letters even before his arrival in Louisiana and continued to do so throughout his stay. He may well have written some preliminary forms of the letters at the times and places indicated, but he certainly edited and revised them before final publication.

Bossu was assigned to the Illinois garrison and traveled with the new commandant of Fort de Chartres, Macarty, up the Mississippi by convoy in the autumn of 1751. The convoy paused for some weeks at the Arkansas Post, a small distance up the Arkansas River from its juncture with the Mississippi.[1] Bossu related that the Arkansaw (Quapaw) Indians adopted him, and he provided a colorful account of the ceremony, which consisted of the painful tattooing of a deer on his thigh. Bossu did not mention the French post, its commandant, garrison, or the French settlers there, giving the impression without explicitly claiming such that he was alone among a tribe virtually unaffected by contact with the Europeans.

When the convoy was thirty leagues south of Fort de Chartres, Macarty went ahead, probably not because he was suffering an attack of gout as Bossu claimed, but rather because of rumors of an Indian uprising. Left behind, Bossu's boat first grounded on a sandbar, and then sank after hitting a partly submerged tree. Bossu wrote that he lost everything he owned.[2]

Although he had written in his account of the trip up the Mississippi that Macarty had gone ahead and left Bossu behind, Bossu later wrote that Macarty sent him ahead to prepare lodgings for troops coming by convoy. Arriving in Illinois, Bossu found the area in an uproar. A small group of Piankashaw and Wea Indians, who had trade relations with the English, attempted to persuade the Illinois to abandon their alliance with the French. This led to a minor confrontation. Bossu's account of the affair contains notable distortions. He dated the climactic action to Christmas Day, apparently in an effort to make it seem more dramatic and romantic; Macarty, the commandant, in his official report indicated that it took place on December 8. Bossu also maintained that it was his clever plan that revealed the Indians' intentions and saved the situation; Macarty did not even mention Bossu in his prosaic report.[3]

In his account of the attack of the Fox and their allies on the Illinois in 1752, Bossu again placed himself in the center of action, rescuing a fifteen-year-old Indian girl. Macarty mentioned Bossu only in regard to the aftermath of the attack.[4] After the events in his first months at Fort de Chartres, Bossu actually told little about his sojourn there, remarking that life was rather peaceful. He provided some personal anecdotes concerning the Illinois but primarily filled his letters with stories derived from other written works.

In mid-1753, Bossu took leave to go to New Orleans, where he sought reimbursement for his losses during his trip to Illinois, and there he met the new governor Kerlérec, who would become Bossu's greatest enemy. Bossu came to detest Kerlérec, and he exhibited that from his very first written mention of the governor, long before he actually became involved in opposition to the governor. Bossu claimed that Kerlérec delayed him in New Orleans until the autumn convoy of 1754 left for Illinois. Again the convoy made slow progress, finally arriving in January 1755, at which time Bossu, probably suffering in part because of his old wound, had to be carried in a litter. He spent some time convalescing at Cahokia. His letters about this period continue to consist largely of stories gleaned from earlier written accounts interspersed with personal anecdotes. He added little about contemporary events in Illinois, although he did provide a short account of an expedition of François Coulon de Villiers, the brother of the ill-fated Joseph Coulon de Villiers de Jumonville, whom George Washington had precipitously attacked and killed. Even this is second-hand; Bossu attended only the dinner before the expedition departed and witnessed the return of François Coulon de Villiers's command.[5]

In late 1756, Bossu left Illinois for France. His health, complicated by his old wound, had not improved. He commanded the convoy going down the Mississippi to New Orleans, and from there he sailed to France in the spring of 1757. After recuperating, Bossu returned to Louisiana late in 1758 on the same ship as the new *commissaire-ordonnateur*, Vincent-Gaspard-Pierre de Rochemore, and it is likely that the two became friendly at this time.

Feuding between governors and *commissaires*, the financial officers of the colony, plagued Louisiana from its earliest days, but none proved more bitter or destructive than that between the governor Kerlérec and Rochemore. Amid the crises of the French and Indian War, their disagreements rapidly graduated from lack of cooperation and recriminations to reciprocal charges of malfeasance and corruption. British sea power largely isolated Louisiana during the war. French ships bearing trade goods necessary to secure Indian alliances did not arrive, and basic provisions were scarce and expensive. Even essential military materials, such as gunpowder, were in short supply. Rochemore regarded Kerlérec's attempts to deal with these problems as usurping his authority. Factions developed around both men. Kerlérec complained bitterly to France about what he termed Rochemore's cabal, a group that included Bossu and other officers.[6]

Shortly after Bossu's return, Kerlérec assigned him to the garrison at Fort Toulouse in Alabama, where Kerlérec appointed as commandant a younger officer inferior in rank to Bossu. Bossu complained, but Kerlérec's only response was to transfer Bossu to the Mobile garrison. Kerlérec acknowledged in a report written in 1758 that Bossu was a brave soldier who had been severely wounded in the service of France and that he was well behaved, but Kerlérec also evaluated him as a "very narrow-minded man, to whom I do not entrust missions." Despite this evaluation, the minister of the marine promoted Bossu to captain in 1759. Bossu then commanded a small convoy to Fort Tombecbé, where he joined the garrison.

In 1762, the growing feud with Kerlérec led to Bossu's recall to France. While his dislike of Kerlérec is everywhere apparent in his writing, Bossu was reticent about the specifics of their dispute, and even his report of his recall explains little: "Kerlérec had used a Spanish schooner to send to the minister charges against Monsieur de Rochemore, *Commissaire Général de la Marine* and *Ordonnateur à la Louisiane*, who was recalled to France by a *lettre de cachet*. Charges were also brought against the officers who accompanied him. I was among them."[7]

In 1759, Rochemore had finally overstepped his authority by issuing treasury bills of exchange, essentially paper money, without royal authorization. The minister severely reprimanded him and granted Kerlérec broad powers over the *commissaire*. Relatives in France were able to delay Rochemore's formal recall, but in 1762, Kerlérec was authorized to order Rochemore to return to France along with eight officers who formed the nucleus of his cabal. One of them was Jean-Bernard Bossu. In France, all were dismissed from royal service.

It appeared that Kerlérec had triumphed, but in reality, the feud, and Bossu's role in it, would long continue. In sending Rochemore and his supporters back to France, Kerlérec made a grave tactical error, for in France they were able to spread their account of events in Louisiana and lobby against Kerlérec.

In the meantime, events that marked the end of French America were playing out. In 1760, the fall of Montréal marked the end of effective resistance to the British conquest of Canada, and France and Britain began long negotiations to conclude the Seven Years' War. In 1763, France, defeated and exhausted, agreed to cede all claims to lands east of the Mississippi to the English, with the exception of New Orleans, which was to go to Spain along with French claims west of the Mississippi. That same year, Kerlérec left office and returned to France, where he was bitterly attacked by Rochemore's circle.

Rochemore died in 1763, but that did not end the feud. If anything, it grew more vitriolic as Rochemore's widow exploited powerful family influence in the cause. The officers who had been expelled from the service on Kerlérec's recommendation vilified him to the government and in public. In 1764, Kerlérec's supporters accused Bossu of having harassed and insulted Kerlérec's wife on the streets of Paris. A government commission began inquiries into the conduct of both Rochemore and Kerlérec in what became known as the "Louisiana Affair." This investigation dragged on for years.[8]

In 1768, Bossu published his first book, *Nouveaux voyages aux Indes Occidentales*. Bossu described his work as written in a "restrained, succinct style," used to convey "simple, unadorned truth," unlike "most travelers, who invent stories and substitute ingenious fables for the truth to make their work more interesting."[9] Although many modern readers have accepted this assurance at face value, Bossu should rather be understood as a typical premodern travel writer, working in a genre dating back to classical antiquity and familiar to a sophisticated eighteenth-century audience. Assurances of the truth were part of the genre, customarily followed by entertaining descriptions of native people, culture, land, climate, resources, plants, and animals, all enlivened by anecdotes about the adventures of the author and others. Premodern travel writers usually did not invent stories but felt free to elaborate and embellish accounts.

Bossu's treatment of the aftermath of the Natchez Indians' massacre of French settlers in 1729 is typical. He had no personal acquaintance with the events, which had occurred long before he came to America, yet he pretended to quote long, elaborate speeches by Indians that neither he nor any other French man could have possibly heard, and he described the massacre in detail unknown to any writer contemporary with the event. He claims the Natchez killed about two thousand French, but this may be merely a misprint for two hundred. His story about Princess Stung Arm is romantic fiction. According to Bossu, she tried to prevent the Natchez massacre, and when that failed, she attempted to confuse the planned date of attack so that the Natchez attacked without allies.[10]

Bossu's treatment of the aftermath of the Villasur massacre follows the same pattern. In 1720, Pedro de Villasur led an expedition from Santa Fe, in what is now New Mexico, to the vicinity of the confluence of the Loup and Platte Rivers, near the site of present-day Columbus, Nebraska. There the Pawnee and Oto attacked the expedition, killing most of the Spanish and some of their Indian scouts.[11] Indians bearing Spanish loot visited Illinois, where Boisbriand was commandant of Fort de Chartres, then under construction. Accounts contemporary with the event are succinct and bare, but Bossu, writing thirty-three years after the event, paints an intimately detailed, colorful word picture:

> The Missouris themselves told all these happenings when they came here wearing the chapel ornaments. The chief wore a beautiful chasuble, and hanging from his neck was a paten, pierced with a nail and serving as a breastplate. Crowned with a feather headdress and a pair of horns, he walked gravely in front of the others. Those who followed him wore chasubles; after them were those dressed in stoles. And then came Indians with maniples around their necks. There came next two or three young men in albs and other in surplices. The acolytes, out of usual order, came at the end of this new-style procession, since they were not dressed up enough. They carried a cross or candelabrum. These people, knowing nothing of the respect due the sacred vessels, hung a chalice around a horse's neck as though it were a bell.[12]

The scene is clearly imaginary. The Pawnee and Oto, not the Missouri, destroyed the Spanish expedition. Villasur built no chapel and had with him only one priest, whose vestment and sacred vessels could not possibly have equipped a procession such as Bossu described. Moreover, Bossu claimed the Indians massacred the entire Villasur expedition except for the priest, who later escaped. In reality, the priest along with Villasur and most of the Spanish soldiers and some of the Indian scouts were killed, but a number of Spanish soldiers and most of the Indian scouts lived to return to Santa Fe. Bossu's account is merely an imaginary elaboration of the earlier written accounts of Pierre-François-Xavier de Charlevoix, Jean-François-Benjamin Dumont de Montigny, and Antoine-Simon Le Page du Pratz.[13] Those earlier written accounts were, in turn, dependent on a muddle of second- and thirdhand reports, rumors, and half truths, all of which grew more picturesque with each retelling. This is typical of Bossu's approach throughout this and his subsequent book.

Bossu also told many other stories that are improbable but just possibly true, such as his account of having in 1751 met an Indian who had seen La Salle when he first traveled down the Mississippi in 1682, sixty-nine years earlier. Still, Bossu was an author of some talent, who could create striking images. Traveling from New Orleans to Illinois, Bossu remarked, "This trip is made by rowing against the current of the winding Mississippi, which flows between two great forests of timber trees as old as the world." In regard to his adoption by the Arkansas Indians, he wrote, "I consider it similar to the honor received by Marshal de Richelieu when his name was inscribed in the golden book among the names of the nobles of the Republic of Genoa."[14]

Bossu's work was well received, but it involved him in further difficulties. Although it is clear in the work that Bossu did not like Kerlérec, his criticisms of the governor are by modern standards rather mild. One sentence, "The new governor says that he has not come all this way just for a change of air,"[15] particularly caused offense. It implied that Kerlérec had set out from the beginning to enrich himself corruptly. Moreover, Bossu's work as printed was not exactly the same as approved by the government censor. As a result, Bossu was sent to the Bastille, though he was released after little more than a month.

In 1769, the government commission's report on the conflict between Kerlérec and Rochemore was finally completed, condemning the actions of the governor and exonerating the *commissaire* and his associates, all of whom sought enormous reparations. Bossu put in a claim for 80,000 livres and requested the Cross of Saint Louis. He and the others were to be disappointed. The commission's report was manifestly the product of the influence of the powerful Rochemore family and so obviously prejudiced and unbalanced that it was largely discounted. Kerlérec was briefly exiled thirty leagues from Paris, and even that was rescinded early in 1770. He started to compose an appeal of the commission's report but died that year before he could complete it. Bossu was restored to the rank of captain and received a pension of 1,080 livres and a bonus of 1,200 livres.[16]

In 1770, Bossu returned to Louisiana in an unsuccessful attempt to recover valuables left behind at the time of his forced departure, and he used the opportunity to compose a second book, *Nouveaux voyage dans l'Amérique Septentrionale.* As in his first book, Bossu retold stories from previously published works, interspersed with personal anecdotes. Most interesting is his lengthy account of a visit to the Arkansas Indians, whom he had visited on his first trip up the Mississippi. They were, he assured his readers, overjoyed to see him again and honored him greatly, though he never explained why the tribe was so happy to see an underofficer of the French marines who had stopped with them for about six weeks fourteen and a half years previously. One may suspect a modicum of exaggeration.

Bossu also visited several other tribes who lived beyond the Arkansas and provided some valuable information about manners and customs. He was, however, not an objective observer. In both books, he idealized Indians, except in regard to their cruelty toward captives and religion, and contrasted their natural simplicity with European immorality and decadence. The influence of Jean-Jacques Rousseau has been suggested in regard to Bossu's attitude toward Indians, but he never mentioned the *philosophe*, and the same sentiments can be found in the work of Antoine-Simon Le Page du Pratz, which Bossu certainly knew and from which he borrowed with a heavy hand.

Bossu's second book seems to have been received with less enthusiasm than the first. Louisiana was already receding from French popular attention. Bossu was back in France by 1771, where he retired on his captain's pension. He died there in 1792.

Appendix: Editions and Translations of Bossu's Books

The full title of Bossu's first book is *Nouveaux voyages aux Indes Occidentales; contenant une Relation des différens Peuples qui habitent les environs du grand Fleuve Saint-Louis, appellé vulgairement le Mississipi; leur Religion; leur gouvernement; leurs moeurs; leurs guerres et leur commerce,* published in two volumes in Paris during 1768. The two-volume work appeared in two editions, identical in all details except that the second bears the words *seconde édition* on the title page and claims to have been published in Amsterdam in 1769.

The first edition was ordered destroyed at the time Bossu was sent to the Bastille and is now rare. It is possible that the second edition was not really published in Amsterdam. To avoided French censors, an author might publish a work abroad or merely print a false title page indicating that it had been printed abroad. The second edition may in fact be the original printing with the substitution of a new title page.

A digital copy is available online at books.google.com, and many on-demand reprints are available. The title may be translated as *Recent Travels in the West Indies, Containing a Description of the Various Peoples Who Inhabit the Vicinity of the Great River Saint Louis, Commonly Called the Mississippi; Their Religion; Their Government; Their Customs; Their Wars; and Their Commerce.* A new edition of the French text, edited by Philippe Jacquin, was published under the title *Nouveaux voyages en Louisiane, 1751–1768,* in 1994.

There have been two English translations, but for accuracy, the original French should always be consulted. The earlier was made by John Reinhold Forester and published in 1771 in two volumes under the title *Travels through That Part of North America Formerly Called Louisiana by Mr. Bossu, Captain of the French Marines.* Forester added to Bossu's text "an abstract of the most useful and necessary articles contained in Peter Loefling's *Travels through Spain and Cumana in South America*" (a reference to Pehr Löfling, *Iter Hispanicum, eller resa til Spanska Länderna uti Europa och America 1751 til 1756,* published posthumously in 1758 by Carolus Linnaeus).

A more recent translation is that by Seymour Feiler, *Jean-Bernard Bossu's Travels in the Interior of North America 1751–1762,* published in 1962. Feiler's translation is much less literal than Forester's and substitutes modern names for Bossu's frequently archaic terms for the names of Indian tribes, places, flora, and fauna. The translation is more immediately accessible, but it substitutes the translator's conclusions for what Bossu actually wrote. The book contains a good index. A German translation also appeared in 1774.

The full title of Bossu's second work is *Nouveaux voyage dans l'Amérique Septentrionale, contenant une collection de lettres écrites sur les lieux par l'auteur, à son ami M. Douin, chevalier, capitaine dans les troupes du roi, ci-devant son camarade dans le Nouveau Monde,* which may be translated as *New Travels in North America, Containing a Collection of Letters Written on Location by the Author, to his Friend Mr. Douin, Chevalier, Captain in the King's Troops, Who Was Earlier His Comrade in the New World.* The title page indicates that the work was printed in Amsterdam during 1777. Again, there is some doubt whether the work was actually printed in Amsterdam or in France with the false ascription to Amsterdam.

An English translation of Bossu's second book was provided by Samuel Dorris Dickinson, published in 1982 under the title *New Travels in North America by Jean-Bernard Bossu, 1770–1771.*

PHILIPPE-FRANÇOIS DE RASTEL DE ROCHEBLAVE:
A MAN OF MANY FLAGS

On October 10, 1765, Captain Thomas Stirling of the 42nd Highlanders, the famous Black Watch, took possession of Fort de Chartres. Pontiac's uprising and other related Indian hostilities toward the British delayed the transfer that had officially been decreed two years previously. The British command in the Illinois Country changed quickly and allowed little consistent or coordinated governance. Major Robert Farmer succeeded Captain Stirling, to be followed by Colonel Edward Cole, then Colonel John Reed, then Lieutenant Colonel John Wilkins, all within five years. Wilkins stayed only two more years before Isaac Hamilton replaced him. He remained just long enough to take most of the troops east, leaving behind Captain Hugh Lord and a mere handful of soldiers. Even they withdrew in 1776, and a former French officer became the sole representative of the British government in Illinois.

Philippe-François de Rastel de Rocheblave was born in France in 1727 to an old noble family, one of twenty-three children. A number of the boys had military careers in North America, as many as seven by one account, though four seems a more likely number.[1] No end of ingenuity has been expended in attempting to figure out their intertwined careers, but no one has produced an entirely satisfactory formulation. The custom of referring to officers in documents only by their last names creates apparently irresolvable ambiguities. Two brothers, Pierre-Louis and Paul, are most often confused with Philippe-François. Pierre-Louis served in Canada until the British conquest and subsequently became the governor of Gorée Island, Senegal, and still later served at Saint-Domingue.[2] It is possible that the Rocheblave active in the Ohio River valley region in the 1750s was Pierre-Louis rather than Philippe-François.[3]

Paul arrived at New Orleans as a cadet in 1752. He spent his career in southern Louisiana, at New Orleans, Pointe Coupée, and Fort Ste. Marie, the artillery post guarding the Mississippi below New Orleans at English Turn. He established a farm in that area. Paul took part in the infamous Kerlérec-Rochemore feud and was identified as a member of Rochemore's cabal. Kerlérec described him as an intelligent person who used his mind for bad purposes, which seems to have meant primarily that he opposed Kerlérec.

In 1760, Paul de Rocheblave quarreled with a member of the Swiss Regiment, Jean-Louis du Billeau, a supporter of Kerlérec. The argument may have begun about money, but the affair was really a manifestation of the Kerlérec-Rochemore feud. The argument degenerated into a fight too disordered to be called a duel. Both were injured, Du Billeau seriously, and each accused the other of dishonorable behavior. Du Billeau complained to Kerlérec, who put Paul in prison, where he passed nearly two years in light confinement. When, in 1762, Kerlérec deported members of the Rochemore cabal, Paul was among them. Back in France, he continued to support Rochemore in the ongoing conflict and in 1764 wrote a memoir about the affair with Du Billeau. The feud created such a scandal that the royal government sent Paul along with several of Rochemore's other partisans to the Bastille in 1765, but the imprisonment was not onerous and did not last long.[4] Older literature sometimes attributed Paul's career in and around New Orleans to Philippe-François.

Under Spanish rule, Paul returned to New Orleans, where in 1771 he stole a pirogue full of trade goods from an English merchant. He pled that he had just found the pirogue floating by itself and unloaded it to protect the goods from loss, but he was less successful in explaining why he had attempted to conceal the goods from the English owner. Convicted of theft, he was exiled from Louisiana for five years. He died at Saint-Domingue in 1787.[5]

Philippe-François first served in Europe, where he held the rank of lieutenant and took part in the famous French victory at Fontenoy in 1745. With the end of the War of the Austrian Succession in 1748, he was reduced to half-pay status.[6] After a short time in the French Antilles, he migrated to America as a member of the marines.[7]

As an officer under the able Métis partisan leader Charles-Michel de Langlade, Rocheblave took part in Braddock's defeat at the Battle of Monongahela in 1755. Although Rocheblave behaved bravely in the battle, an incident in the aftermath has contributed to misgivings about his character. After the battle, one of Langlade's men, named La Choise, came across the corpse of a well-dressed British officer who carried a rich purse. Rocheblave came upon the scene at about the same time and claimed a share of the officer's money. The two argued, but La Choise refused to share and kept the purse. The next morning, La Choise was discovered murdered, and the purse with its contents was missing. There was no proof that Rocheblave had done the deed, but suspicion endured.[8]

Rocheblave continued to fight along the Ohio River valley front until its collapse in 1759. He took part in the ill-fated attempt to relieve the siege of Fort Niagara in 1759, but he remained behind the main force in charge of the detachment guarding the bateaux and canoes, and thus he was not present at the French defeat at La Belle Famille.

Philippe-François de Rocheblave next appeared in Illinois in 1760, when Neyon de Villiers appointed him commandant of the small Fort Massiac on the lower Ohio River.[9] He seems to have remained there only a short time. In 1763, Rocheblave married Marie-Michel Dufresne, daughter of a militia officer at Kaskaskia, where he was serving as town commandant. In the same year, Neyon de Villiers left Fort de Chartres for New Orleans, and Rocheblave was among the forty officers and men Neyon left behind. Rocheblave formally retired from the French marines in 1764.[10] He remained at Kaskaskia, where he engaged in trade, apparently without great success.

When the British finally took control of Fort de Chartres in 1765, the last French commander, Louis Groston de St. Ange de Bellerive, crossed over the Mississippi to St. Louis and assumed command. France had ceded the west side of the river to Spain, but Spain had not yet taken possession. Late in 1765 or at the beginning of 1766, Rocheblave, too, moved to the Spanish side of the Mississippi, where St. Ange apparently appointed him the commandant of Ste. Geneviève. Many of the French inhabitants of Illinois had also migrated to Ste. Geneviève or St. Louis on the Spanish side of the river. In 1765, Ste. Geneviève was certainly larger than St. Louis, founded just the preceding year, but St. Louis was the better location for trade and administration. Ste. Geneviève would remain primarily a farm town.[11]

The chief reason that Spain had accepted the former French territory west of the Mississippi was fear of Anglo-American expansionism, but Spain was not able to assume firm control of that vast territory. Spain's own weakness and parsimony played a role in this, as did the abortive attempt in New Orleans to oppose the Spanish assumption of power. From 1765 to 1770, the administration of the territory was managed by French officers. The first Spanish official arrived in St. Louis in 1767 but soon departed. Permanent Spanish government, established in 1770, consisted of only a few bureaucrats and a few dozen troops, more a gendarmerie than a military force. Former French officers still held positions of importance under a thin veneer of Spanish officials.

In 1768, Don Antonio de Ulloa, the first governor of Spanish Louisiana, described Rocheblave as commandant at Ste. Geneviève, adding that he "finds himself serving at present without a salary."[12] Rocheblave took his oath to Spain seriously and served conscientiously, but he also quarreled with the British commandant of Fort de Chartres about the behavior of British soldiers and clashed with Don Francisco Ríu, commander of the first Spanish expeditionary force to reach Spanish Illinois. By the end of 1769, Rocheblave had become the subject of negative reports in New Orleans, and in June 1770, he was replaced as town commandant by Louis Dubreuil de Villars, another former French officer who had entered Spanish service.[13] Rocheblave and his family continued to reside at Ste. Geneviève until late 1775 or early 1776, when he crossed over to the British side of the river. Madame Rocheblave sold the family's holdings at Ste. Geneviève in 1777. By that time, Philippe-François had commenced a new career on the eastern, British side of the river.

The British garrison in Illinois was never large, and much of it was recalled in 1772, leaving only Captain Lord with a small detachment of the 18th Regiment, the Loyal Irish. The Mississippi River finally consumed the river wall of Fort de Chartres that year, rendering the fort useless. Lord and his troops housed themselves in the old Jesuit house in Kaskaskia, which they surrounded with a palisade. They named the post Fort Gage. There Rocheblave met and apparently befriended Lord.

In 1776, as part of a redeployment to deal with the revolt of the colonies, Lord and his troops were withdrawn from Illinois and sent to Detroit. Lord left his possessions and family behind in Rocheblave's care, and the British commissioned Rocheblave to watch over their interests in Illinois. He was to report on the actions of the Spanish, deal with the Indians, call out the militia if necessary, announce proclamations, and deal with passports. General Carleton in Québec granted him only two hundred pounds per year, indicating that Rocheblave was expected to act merely as a caretaker.

Rocheblave had grander ideas, seeing himself as fully the commandant of Illinois. He acted to alleviate conditions caused by the poor harvests of 1776 and 1777, issuing a proclamation that debts due in grain could be paid in silver or peltry, except if such debts were due to inhabitants who needed the grain to subsist or as seed grain. Other creditors who wanted grain rather than silver or pelts would have to wait until the next harvest.[14] English merchants complained that Rocheblave favored the French, but that was to be expected. The French had previously complained that British administrators had favored the English. Rocheblave complained about both:

> I was in command formerly in these parts for three years and during that time I did not have to decide more than one legal case a week. . . . At present one is obligated every day to imprison men, who demand that if the English law is favorable to them it should be followed. On another occasion the very next day, the same people will demand the old French laws which have always been followed. If I were not a little crazed already, I be- lieve they would cause me to become entirely so.[15]

Rocheblave also reported on the Spanish on the western side of the Mississippi, the American James Willing's predatory raid down the Mississippi, and Indian affairs. The British hoped he might stir up the Indians on the Ohio River against the American rebels, and the Americans thought he had, but Rocheblave's lack of resources forestalled any such activity.[16] Rocheblave was also acutely conscious that he had little chance of defending Illinois should American rebels move against it, and he repeatedly appealed to the British command in Québec for troops and resources, which were not forthcoming. He also spent far more than the meager allowance provided by the English, and he would have to beg and petition for years to recoup his expenditures.

Throughout his short tenure, two years, as de facto commandant of the British Illinois Country, Rocheblave seems to have acted consistently and ably in British interests, as he had earlier in Spanish interests. Although he exceeded his role (and expenses) as initially envisioned by his British superiors, his actions showed good judgment and were worthy of sup- port. If his recommendations had been followed, Illinois may well have remained in British hands at the conclusion of the American Revolution.

When the British government in Québec initially refused to honor his expenses, Rocheblave appealed the ruling, but before he received a reply, events took his life in yet another new direction. On July 4, 1778, George Rogers Clark captured Kaskaskia, Philippe-François de Rocheblave, and all of Illinois without a fight. In a letter to the Spanish governor at New Orleans, the Spanish commandant of St. Louis, Don Fernando de Leyba, related Rocheblave's defiant declaration to Clark: "I am in your hands, do with me what you wish, the fear of death will not make me change my way of thinking. The King of Great Britain is my Prince. He has nourished me, and I have sworn fidelity to him."[17]

Rocheblave languished in captivity at Kaskaskia for a month or so before Clark sent him to Virginia. He was greatly concerned for his family and that of Captain Lord, who were left behind at Kaskaskia, and he besieged the British authorities then and later with pleas to support them. At Williamsburg, Rocheblave had the parole of the town. According to the understanding of Virginian authorities, he violated that parole and escaped to New York in the autumn of 1778. Rocheblave, relying on a sophistic argument that would have delighted a Jesuit, maintained he had honorably observed the terms of the parole and had escaped only when circumstances not of his making freed him from those restraints.

Rocheblave remained in New York until 1781, when he traveled to Québec. There he plied the British administration with plans to reconquer Illinois, which came to nothing, and pleas for payments for his expenses in Illinois and during captivity, as well as back pay of his salary as commandant. He obtained some money, never as much as he felt due him, and a grant of a small trading privilege at posts on the Great Lakes, but his commercial venture seems to have brought little profit. When Rocheblave presumed to make drafts on the government account at Mackinac without authorization, he received an official rebuke. In 1782–83, Rocheblave traveled to Illinois and then Québec, where he presented plans for a British conquest of all the lands once included in French Louisiana and petitions for compensation of his losses in Illinois. All were ignored. This seems to have embittered him toward the British in Canada, and by 1785, he began to associate with French Canadians who disliked British rule, earning the distrust of British officials.

In the 1780s, Rocheblave and his family settled first in Montréal and then at Varennes, a suburb of Montréal. He was somewhat involved in the fur trade and entered Canadian politics, serving in the Lower Canadian House of Assembly from 1792 until his death in 1802.

Rocheblave has been dismissed as a mercenary character who changed his loyalties to suit his personal interests, but such an interpretation is imbued with anachronistically modern nationalism and fails to see him in the context of his time and culture. Rocheblave was a man of the *ancien régime*. From an aristocratic family, he had an aristocratic upbringing and sensibilities. His perception of the world was primarily hierarchical, with highest loyalty due to the king. Nationalism was nascent, but not yet fully formed, and manifest primarily in the person of the king. A younger son, Rocheblave had his aristocratic name but neither title nor resources. From a very large family, he had to make his way in the world with no or little help, and his career as a military officer depended on the king.

When France left America, Rocheblave was left behind, and he felt he had been abandoned by his king.[18] He sought a new prince in the Spanish monarch, but when it became apparent he was not trusted or appreciated by Spanish officials, he sought yet another prince, the British king. He was defiantly loyal when confronted by George Rogers Clark, and his enthusiasm for the British waned only when he again felt underappreciated and cheated of his due.

If Rocheblave was sometimes domineering and overbearing in his roles as commandant, that too may be attributed to his hierarchical view of the world: he saw himself as an aristocrat dealing with social and intellectual inferiors. The circumstances of his commands, beset with insufficient resources in rapidly evolving circumstances, also contributed to his frustration. Too, American writers have seldom been kind to those who opposed the Revolution.

Afterword

IN 1763, THE French monarchy surrendered sovereignty of Illinois east of the Mississippi to England and of the lands west of the Mississippi to Spain. Neither power long retained their new possessions. Freed from the exaggerated but real and long-enduring fear of the French, the English colonists grew increasingly willing and even eager to resist the economic and political impositions of the motherland. The end of the French and Indian War made the American Revolution almost inevitable.

Recent studies have largely erased the image of the Spanish administration of Upper Louisiana as inept and tyrannous, but it is true that Spain held its northern lands only lightly, with few administrators and token military forces. Unable to resist the demands of Napoleon, Spain ceded Louisiana back to France, and facing renewed war with Britain, France passed the lands on to the United States. Apparently, in less than a generation, the political map of North America had been altered virtually beyond recognition.

Almost unseen and unrecognized amid all the changes, old patterns and relationships endured. Robert Englebert has emphasized that the connections of the French "water world," the lakes, rivers, portages, and settlements that bound French America together, continued to exist and link Canada through Illinois on down to New Orleans regardless of national boundaries (and modern national narratives). One example among many suffices here: Pierre Menard (1766–1844), born near Montréal, came to Illinois from Canada in 1786, long after the end of French sovereignty. By the early 1790s, Menard had established a successful trading business at

Kaskaskia and had become a respected leader among the French, Anglo-Americans, and Indians. Menard served as the president of the Illinois Territorial Council from 1812 to 1818, preparing the territory for statehood, and when Illinois was admitted as a state in 1818, Pierre Menard became the first lieutenant governor. His pleasant home, incorporating many elements of the French southern Louisiana style, is preserved as a state historic site. Others of French descent continued to come south along the long-established routes from Canada and often returned to renew family relationships, make business connections, and find marriage partners. The French connection continued to exist and shape mid-America long after Fort de Chartres had fallen into ruins.

Notes

Lexicon

Bibliography

Index

Notes

PREFACE

1. E.g., C. J. Ekberg, *Stealing Indian Women: Native Slavery in the Illinois Country* (Urbana: University of Illinois Press, 2007); and S. White, *Wild Frenchmen and Frenchified Indians: Material Culture and Race in Colonial Louisiana* (Philadelphia: University of Pennsylvania Press, 2012).

PART I. FRENCH ILLINOIS

1. For an excellent ecological approach to the history of French Illinois, see M. J. Morgan, *Land of Big Rivers: French and Indian Illinois, 1699–1778* (Carbondale: Southern Illinois University Press, 2010).

2. E. J. Blasingham, "The Depopulation of the Illinois Indians," pt. 1, *Ethnohistory* 3, no. 3 (Summer 1956): 193; J. Scott, *The Illinois Nation*, pt. 1 (Streator, IL: Streator Historical Society, 1973), 1.

3. E. J. Blasingham, "The Depopulation of the Illinois Indians," pt. 2, *Ethnohistory* 3, no. 4 (Autumn 1956): 361–67; D. J. Costa, "On the Origins of the Name 'Illinois,'" *Society for the Study of the Indigenous Languages of the Americas Newsletter* 25, no. 4 (2007): 9–12.

4. Blasingham, "Depopulation," pt. 2, 361–65.

5. R. G. Thwaites, ed., *The Jesuit Relations and Allied Documents: Travels and Explorations of the Jesuit Missionaries in New France, 1610–1791*, vol. 59 (Cleveland: Burrows, 1896–1901), 124; concerning French and Indian mutual cultural interactions in general, see White, *Wild Frenchmen*.

6. A. Pénicaut, *Fleur de Lys and Calumet: Being the Pénicaut Narrative of French Adventure in Louisiana*, trans. and ed. R. G. McWilliams (1953; repr., Tuscaloosa: University of Alabama Press, 1988), 116, 137.

7. Thwaites, *Jesuit Relations*, vol. 66, 240.

8. White, *Wild Frenchmen*, 112–42.

9. [Bernard] Diron d'Artaguiette, "Journal of Diron d'Artaguiette, Inspector General of Louisiana, 1722–1723," in *Travels in the American Colonies*, ed. N. D. Mereness (New York: Macmillan, 1916), 71.

10. M. E. Good, *Guebert Site: an 18th Century Historic Kaskaskia Indian Village in Randolph County, Illinois* (Wood River, IL: Central States Archaeological Societies, 1972).

11. Vaudreuil to Macarty, 28 April 1752, Vaudreuil Papers, Huntington Manuscripts, Loudoun Collection, Huntington Library, San Marino, CA, 365; translation in T. C. Pease and E. Jenison, *Illinois on the Eve of the Seven Years' War, 1747–1755*, Collections of the Illinois State Historical Library, vol. 29; French Series, vol. 3 (Springfield: Trustees of the Illinois State Historical Library, 1940), 620.

12. 1732 census, Archives Nationales d'Outre-Mer (formerly Archives Nationales Coloniales), Aix-en-Provence, France (hereafter cited as ANC), G1.464, as summarized in M. C. Norton, *Illinois Census Returns 1810, 1818* (Collections of the Illinois State Historical Library, vol. 24, Statistical Series, vol. 2; Springfield: Trustees of the Illinois State Historical Library, 1935), xxii–xxv; N. M. Belting, *Kaskaskia under the French Regime*, University of Illinois Studies in the Social Sciences, vol. 29, no. 3; Urbana: University of Illinois Press, 1948), 38; C. R. Maduell Jr., ed. and trans., *The Census Tables for the French Colony of Louisiana from 1699 through 1732* (Baltimore: Genealogical Pub. Co., 1972), 150; R. de Berardinis, trans., "The 1732 French Census of Illinois," *Illinois State Genealogical Quarterly* 32, no. 3 (Fall 2000): 155–64. There are evident errors in the original manuscript, which led to slight differences in the numbers being accepted by different editors. I have followed Berardinis.

13. There are two extant copies of the 1752 census. One is in the Vaudreuil Papers, the personal and private papers of Pierre de Rigaud de Vaudreuil, who was governor of Louisiana from 1743 to 1753 and was then transferred to Canada, where he served as governor from 1755 to 1760. See B. Barron, *The Vaudreuil Papers: A Calendar and Index of the Personal and Private Records of Pierre de Rigaud de Vaudreuil, Royal Governor of the French Province of Louisiana, 1743–1753* (New Orleans: Polyanthos, 1975), xi–xiii, 155; Vaudreuil Papers, 426, 1–7. On the voyage from Louisiana to Canada, the French ship carrying Vaudreuil's brother and the chest of his papers was captured by the British. The papers passed into the hands of Major General John Campbell, earl of Loudoun, the last British colonial governor of America, and remained in the hands of the Loudoun descendants until 1923, when Henry E. Huntington acquired them for the Huntington Library and Art Gallery in San Marino, California, where they remain today. The other copy is in the papers of William Pitt the Elder, the first earl of Chatham, and is in the British Public Record Office, Chatham mss, bundle 95.4. It seems to be a poor copy made from the original now in the Huntington Library. Norton, *Illinois Census*, xxvi–xxvii, is derived from the

inferior Pitt manuscript. Belting, *Kaskaskia*, 39, and R. de Berardinis, trans., "The 1752 French Census of Illinois," *Illinois State Genealogical Quarterly* 32, no. 4 (Winter 2000): 195–203, are derived from the Huntington manuscript. The Berardinis version is more accurate.

14. The Louisiana Code Noir was largely based on Louis XIV's Code Noir of 1685 for the French Caribbean colonies. C. J. Ekberg, G. Kilman, and P. Lebeau, trans. and eds., *Code Noir: The Colonial Slave Laws of French Mid-America*, Extended Publication no. 4 (Naperville, IL: Center for French Colonial Studies, 2005), C. J. Ekberg, "Black Slavery in Illinois, 1720–1765," *Western Illinois Regional Studies* 12, no. 1 (Spring 1989): 5–19; C. Ekberg, *Colonial Ste. Genevieve: An Adventure on the Mississippi Frontier*, 2nd ed. (Tucson, AZ: Patrice Press, 1996), 196–238.

15. The word *maroon* comes from the Spanish *cimarrón*, meaning fugitive, with the extended meaning of escaped slaves who formed independent communities. Joseph Gagné suggests to me that the name might be derived from the French *marron*, citing the entry in the *Dictionnaire de l'Académie française*, 4th ed. (Paris: Chez la Vve B. Brunet, 1762): "*On dit dans les Colonies d'Amérique, qu'Un Nègre est marron, qu'il est devenu marron, pour dire, qu'il s'est enfui, qu'il s'est retiré dans les bois, dans les déserts, pour y vivre en liberté. Il se dit aussi des animaux, qui de domestiques sont devenus sauvages.*" [It is said in the colonies of America that a Negro is a *marron*, that he has become a *marron*, that is to say, he fled, he withdrew into the woods, into the deserts, to live there in freedom. It is said also of animals that were domestic and became wild.]

16. Ekberg, *Ste. Genevieve*, 234.

17. D. Hardcastle, "The Military Organization of French Colonial Louisiana," in *Proceedings of the Gulf Coast History and Humanities Conference*, ed. W. S. Coker, vol. 7, *The Military Presence on the Gulf Coast* (Pensacola, FL: Gulf Coast History and Humanities Conference, 1978), 1–20; reprinted in *The Louisiana Purchase Bicentennial Series in Louisiana History*, ed. G. R. Conrad, vol. 1, *The French Experience in Louisiana* (Lafayette: Center for Louisiana Studies, University of Southwestern Louisiana, 1995), 345–59.

18. Hardcastle, "Military Organization," 348–49; C. A. Brasseaux, *France's Forgotten Legion: Service Records of French Military and Administrative Personnel Stationed in the Mississippi Valley and Gulf Coast Region, 1699–1769* (Baton Rouge: Louisiana State University Press, 2000), CD-ROM (hereafter cited as *FFL*), introduction; D. J. Lemieux, "Some Legal and Practical Aspects of the Office of *Commissaire-Ordonnateur* of French Louisiana," *Louisiana Studies* 14 (1975), 379–93, reprinted in Conrad, *Louisiana Purchase*, 1:395–407, particularly emphasizing the differences between the *intendant* in France and the *commissaire-ordonnateur* in Louisiana.

19. A. Balvay, *L'Épée et la Plume: Amérindiens et soldats des troupes de la marine en Louisiane et au Pays d'en Haut (1683–1763)* [The sword and the pen: American

Indians and soldiers of the Troupes de la Marine in Louisiana and le Pays d'en Haut]. (Québec: Les Presses de l'Université Laval, 2006), 345.

20. Older literature refers to three successive Forts de Chartres. In a recent reexamination of the literary sources, Brown and Mazrim argue that there were four forts, and their conclusion has been brilliantly confirmed by their excavations at the site of the third fort. M. K. Brown and R. Mazrim, "Revisiting the Forts and Village at Chartres in the Illinois Country," *Illinois Archaeology* 22, no. 1 (2010): 134–47. This section is largely dependent on their research and conclusions.

21. Brasseaux, *FFL*, introduction.

22. R. D. Edmunds and J. L. Peyser, *The Fox Wars: The Mesquakie Challenge to New France* (Norman: University of Oklahoma Press, 1993).

23. Périer and La Chaise, response article by article to a letter of the Company of 27 October 1727, ANC, C13A.11.89v; Belting, *Kaskaskia*, 18.

24. ANC, C13B.581; Brown and Mazrim, "Revisiting,"137.

25. Bienville and Salmon to minister, 8 April 1734, ANC C13A.18.86v–87; translation in D. Rowland and A. G. Sanders, *Mississippi Provincial Archives*, vols. 1–3 (Jackson: Press of the Mississippi Department of Archives and History, 1927–32), and vol. 4, rev. and ed. P. K. Galloway (Baton Rouge: Louisiana State University Press, 1984), 3:667.

26. "Fort de Chartres," From Kaskaskia to Sangamo: Dispatches from the Archaeological History of the Illinois Country, 1600–1850, accessed October 14, 2013, http://illinoiscountryarchaeology.blogspot.com/search/label /Fort%20de%20Chartres.

27. Macarty to Vaudreuil, 20 January 1752, Vaudreuil Papers, 328; translation in Pease and Jenison, *Illinois on the Eve*, 440–41.

28. P. Pittman, *The Present State of the European Settlements on the Mississippi* (London: J. Nourse, 1770), 45–46.

29. J. Wallace, "Fort de Chartres: Its Origin, Growth and Decline," *Transactions of the Illinois State Historical Society* (1903): 105–17. Although the article contains a number of errors in regard to the history of Fort de Chartres, it gathers together accounts of the state of the fort written after its abandonment, well into the nineteenth century, and was important in creating interest in preserving the site and the few visible remnants of the fort.

30. R. Englebert, "Beyond Borders: Mental Mapping and the French River World in North America, 1763–1805" (PhD diss., University of Ottawa, 2010).

31. Fundamental works on convoys are M. K. Brown, *The Voyageur in the Illinois Country: The Fur Trade's Professional Boatman in Mid America*, Extended Publication Series, no. 3 (Naperville, IL: Center for French Colonial Studies, 2002); and N. M. Miller Surrey, *The Commerce of Louisiana during the French Regime, 1699–1763* (New York: Columbia University Press, 1916), 1–81.

32. Jean-Bernard Bossu, *Nouveaux voyages aux Indes Occidentales; contenant une Relation des différens Peuples qui habitent les environs du grand Fleuve Saint-Louis, appellé vulgairement le Missisipi; leur Religion; leur gouvernement; leurs moeurs; leurs guerres et leur commerce* [New voyages to the West Indies; containing a relation of the different peoples who live near the great River St. Louis, commonly called the Mississippi; their religion; their government; their manners; their wars and their trade] (Paris: Chez Le Jay, 1768), 1: 37–38.

33. Diron d'Artaguiette, "Journal," 40–67.

34. M. de Villiers de Terrage, *The Last Years of French Louisiana*, ed. C. A. Brasseaux and G. R. Conrad, ann. C. A. Brasseaux, trans. Hosea Phillips (Lafayette: Center for Louisiana Studies, University of Southwestern Louisiana, 1982), 133 n4.

35. Bienville to minister, 20 August 1735, ANC, C13A.20.152–59.

36. Villiers de Terrage, *Last Years*, 165.

37. L. C. Dean and M. K. Brown, comp., Kaskaskia Manuscripts, 1714–1816: A Calendar of Civil Documents in Colonial Illinois (Chester, IL: Randolph County Archives, 1981), Ks. Ms. 37:5:4:2.

38. Antoine-Simon Le Page du Pratz, *Histoire de la Louisiane* [History of Louisiana], vol. 1 (Paris: De Bure, 1758), 331. Shipped in the spring, the flour would have been from the 1747 crop. The crop was actually poor in 1748.

39. Ekberg, *Ste. Genevieve*, 143–51, provides an overview of lead production from the beginning of the eighteenth century to the War of 1812.

40. Brown, *Voyageur*, 19.

PART 2. COMMANDANTS OF FORT DE CHARTRES

First Commandant: Pierre-Sidrac Dugué de Boisbriand (1718–24)

1. On Boisbriand's arrival in Louisiana, D. E. Pusch, "Founders of Louisiana: The First Two Ship Lists of 1699," *Mississippi Valley Mélange* 7 (2012): 2–31.

2. On Cadillac's charge of insolence against Vitrac, Adjudication of the Council of the Marine in regard to the letters of La Mothe-Cadillac of 9 February and 1 September 1716, ANC, C13A.4.281. On Cadillac's complaint that Bienville and Boisbriand had formed an officers' cabal to support Vitrac, La Mothe-Cadillac to Minister, February 2, 1716, ANC, C13A.4.571–72.

3. Bienville replaced Cadillac as acting governor and in turn was succeeded by Jean-Michel de L'Epinay et de Longueville in 1717, but in early 1718, L'Epinay was recalled and Bienville again became governor. In 1717, Boisbriand was named commandant of Mobile, but he served only briefly. He visited France that same year, returning to Louisiana early in 1718 as the king's lieutenant and member of the Superior Council of Louisiana, before becoming the commandant of the Illinois Country.

4. The Canadian administration bitterly opposed the annexation of Illinois to Louisiana and continued to campaign for its reassignment to Canada in the last years of the French regime in America. For a history of the controversy, see G. R. Conrad, "Administration of the Illinois Country: The French Debate," *Louisiana History* 36, no. 1 (Winter 1995): 31–53.

5. Kaskaskia was founded in 1703 when the Kaskaskia Indians moved there, accompanied by Jesuit missionaries and a few French traders who had married into the tribe. In subsequent years, more French settled at Kaskaskia and turned increasingly to farming.

6. M. K. Brown, *History as They Lived It: A Social History of Prairie du Rocher, Ill.* (Tucson: Patrice Press, 2005), 68–71.

7. E. S. Mills, "Parallel Lives: Philippe de La Renaudière and Philippe (de) Renault, Directors of the Mines, Company of the Indies," *Natchitoches Genealogist* 22 (April 1998): 3–18 sorts out the careers of the two like-named directors of mines in Illinois in the early eighteenth century, often confused with one another or even both assumed to be the same individual in earlier literature. For the career of Renault, see also M. Giraud, *A History of French Louisiana*, vol. 5, *The Company of the Indies, 1723–1731*, trans. B. Pearce (Baton Rouge: Louisiana State University Press, 1991), 441–44.

8. Dutisné became the second and fifth commandant of Fort de Chartres. His biography appears later in this book. On the Villasur expedition, M. de Villiers du Terrage, "Le massacre de l'expedition espagnole du Missouri (11 août 1720)," *Journal de la Société des Américanistes de Paris*, n.s., 13 (1921): 239–55, which contains a French translation of the surviving fragments of a diary of a Spanish corporal who took part in the expedition. It is clear that Boisbriand had only confused, incomplete, and in part false information about the event. For unique hide paintings that portray the massacre, see G. Hotz, *The Segesser Hide Paintings: Masterpieces Depicting Spanish Colonial New Mexico*, trans. J. Malthaner (Santa Fe: Museum of New Mexico Press, 1991); T. E. Chavez, *A Moment in Time: The Odyssey of New Mexico's Segesser Hide Paintings* (Los Ranchos, NM: Rio Grande Books, 2012).

9. F. Norall, *Bourgmont, Explorer of the Missouri, 1698–1725* (Lincoln: University of Nebraska Press, 1988), 40–42.

10. Edmunds and Peyser, *Fox Wars*, 94–103; on the Kaskaskia resident killed "two steps from the village," Kaskaskia Parish Records, Family Search Historical Record Collections, First Book, 8, accessed May 12, 2014, https://familysearch.org/search/collection/show#uri=http://familysearch.org/searchapi/search/collection/1388122.

11. For a description of the Indians' trip to Paris, see the chapter on Étienne de Véniard de Bourgmont and Ignon Ouaconisen.

12. Jean-Bernard Bossu, *Nouveaux voyage dans l'Amérique septentrionale, contenant une collection de lettres écrites sur les lieux par l'auteur, à son ami M. Douin, chevalier,*

capitaine dans les troupes du roi, ci-devant son camarade dans le Nouveau Monde [New travels in North America, containing a collection of letters written on location by the author, to his friend Mr. Douin, chevalier, captain in the king's troops, who was earlier his comrade in the New World] (Amsterdam: Chez Changuion, 1777), 227–28.

Second and Fifth Commandant: Claude-Charles Dutisné (1724–25, 1729–30)

1. In addition to the usual sources, M. Piper, "Tarnished Galahad: The Short and Dynamic Career of Claude-Charles DuTisné," *Journal of the Early Americas* 2, no. 3 (June–July 2012), 26–31; M. M. Wedel, "Claude-Charles Dutisné: A Review of His 1719 Journeys," pts. 1 and 2, *Great Plains Journal* 11, no. 1 (1972): 4–25, 12, no. 2 (1973): 147–73; and H. H. Cruzat, "Letters of Sieur Terrisse de Ternan," *Louisiana Historical Quarterly* 3, no. 4 (1920): 509–42 (hereafter cited as *LHQ*). Brasseaux, *FFL*, "Dutisné" mistakenly reported that Dutisné died at the hands of the Chickasaw in 1736, but it was Dutisné's son who was killed.

2. C. J. Russ, "Dutisné," *Dictionary of Canadian Biography*, accessed February 27, 2014, http://www.biographi.ca/en/bio/dutisne_claude_charles_2E.html; R. P. L. LeJeune, *Dictionnaire Général de biographie, histoire, littérature, agriculture, commerce, industrie et des arts, sciences, mours, coutumes, institutions politiques et religuses du Canada* [General dictionary of biography, history, literature, agriculture, commerce, industry and the arts, sciences, mores, customs, political and religious institutions of Canada] (Ottawa, 1931), 2:720–21; Vaudreuil to Minister, 19 October 1705, ANC, C11A.22.251v.

3. Le Page du Pratz, *Histoire*, 2:298–304. Even if the colorful story of his confrontation with the Indians is true, Dutisné's promotion was probably more due to the need to fill a vacancy in the rank. Bossu, *Nouveaux voyages aux Indes Occidentales*, 1:231–33, retells the story, with characteristic unreliable elaborations.

4. Cadillac claimed the location was lost because a Spaniard and two Indians who had accompanied him on the trip had died on the way back. Adjudication of the Navy Council in regard to Cadillac's letters of 15, 23, 24, and 26 July and 9 October 1716, ANC, C13A.4.381.

5. E.g., Wedel, "Dutisné," pt. 1, 4–9 provides an excellent account of this episode and adopts this interpretation.

6. In 1716, Cadillac included Dutisné among the officers he claimed were conspiring against him. Cadillac to Council of the Marine, 22 June 1716, ANC, C13A.4.605.

7. Pénicaut, *Fleur de Lys*, 215 has Dutisné coming directly from Natchitoches to Natchez, where he joined Boisbriand and proceeded directly to Illinois. Pénicaut routinely suppressed personal material, except in the case of his hero, Louis Juchereau de St. Denys.

8. Father Raphaël to the Abbé Raguet, 28 December 1726, ANC, C13.10.49–50v; *MPA*, 2:525–28.

9. E.g., M. Allain, "Louisiana Women Criminals during the French Colonial Period," *Le Journal* 16, no. 1 (Winter 1999), reprinted in *French Colonial Studies: Le Pays des Illinois: Selections from Le Journal, 1983–2005*, ed. M. K. Brown and H. R. Williams, Extended Publications Series, no. 6 (Naperville, IL: Center for French Colonial Studies, 2006), 103–8. See also the chapter on Alphonse de La Buissonnière and Marie-Thérèse Trudeau.

10. A. Balvay, "The French and the Natchez: A Failed Encounter," in *French and Indians in the Heart of North America, 1630–1815*, ed. R. Englebert and G. Teasdale (East Lansing: Michigan State University Press, 2013), 144–47.

11. On Dutisné's wound, Diron to Périer, 1 October 1729, ANC, C13A.12.178.

Third Commandant: Jean-Charles de Pradel (Interim 1725)

1. Jean-Charles de Pradel must be distinguished from Jean-Baptiste de Pradel. Jean-Charles de Pradel died in 1764; see A. Baillardel and A. Priolt, *Le Chevalier de Pradel* (Paris: Maisonneuve Frères, 1928); and G. C. H. Kernion, "The Chevalier de Pradel," *LHQ* 12, no. 2 (1929): 238–54. Jean-Baptiste de Pradel was active in Louisiana at least as late as 1773; see L. L. Porteous, "Index to the Spanish Judicial Records of Louisiana, LXXX," *LHQ* 28, no. 2 (1945): 602–3.

2. For a full description of this incident, see C. J. Ekberg and S. Person, *St. Louis Rising: The French Regime of Louis St. Ange de Bellerive* (Urbana: University of Illinois Press, 2015), 18–19; Norall, *Bourgmont*, 42–44.

3. On the warfare between the Fox and the Illinois and French in Illinois, Edmunds and Peyser, *Fox Wars*, 87–118. On Pradel's problems with Plé, C. W. Alvord, *The Centennial History of Illinois*, vol. 1, *The Illinois Country, 1673–1818* (Chicago: A. C. McClurg & Co., 1922), 157. Brown, *History*, 24, 62 notes that Plé was a pit sawyer and suggests the dispute may have been over lumber for Fort de Chartres. Abstract of the Letters from the Council of Louisiana to the Directors of the Company of the Indies, November 17, 1725, ANC, C13A.9.245; *MPA*, 2:498 (giving date as November 7, 1725).

4. Baillardel and Priouly, *Chevalier de Pradel* contains a wealth of correspondence between Pradel and his family, primarily in regard to his business ventures, and an effusive and excessively laudatory overview of his career. For a review and summary of this work, see Kernion, "Chevalier de Pradel."

5. My thanks to Mike Piper for his appreciation of Pradel's family situation.

Fourth Commandant: Pierre-Charles Desliette (1725–29)

1. *Alphabet Laffilard*, accessed August 18, 2015, http://anom.archivesnation-ales.culture.gov.fr/ark:/61561/tu24uvvsy, 459.

2. C. J. Russ, "Tonty de Liette (Deliette, Desliettes), Charles-Henri-Joseph de," *Dictionary of Canadian Biography*, accessed October 7, 2013, http://www.biographi.ca/en/bio/tonty_de_liette_charles_henri_joseph_de_3E.html; Brasseaux, "Delisle," *FFL*.

3. Russ, "Tonty de Liette."

4. P.-F.-X. de Charlevoix, S.J., *Histoire et description générale de la Nouvelle-France* (Paris: Chez Rollin Fils, 1744), 2:460. Russ suggests that the Desliette who died in 1721 may have been one of the sons of Alphonse de Tonty or a like-named, but otherwise unattested, son of Pierre-Charles Desliette, perhaps by an Illinois woman. C. J. Russ, "Liettes, Pierre-Charles de (di Lietto, Deliette, Desliettes)," *Dictionary of Canadian Biography*, accessed October 7, 2013, http://www.biographi.ca/en/bio/liette_pierre_charles_de_2E.html. Pierre-Charles Desliette described himself as having been very young in 1687. Pierre Deliette, "Memoir of De Gannes Concerning the Illinois Country," in *The French Foundations, 1680–1693*, ed. T. C. Pease and R. C. Werner, Collections of the Illinois State Historical Library, vol. 23; French Series, vol. 1 (Springfield: Illinois State Historical Library, 1934), 307.

5. Russ, "Liettes, Pierre-Charles de."

6. Deliette, "Memoir of DeGannes," 302–95.

7. *Alphabet Laffilard*, accessed August 18, 2015, http://anom.archivesnationales.culture.gov.fr/ark:/61561/tu24uvvsy, 459.

8. M. K. Brown and L. C. Dean, *The Village of Chartres in Colonial Illinois, 1720–1765* (1977; repr., Baton Rouge, LA: Provincial Press, 2010), 20, no. D-29, a document attesting to Desliette as commandant in Illinois in 1726.

9. Edmunds and Peyser, *Fox Wars*, 111. It was customary for Indians to terminate a raid after a single strike, no matter how small. Pouchot describes this characteristic of Indian warfare with insight. P. Pouchot, *Mémoires sur la dernière guerre de l'Amerique Septentrionale entre la France et l'Angleterre* [Memoirs on the last war in North America between France and England] (Yverdon, 1781), 3:349–50.

Sixth Commandant: Robert Groston de St. Ange (1730–33)

1. Ekberg and Person's *St. Louis Rising* provides by far the best synopsis of the lives of Robert Groston and his son Louis Groston de St. Ange de Bellerive. Ekberg and Person prefer the spelling Grotton. I have retained Groston, as it has been most often used in modern literature. Both forms, as well as Groton, appear in contemporary documents.

2. Charlevoix, *Histoire*, 3:390.

3. For a fuller treatment, see the chapter on Étienne Véniard de Bourgmont and the literature cited there.

4. Périer to Minister, 1 April 1729, ANC, C13A.12.16.

5. Belting, *Kaskaskia*, 98–99; Father Tartarin to an unknown recipient, ca. 1738, ANC, 13A.23.243–44.

6. For the best account of the massacre of the Fox in 1730, see Edmunds and Peyser, *Fox Wars*, 119–57.

7. Brown and Mazrim, "Revisiting," 134–47.

8. Salmon to Minister, 17 July 1732, ANC, C13.15.167–68.

Seventh Commandant: Pierre d'Artaguiette d'Itouralde (1733–36)

1. D'Artaguiette Family Tree, *Amitiés Vendée-Louisiane*, accessed June 16, 2013, http://www.vendeelouisiane.fr/images/stories/famille%20dartaguiette%20%20des%20ocars.pdf.

2. E.g., Brasseaux, "D'Artaguiette d'Itouralde," *FFL*, confuses Bernard with Pierre.

3. ANC, C13C.2.18–269; translation in Diron d'Artaguiette, "Journal," 15–92.

4. Recommendations for the replacement of military officers in Louisiana, 8 September 1733, ANC, D2C.50.39.

5. Bienville and Salmon to Minister, 3 May 1735, ANC, C13A.20.83–93.

6. "List of the troops and militia who made the campaign against the Chicka-saws in 1736," ANC, F3.24.243. This lists only the troops and militia members from southern Louisiana in the campaign. Two days before the battle, Bienville left 30 men behind at a hastily constructed small fort, 20 to guard the boats and baggage, and 10 sick, giving him an effective force of 514 men. In addition, the Choctaw warriors numbered about 600, but they took little part in the battle, at least until the last stage, according to Bienville. "Account made by Bienville of his Expedition against the Chickasaws," ANC, F3.24.264–73. Texts and translation in C. Dunn and E. Dunn, trans., "Indiana's First War," *Indiana Historical Society Publications* 8, no. 2 (1924): 74–107.

7. I have followed the dates and numbers of troops given in an anonymous account that seems to represent the official report, probably derived from several primary accounts: "Account of the Battle Fought by D'Artaguiette with the Chicka-saws," ANC, F3.24.258–63. An account of d'Artaguiette's campaign by a soldier who went by the nickname of "Parisien" and held the rank of *anspessade* (lance corporal) differs somewhat in regard to numbers of troops and dates: "Account of the March and Defeat of d'Artaguiette, by Parisien," ANC, F.3.24.256–57. Text and translations of both accounts in Dunn and Dunn, "Indiana's First War," 106–23, 128–33.

8. For the best account of Bienville's campaign, see J. R. Atkinson, *Splendid Land, Splendid People: The Chickasaw Indians to Removal* (Tuscaloosa: University of Alabama Press, 2004), 42–61.

9. "Report of de Richar[d]ville on d'Artaguiette's Engagement against the Chickasaws," ANC, F3.24.252–54; text and translation in Dunn and Dunn, "Indiana's First War," 132–43.

10. Sam Eveleigh to Herman Verelst, 29 June 1736, in *The Colonial Records of the State of Georgia*, ed. A. D. Candler, vol. 21, *Original Papers, 1735–1737* (Atlanta: Chas. P. Byrd, State Printer, 1910), 175–78, giving an account of the battle by William McMullin, an English trader, who reported about twenty-five French

and ten French-allied Indians killed, in addition to twenty-three [*sic*; the actual number was twenty-two] French and two Indians taken captive. Nineteen of the captive French and one of the Indians were subsequently burned.

11. "Account by Parisien," ANC, F.3.24.256–57. Text and translation in Dunn and Dunn, "Indiana's First War," 128–29.

12. Ibid.; Atkinson, *Splendid Land*, 68–69.

Eighth Commandant: Claude-Alphonse de La Buissonnière (1736–40)

1. The first name Claude is attested in a single source: Dean and Brown, Kaskaskia Manuscripts, 40:3:16:1. Otherwise, he was universally known as Alphonse de La Buissonnière.

2. [Charles Théveneau de Morande?], *Le Porte-feuille de Madame Gourdan dite la Comtesse* [The portfolio of Madame Gourdan, called the countess] (Spa, 1783). Works that would attract unfavorable attention from the censor were often published anonymously and printed either outside France or within France secretly with false information on the title page indicating foreign origin.

3. List of officer stationed in Louisiana, ca. 6 March 1730, ANC, D2C.51.91.

4. Périer's comments on Louisiana officers, 1732, ANC, D2C.50.20 vo, 23, 28.

5. Bienville to Minister, 29 June 1736, ANC, C13A.21.181–82; translation in *MPA* 3:686.

6. Either the old Fort d'Orléans or a newer fort, perhaps by the same name, built by the mouth of the Kaw River. Bienville to Minister, 29 June 1736, ANC, C13A.21.184–184v; translation in *MPA* 3:688.

7. Bienville to Minister, 5 September 1736, ANC, C13A.21.219; translation in *MPA* 1:327.

8. Ibid., C13A.21.220–220v; translation in *MPA* 1:328.

9. For the best general account of the campaign, see Atkinson, *Splendid Land*, 63–73.

10. M. K. Brown, "Allons, Cowboys!," *Journal of the Illinois State Historical Society* 76 (Winter 1983): 273–82.

11. N. W. Caldwell, "The Chickasaw Threat to French Control of the Mississippi in the 1740s," *Chronicles of Oklahoma* 16, no. 4 (December 1938): 469. This was a smaller contingent than in the first campaign against the Chickasaw. Memories of the losses of 1736 may have discouraged participation.

12. Brown, "Allons, Cowboys!," 280–81.

13. Bienville was ordered to put the colony in order. He was then allowed to request retirement. In 1743, he departed Louisiana never to return, more than forty years after his first arrival.

14. Service records, 14 June 1740, ANC, C13A.25.86.

15. Salmon to Minister, 26 April 1741, ANC, C13A.26.142; Beauchamp to Minister, 25 April 1741, NAC C13A.26.207–207v; translation in *MPA* 4:183.

16. Beauchamp to Minister, 25 April 1741, ANC, C13A.26.207–207v; translation in *MPA* 4:183; Salmon to Minister, 26 April 1741, ANC, C13A.26.142. De La Loëre's illness may not have been related. He suffered three attacks of "apoplexy," usually interpreted as stroke, though the diagnosis was certainly not made by a medical professional and could have represented any illness with a sudden onset. De La Loëre recovered and served another seven years at Fort de Chartres before his death.

17. Beauchamp to Minister, 25 April 1741, ANC, C13A.26.207–207v; translation in *MPA* 4:183.

Ninth and Eleventh Commandant: Jean-Baptiste Benoist de St. Clair (1740–42, 1749–51)

1. His name also appears as both Benoist de St. Clair and Benoist de Ste. Claire, as well as half a dozen certainly corrupt forms. St. Clair is the preferable form. The name may be derived from Saint Claire of Assisi, a woman follower of Saint Francis of Assisi, but the many locations in France use the form St. Clair.

2. On duels and dueling culture in eighteenth-century France, R. A. Nye, *Masculinity and Male Codes of Honor in Modern France* (New York: Oxford University Press, 1993), 24–46.

3. M. Giraud, *A History of French Louisiana*, vol. 2, *Years of Transition, 1715–1717*, trans. B. Pearce (Baton Rouge: Louisiana State University Press, 1993), 76, 86–87; Adjudication of the Council of the Marine in regard to several letters of La Mothe-Cadillac of 15, 23, 24, and 26 July and 9 October 1716, ANC C13A.4.384; Adjudication of the Council of the Marine in regard to a letter of Crozat, 10 October 1716, ANC C13A.4.417–18.

4. Abstract of a letter of the Superior Council of Louisiana to the Directors of the Company, 23 April 1725, ANC, C13A.9.129–29v; trans. *MPA* 2:460–61.

5. Périer, List of officers maintained in the province of Louisiana, 1 April 1730, ANC, D2C.50.9; Périer's observations, 1732, ANC, D2C.50.21v; Bienville to Minister, 16 April 1735, ANC, D2C.51.127.

6. Bienville, Recommendations for the replacement of officers, 15 October 1736, ANC, D2C.51.140; Notified of promotion, Minister to Benoist, 5 November 1736, ANC, B.64.528; Commanding Fort Tombecbé, 17 June 1737, ANC, 13A.22.99v; Proposal to send Benoist to Illinois, Bienville to Minister, 29 June 1736, ANC, 13A.21.182; trans. *MPA* 3:686. Benoist seems to have arrived in Illinois in 1739 after a leave of absence.

7. Diron d'Artaguiette to Minister, 24 October 1737, ANC, C13A.22.234; trans. *MPA* 4:143. In another letter, Bienville indicates that this was a weak attack and the garrison of forty-five men, not counting officers, was quite able to defend the post. Bienville to Minister, 17 June 1737, ANC, 13.22.99v.

8. Bienville to Minister, 30 July 1742, ANC, C13A.27.81–84v.

9. Catherine Beaudreau had eight children with Étienne Langlois, a landowner and merchant in Illinois. Étienne was probably the militia lieutenant Langlois who was killed in the Chickasaw campaign in 1736. Catherine then married Urbain Gervais, but he too was long dead by 1745. She signed her letters Widow Gervais. For the correspondence between Benoist and Gervais, see H. H. Cruzat, "Records of the Superior Council of Louisiana, XLVIII," *LHQ* 13, no. 4 (1930), 675; "LIII," *LHQ* 15, no. 1 (1932), 140–41, 143; "LIV," *LHQ* 15, no. 3 (1932), 520–21, 524–25; "LV," *LHQ* 15, no. 4 (1932), 664, 672–73; "LXIV," *LHQ* 18, no. 3 (1935), 709; and "LXXI," *LHQ* 20, no. 2 (1937), 495–96, 507 (this last, unaddressed letter was perhaps to a different person).

10. On Benoist's case to recover debts from the Gervais estate, Cruzat, "Records of the Superior Council of Louisiana, LXX," *LHQ* 20, no. 1 (1937), 237; "LXXIV," *LHQ* 21, no. 1 (1938), 306–7, 318; "LXXV," *LHQ* 21, no. 2 (1938), 576–78, 581, 584–85; "LXXVI," *LHQ* 21, no. 3 (1938), 880, 886–87.

11. This episode is treated more fully in the chapter on Jean-Jacques de Macarty Mactique.

12. On the convoy, S. Faye, "The Arkansas Post of Louisiana: French Domination," *LHQ* 26, no. 3 (1943), 711–12; Vaudreuil to Benoist, 25 December 1752, Vaudreuil Papers, 420; translation in Pease and Jenison, *Illinois on the Eve*, 799–801.

Tenth Commandant: Jean-Gaspard de Bertet de La Clue (1742–49)

1. M. Verge-Franceschi, *Le Lieutenant général des Armées navales Jean-François de Bertet de La Clue-Sabran (1696–1764)*, accessed March 10, 2013, https://www.departemento6.fr/documents/Import/decouvrir-les-am/rr90-1985-04.pdf. As a young sailor, Jean-François de Bertet de La Clue-Sabran sailed from France to Dauphin Island. He wrote an interesting and important log of the journey and account of the island: *A Voyage to Dauphin Island in 1720: The Journal of Bertet de la Clue*, trans. and ed. F. Escoffier and J. Higginbotham (Mobile, AL: Museum of the City of Mobile, 1974). His experience may have influenced his brother's decision to come to Louisiana.

2. For records of the ages, services, and aptitudes of the officers serving in Louisiana 1740, see ANC, C13A.25.86v.

3. Bienville to Minister, 4 February 1743, ANC, 13A.28.31–40.

4. The chief was called La Demoiselle by the French, but his native name was Memeskia. He was also known as Old Briton by the British.

5. Pease and Jenison, *Illinois on the Eve*, xxiv–xxv; Vaudreuil to Minister, 24 May 1748, ANC, C13A.32.63–64.

6. De Guyenne to Vaudreuil, 10 September 1752, Vaudreuil Papers, 312; translation in Pease and Jenison, *Illinois on the Eve*, 720. This Rouensa was not, of course, the Rouensa who was chief in the late seventeenth century and the father

of Marie Rouensa-8cate8a, though perhaps he was a descendant. The names of prominent chiefs were often passed down through the generations.

7. Fort de La Trinité, also known variously as the Trinité Post, the Post of the Missouri, or Fort de Cavagnal (or Cavagnial or Cavagnolle), was established on the Missouri River in the vicinity of Kansas City, Missouri, and Fort Leavenworth, Kansas. It was abandoned about 1764, and although the ruins were visible into the early nineteenth century, its exact location is now unknown.

Twelfth Commandant: Jean-Jacques de Macarty Mactique (1751–60)

1. An annotated list of officers in Louisiana (8 April 1737, ANC, D2C.51.106) gives Macarty's age as twenty-nine, and a similar list from three years later (15 June 1740, ANC, C13A.25.89–89v) gives his age as thirty-four. Concerning Macarty's bibliography in general, see W. P. McCarthy, "The Chevalier Macarty Mactigue," *Journal of the Illinois State Historical Society* 61, no. 1 (Spring 1968), 41–57. Both forms of the name, Mactique and Mactigue, were used commonly.

2. Périer to Minister, 6 March 1733, ANC, C13A.16.201–5.

3. The story that Jean-Jacques Macarty's home served as Andrew Jackson's headquarters during the Battle of New Orleans in 1815 is a myth. The house used by Jackson was built by Edmond Macarty after 1807.

4. For instance, a letter from Jean-Jacques Macarty Mactique to Claude-Joseph Favrot, 14 April 1758, begins, "I, Jean-Jacques de Macarty, knight of the Royal and Military Order of Saint Louis, major, commandant in the country of Illinois." Louisiana Digital Library, accessed August 19, 2013, http://louisdl. louislibraries.org/cdm/ref/collection/LPC/id/279.

5. An annotated list of officers in Louisiana, 15 June 1740, ANC, C13A.25.89–89v, has "very well behaved"; a similar list, 29 August 1758, ANC, D2C.52.40v, says "precise and dignified." Barthélemy-Daniel de Macarty was the grandfather of the infamous Madame Lalaurie of New Orleans. C. M. Long, *Madame Lalaurie: Mistress of the Haunted House* (Gainesville: University Press of Florida, 2012).

6. Barron, *Vaudreuil Papers*. Many of the most important of Macarty's post papers are transcribed and translated in Pease and Jenison, *Illinois on the Eve*.

7. See the chapter on Jean-Bernard Bossu for more details.

8. "The post is the most troublesome in the colony; the number of voyageurs from all parts, the discipline of the troops, public welfare, governing the Indians—the most essential and most extensive part. One man alone cannot suffice." Macarty to Minister, 1 June 1752, ANC, C13A.36.311v. Pease and Jenison, *Illinois on the Eve*, 644, translates "embarrassans" as "embarrassing." "Troublesome" certainly conveys the meaning more clearly.

9. Vaudreuil to Minister, 10 October 1751, ANC, 13A.35.167–68; translation in Pease and Jenison, *Illinois on the Eve*, 401–2.

10. Macarty to Minister, 1 February 1752, ANC, C13A.36.307–307v. For a more detailed, rambling account of the incident and its aftermath, see Macarty to Vaudreuil, 20 January 1752, Vaudreuil Papers 328. Translations in Pease and Jenison, *Illinois on the Eve*, 478–79, 432–59.

11. Bossu, *Nouveaux voyages aux Indes Occidentales*, 1:128–34.

12. Ibid.

13. Ibid., 1:148, says there were six Fox. La Jonquière wrote that there were seven, identifying them as Fox, Sauk, and Sioux, of whom six were killed. He mentioned that one of the dead was a son of the Fox chief Pemoussa. La Jonquière to Minister, 25 September 1751, ANC, C11A.97.82. Macarty wrote that seven Fox were killed, probably forgetting about the escapee. Macarty to Vaudreuil, 2 September 1752, Vaudreuil Papers, 376. Translations in Pease and Jenison, *Illinois on the Eve*, 361, 654.

14. According to Edmunds and Peyser, *Fox Wars*, 199–200, by 1750 most of the Fox were living on the lower Rock River, near modern Rock Island, but Bossu, *Nouveaux voyages aux Indes Occidentales*, 1:150, wrote that the attack came down the Wisconsin River, entering the Mississippi well north of the Rock River. It is not apparent how Bossu could have had exact knowledge of the route of the raiders. His account is probably mere supposition based on the earlier location of the Fox.

15. La Jonquière to Minister, 25 September 1751, ANC, C11A.97.82; Macarty to Vaudreuil, 7 December 1752, Vaudreuil Papers, 412. Translations in Pease and Jenison, *Illinois on the Eve*, 361, 750.

16. Macarty wrote that the attackers consisted of Fox, Sioux, Sauk, Potawatomi, Winnebago, and Menominee but did not mention the Kickapoo. Macarty to Vaudreuil, 2 September 1752, Vaudreuil Papers, 376. Another account attributed the attack to Fox, Sauk, Sioux, and Menominee. Pierre de la Rue, l'abbé de l'Isle Dieu to Minister, 5 September 1753, ANC, C11A.99.199–200. Translations in Pease and Jenison, *Illinois on the Eve*, 654, 831–32. It would not be unusual for a large war party to include a few individuals from other tribes along with the main participants.

17. Bossu, *Nouveaux voyages aux Indes Occidentales*, 1:150. References to Bossu's accounts of the raid in 1752 in the following paragraphs, ibid., 1:148–59.

18. "Adanville," more properly Adamville, was commandant at the Peoria Post, appointed by Macarty. Bossu, *Nouveaux voyages aux Indes Occidentales*, 1:150, indicated that all came by canoe. According to Macarty, a portion moved on foot. Macarty to Vaudreuil, 2 September 1752, Vaudreuil Papers, 376. References to Macarty's accounts of the raid in 1752 in the following paragraphs are from ibid.; translation in Pease and Jenison, *Illinois on the Eve*, 654–55.

19. Both Macarty and de Guyenne reported that the attack took place on June 1, 1752, but Bossu stated that the attack took place on Corpus Christi Day, June 6. Bossu's date of June 6 is an evident mistake. Corpus Christi is a movable feast that is held on the Thursday after Trinity Sunday. In 1752, that was June 1. June 6 fell on a Tuesday that year and could not have been Corpus Christi. Macarty to Vaudreuil, 2 September 1752, Vaudreuil Papers, 376, translation in Pease and Jenison, *Illinois on the Eve*, 654–55; De Guyenne to Vaudreuil, 10 September 1752, Vaudreuil Papers, 312, translation in Pease and Jenison, *Illinois on the Eve*, 718; Bossu, *Nouveaux voyages aux Indes Occidentales*, 1:151.

20. Bossu, *Nouveaux voyages aux Indes Occidentales*, 1:152–53. Bossu claimed that he was able to save a fifteen-year-old Illinois girl who was bringing him strawberries when the attack began. She ran into his arms, he wrote, and the pursuing enemy dared not fire at her for fear of hitting him. It may be doubted whether this romantic vignette is true.

21. Ibid.; Macarty to Vaudreuil, 2 September 1752, Vaudreuil Papers, 376; translation in Pease and Jenison, *Illinois on the Eve*, 655.

22. Bossu, *Nouveaux voyages aux Indes Occidentales*, 1:154.

23. Macarty to Vaudreuil, 2 September 1752, 655–57.

24. De Guyenne to Vaudreuil, 10 September 1752, Vaudreuil Papers, 312; translation in Pease and Jenison, *Illinois on the Eve*, 721–22.

25. Ibid.

26. Bossu, *Nouveaux voyages aux Indes Occidentales*, 1:154–59. On the Illinois being terrified, Macarty to Vaudreuil, 2 September 1752. The Kaskaskia tribe, through not attacked, was also terrified. Pierre de la Rue, l'abbé de l'Isle Dieu to Minister, 5 September 1753.

27. Macarty reported that Marin *fils* returned five Illinois women to Macarty and Adamville saved a Sauk warrior. Macarty to Vaudreuil, 7 December 1752, Vaudreuil Papers, 412. Later, Duquesne reported the number of Illinois women Marin *fils* ransomed as four. Duquesne to Minister, 31 October 1753, ANC, C11A.99.114. Macarty also wrote that Adamville got the Sauk to release one Michigamea man, three women, and one child. Macarty to Vaudreuil, 2 September 1752, Vaudreuil Papers, 376. Translations in Pease and Jenison, *Illinois on the Eve*, 752–53, 850, 664.

28. Bossu, *Nouveaux voyages aux Indes Occidentales*, 1:81; M. K. Brown, "The Search for the Michigamea Indian Village," *Outdoor Illinois* (March 1972), 19, 26; C. E. Orser Jr., "The Kolmer Site: An Eighteenth Century Michigamea Village" (master's thesis, Wayne State University, Detroit, 1975); R. E. Hauser, "The Fox Raid of 1752: Defensive Warfare and Decline of Illinois Indian Tribe," *Illinois Historical Journal* 86 (1993): 220.

29. Macarty and Buchet to Vaudreuil, 15 January 1752, Macarty to Vaudreuil, 20 January 1752, Vaudreuil to Macarty, 25 April 1752, and Macarty to Vaudreuil,

2 September 1752, Vaudreuil Papers, 327, 328, 360, 376. Translations in Pease and Jenison, *Illinois on the Eve*, 423–26, 440–45, 598–99, 691–95. Also, Brown and Mazrim, "Revisiting," 137–38.

30. Although Ste. Geneviève was still very small in 1752, Macarty clearly recognized its great economic potential: "Ste. Geneviève will become more considerable than this place [Kaskaskia]. There are at present twenty-seven habitants who have lands and whose lands include four score thirteen arpents frontage. This place reports of its lands that they are more extensive, more fertile, and better." The twenty-seven did not consist of the entire population, just the landholders. Macarty to Vaudreuil, 2 September 1752, Vaudreuil Papers, 376; translation in Pease and Jenison, *Illinois on the Eve*, 693. For Ste. Geneviève in general, see Ekberg, *Ste. Genevieve*.

31. Kerlérec to Minister, 20 August 1753, ANC, C13A.37.72–73; translation in Pease and Jenison, *Illinois on the Eve*, 827–29.

32. Kerlérec's only criticisms were that Macarty was not good in dealing with Indians and that, early in his tenure, he should have been more tactful in dealing with the French inhabitants of Illinois. Service Records, ANC, D2C.50.62vo; Vaudreuil to Macarty, 28 April 1752, Vaudreuil Papers, 365; translation in Pease and Jenison, *Illinois on the Eve*, 619–20.

33. Pierre de la Rue, l'abbé de l'Isle Dieu, to Minister, 29 October 1754, ANC, C11A.99.481; translation in Pease and Jenison, *Illinois on the Eve*, 914–15.

34. Michel Baudouin, Jesuit Superior of the Louisiana Mission, to Pierre de la Rue, l'abbé de l'Isle Dieu, 28 June 1754, ANC, C11A.99.478; translation in Pease and Jenison, *Illinois on the Eve*, 869–78.

35. E.g. Vaudreuil to Macarty, 28 April 1752, and Macarty to Vaudreuil, 6 September 1752, Vaudreuil Papers, 378. Translations in Pease and Jenison, *Illinois on the Eve*, 620–21, 703.

36. Macarty to Vaudreuil, 18 March 1752, and Macarty to Vaudreuil, 27 March 1752, Vaudreuil Papers, 338–39. Translations in Pease and Jenison, *Illinois on the Eve*, 524–27, 532, 552. Macarty's dispatch for La Mazelière in regard to the legal procedure against the twenty-one Illinois deserters, before 28 September 1752, ANC, C13A.36.102–17.

37. Vaudreuil to Macarty, 28 April 1752, Vaudreuil Papers, 365; translation in Pease and Jenison, *Illinois on the Eve*, 618–20.

38. Because of the 1752 crop failure, wheat was abundant but of poor quality, infected with rust. Macarty to Vaudreuil, 2 September 1752, Vaudreuil Papers, 376. D'Orgon passed on information from Macarty reporting that the corn crop was lost. D'Orgon to Vaudreuil, 7 October 1752, Vaudreuil Papers, 399. On the 1753 crop failure, Kerlérec to Minister, 20 August 1753, ANC, C13A.37.71–71v. A boat conveying supplies faced dangers along the river route and was attacked, resulting in eight dead, one wounded, and a girl kidnapped. Macarty to Minister,

20 May 1753, ANC, C13A.37.188–89. Translations in Pease and Jenison, *Illinois on the Eve*, 686, 735–50, 814–16.

39. Duquesne to Minister, 31 October 1753, ANC, C11A.99.115v–18; translation in Pease and Jenison, *Illinois on the Eve*, 845–47.

40. Villiers du Terrage, *Last Years*, 65.

41. Dumas to Macarty, 10 November 1755, ANC, C13A.39.172–75.

42. G. C. Din, "François Coulon de Villiers: More Light on an Illusive [*sic*] Historical Figure," *Louisiana History* 41, no. 3 (Summer 2000): 345–57. In addition to an overview of Villiers's life, Din provides a translation of a letter from Bernardo de Gálvez to José de Gálvez, 21 March 1777, and the accompanying petition of Villiers to the Spanish king requesting appointment to the Spanish Army, which consists of a memoir of his entire military service from 1720, when he first entered French service as a cadet.

43. The numbers killed and captured vary slightly in different sources. Kerlérec reported English casualties as two officers and six enlisted men killed, and thirty soldiers, three women, and seven children captured. Kerlérec to Minister, 23 January 1758, ANC, C13A.40.24–26.

44. Francis Parkman's influential *Montcalm and Wolfe*, relying entirely on English reports, seems largely responsible for promulgating the massacre story, which can still be found online. F. Parkman, *Montcalm and Wolfe* (1884; repr., Boston: Little, Brown and Co., 1914), 1:423.

45. Death of the sergeant was widely reported, e.g., Bossu, *Nouveaux voyages aux Indes Occidentales*, 1:214. On transport of the prisoners to Fort de Chartres and ransom of the prisoners from Indians, ibid. On transport of prisoners to New Orleans, Layssard to Minister, 22 November 1758, ANC, C13A.40.335–38.

46. In his memoir, Villiers calls Grant "Crane," having misunderstood or misremembered the name. Din, "François Coulon," 355.

47. Villiers in his memoir records the name as "Royal Fort Annon." Ibid., 355.

48. On the siege and conquest of Fort Niagara and the battle at La Belle Famille, F. Anderson, *Crucible of War: The Seven Years' War and the Fate of Empire in British North America, 1754–1766* (New York: Alfred A. Knopf, 2000), 335–37; B. L. Dunnigan, *Siege—1759: The Campaign against Niagara*, rev. ed. (Youngstown, NY: Old Fort Niagara Association, 1996). For Macarty's report of the casualties, Macarty to Kerlérec, 30 August 1759, ANC, C13A.41.103–7.

49. Both recovered from their wounds, and after a year and a half as prisoners, both were exchanged, went to France, and then to New Orleans. Aubry became acting governor of Louisiana in 1765, succeeding Jean-Jacques Blaise d'Abbadie upon his death. He perished in a shipwreck while returning to France in 1770. François Coulon de Villiers served as commandant at Natchitoches during the transition from French to Spanish rule and hoped then to enter the Spanish Army in New Orleans. Villiers maintained in his memoir that because of a

confusion of names, the post was awarded to Baltazar de Villiers, no relation, a considerably junior officer. Din, "François Coulon," 351–52. Baltazar de Villiers was an able, highly respected officer who went on to serve well as commandant of the Arkansas Post, so the decision may not have been an error. M. S. Arnold, *Colonial Arkansas 1686–1804: A Social and Cultural History* (Fayetteville: University of Arkansas Press, 1991), 17, 117–18, *et passim*. Coulon de Villiers's attempts to have the decision changed failed, but he entered the civil service, serving several terms as *alcalde* and probate judge. He continued to live in New Orleans until his death in 1794.

50. B. Fortier, "New Light on Fort Massac," in *Frenchmen and French Ways in the Mississippi Valley*, ed. J. F. McDermott (Urbana: University of Illinois Press, 1969), 57–71. "Massac" is an American corruption of "Massiac."

51. Ibid., 62.

52. Kerlérec to Minister, 12 December 1758, ANC, C13A.40.140; *MPA* 5:207–8.

53. By the time of the construction of the fort, the marquis de Massiac had been replaced as the minister of the marine, but word had not yet reached Illinois.

54. Villiers du Terrage, *Last Years*, 124.

55. Ibid., 141.

56. Rochemore to Minister, 27 August 1760, ANC, C13A.42.151.

57. G. Lugano, "Records of the Superior Council of Louisiana, LXXXVII," *LHQ* 24, no. 2 (1941), 586–88.

58. Thwaites, *Jesuit Relations*, 70:285: Father François-Philibert Watrin, "Bannissement des Jésuites de la Louisiane." The expulsion of the Jesuits was a complex legal and legislative procedure begun in 1761, the last elements of which were not fully promulgated in Louisiana until 1764. The Jesuit possessions in Illinois were confiscated and sold, and the Jesuits were sent down to New Orleans in 1763.

59. C. W. Alvord and C. E. Carter, eds., *The Critical Period 1763–1765*, Collections of the Illinois State Historical Library, vol. 10, British Series, vol. 1 (Springfield: Trustees of the Illinois State Historical Library, 1915), 183; Villiers du Terrage, *Last Years*, 212; D'Abbadie to Minister, 20 April 1764, ANC, C13A.44.88.

60. La Jonquière to Minister, 25 September 1751, ANC, C11A.97.82; translation in Pease and Jenison, *Illinois on the Eve*, 361.

61. Bossu, *Nouveaux voyages aux Indes Occidentales*, 1:148–54. Bossu mistakenly dates to 1752 the initial raid, which actually took place in 1751.

62. On the event in December 1751, Macarty to Vaudreuil, 20 January 1752, Vaudreuil Papers, 328; and Macarty to Minister, 1 February 1752, ANC, C13A.36.307. On the attack on 1 June 1752, Macarty to Vaudreuil, 2 September

1752, Vaudreuil Papers, 376. Translations in Pease and Jenison, *Illinois on the Eve*, 432–35, 478–79, 654–56. An earlier account, written by Macarty to Vaudreuil on 2 June 1752, has not survived.

63. Pierre-Paul de La Marque de Marin was in charge of La Baye and the Post of the Sioux in partnership with La Jonquière and the corrupt *intendant* of New France, François Bigot. This was the territory occupied by the Fox and their allies. La Baye referred specifically to Green Bay but more generally to all the French posts between Green Bay and the Falls of St. Anthony. The Post of the Sioux was located on Lake Pepin, near Frontenac, Minnesota.

64. Hauser, "Fox Raid," 220–23.

65. Macarty to Vaudreuil, 2 September 1752: Vaudreuil Papers, 376; translation in Pease and Jenison, *Illinois on the Eve*, 663–64; Bossu, *Nouveaux voyages aux Indes Occidentales*, 1:153–54.

66. Macarty to Vaudreuil, 2 September 1752; translation in Pease and Jenison, *Illinois on the Eve*, 668–69, 672, 685.

67. Hauser, "Fox Raid," 222.

68. De Guyenne to Vaudreuil, 10 September 1752, Vaudreuil Papers, 312; translation in Pease and Jenison, *Illinois on the Eve*, 718.

69. Hauser, "Fox Raid," 222; Michel Baudouin to Pierre de la Rue, 28 June 1754.

Thirteenth Commandant: Pierre-Joseph Neyon de Villiers (1760–63)

1. For a more detailed account of this affair, see the chapter on Jean-Jacques de Macarty Mactique, the previous commandant.

2. The confusion between Pierre-Joseph Neyon de Villiers and François Coulon de Villiers was understandable in early historical works, written when relatively few primary sources were available. The careers of both men are now much more fully documented, but the old misattribution persists in some modern written accounts and websites. François Coulon de Villiers's wartime career is covered more fully in the chapter on Macarty and in Din, "François Coulon," 345–57.

3. Villiers du Terrage, *Last Years*, 147. Neyon's career was interwoven with that of his brother-in-law, Kerlérec. Marc de Villiers du Terrage, a relative of Kerlérec's, wrote *The Last Years of French Louisiana* in large part to vindicate Kerlérec's administration, in the course of which he presents an excessively positive portrait of Neyon.

4. Kerlérec to Minister, 1 March 1761, ANC, C13A.42.208v.

5. In Villiers du Terrage, *Last Years*, 165 n9, editor C. A. Brasseaux indicates that Fazende's name was René-Jean-Gabriel, but in *France's Forgotten Legion*, "Fazende," Brasseaux gives his name as Antoine.

6. Service records, 1758, ANC, D2C.50.73.

7. Villiers du Terrage, *Last Years*, 165.

8. Joseph Gagné has written a complete study of the retreats of La Chapelle from Detroit and Beaujeu from Michilimackinac, their subsequent interactions with Neyon de Villiers, La Chapelle's eventual vindication, and Beaujeu's subsequent career in the Illinois Country. J. F. Gagné, "'Fidèle à Dieu, à la France, et au Roi': Les retraites militaires de La Chapelle et de Beaujeu vers la Louisiane après la perte du Canada, 1760–1762" ["Faithful to God, to France, and to the king": Military retreats of La Chapelle and Beaujeu toward Louisiana after the loss of Canada] (master's thesis, Université Laval, 2014), http://www.theses.ulaval.ca/2014/30241/30241.pdf. L. P. Kellogg translated the account of La Chapelle's retreat and a summary account of his final exoneration, but she left much of the account of events after La Chapelle's arrival in New Orleans untold. L. P. Kellogg, "La Chapelle's Remarkable Retreat through the Mississippi Valley, 1760–61," *Mississippi Valley Historical Review* 22 (1935): 63–81. Kellogg's translation is based on the publication of La Chapelle's memoir in Baron Passerat de La Chapelle, "Le Baron Pierre Passerat de La Chapelle. Conférence faite à la Société d'Histoire du Canada par M. le Baron de La Chapelle," pts. 1 and 2, *Nova Francia* 7, no. 1 (January–June 1932): 81–135; 7, no. 2 (July–December 1932): 178–210. The summary of events presented here does little justice to the full story presented in Gagné's work, which is based on many unpublished documents in addition to La Chapelle's memoir. An enhanced version is to be published in 2016.

9. The letter is quoted in La Chapelle's memoir, a translation of which is in Kellogg, "La Chapelle's Remarkable Retreat," 65.

10. Buffalo Rock, the site of La Chapelle's fort, is only a few miles from the modern town of Ottawa, Illinois, the name of which is a coincidence and has nothing to do with the short-lived fort. The surface of Buffalo Rock was strip-mined in the nineteenth century, destroying any trace of the occupation by La Chapelle's men.

11. Joseph Gagné has not been able to confirm that Beaujeu did receive orders from Vaudreuil, although it seems likely.

12. La Chapelle indicated subtly that he was aided in hiding original documents and obtaining replacement writing materials by officers sympathetic to his cause, but he recorded no names besides the Chevalier de Pradel.

13. D. D. Ruddy, "Louis Liénard de Beaujeu de Villemonde," *Dictionary of Canadian Biography*, accessed December 9, 2013, http://www.biographi.ca/en/bio.php?id_nbr=2507.

14. Attempts were made to blacken La Chapelle's reputation by accusing him of misdeeds in Canada. These accusations were taken seriously by Villiers du Terrage in *Last Years*, 167–68, but the miscreant was a different La Chapelle, not even a relative. Regarding La Chapelle's subsequent career, see L. Phelps

Kellogg, "Passerat de La Chapelle in the American Revolution," *Mississippi Valley Historical Review* 25, no. 4 (March 1939): 535–38.

15. K. W. Seineke, *The George Rogers Clark Adventure in the Illinois and Selected Documents of the American Revolution at the Frontier Posts* (New Orleans: Polyanthos, 1981), 43.

16. C. A. Brasseaux and M. K. Le Blanc, "Franco-Indian Diplomacy in the Mississippi Valley, 1754–1763: Prelude to Pontiac's Uprising?," *Journal de la Société des Américanistes de Paris* 68, no. 1 (1982): 59–70. This article has not enjoyed the full recognition it deserves.

17. Ibid.

18. Ekberg has suggested that d'Abbadie knew about the treaties of November 1762 and February 1763 ceding the colony when he left for Louisiana in the spring of 1763 and that he probably gossiped about them when he arrived in New Orleans. C. J. Ekberg, "The Exclusive Maxent-Laclède Trading Grant," *Missouri Historical Review* 106 (July 2012): 195 n7.

19. Lugano, "Records of the Superior Council of Louisiana, XCIV," *LHQ* 26, no. 1 (1943): 249–50.

20. Neyon de Villiers to Kerlérec, 1 December 1763, quoted by Villiers du Terrage in *Last Years*, 203–6.

21. On the transfer of cannons from Fort Massiac to Ste. Genevieve, ANC, C13A.43.353–65. Several useless cannons were left behind at Fort Massiac. Controversy arose between the French and British about the ownership of the cannons in French forts in general. Neyon made no effort to secure the cannons of Fort de Chartres. St. Ange transferred cannons from Fort de Chartres to the west bank of the Mississippi in 1765, leaving a few behind for the convenience of the British according to orders.

22. Villiers du Terrage, *Last Years*, 218–19.

23. Ibid., 218 n30.

24. "The Journal of M. Dabbadie, 1763–1764," trans. in Alvord and Carter, *Critical Period*, 1:189–90.

Fourteenth and Last French Commandant: Louis Groston de St. Ange de Bellerive (1764–65)

1. For a full treatment of the St. Ange family, and particularly Louis Groston de St. Ange de Bellerive, see Ekberg and Person, *St. Louis Rising*. For greater detail about Louis's association with Bourgmont, see the chapter on the sixth commandant, Robert Groston de St. Ange.

2. See the chapter on Robert Groston de St. Ange.

3. Bienville to Minister, 29 June 1736, ANC, C13A.21.184–184v; translation in *MPA* 3:688.

4. See the chapter on Robert Groston de St. Ange.

5. Bienville recommendations for replacements, 15 October 1736, ANC, D2C.50.45 and D2C.51.151v; Bienville to Minister, 29 June 1736, ANC, C13A.21.184; Summary of the ages, services and aptitudes of the officers serving in Louisiana, ANC, C13A.25.91.

6. Brasseaux, "Groston de Saint Ange de Bellerive," *FFL*. The records indicate that St. Ange was promoted to half-pay status in both 1738 and 1748, the second occasion probably made necessary by the army reform after the end of King George's War in 1748, which would have invalidated the earlier appointment.

7. General Haldimand to Lord Dartmouth, 5 January 1774, *Sir Frederick Haldimand: Unpublished Papers and Correspondence 1758–1784* (London: World Microfilm Publications, 1977), reel 14.

8. Daniel Blouin, Mémoire, 9 July 1771, in Thomas Gage Papers, 138.16, Clements Library, Ann Arbor, MI.

9. Summary of the ages, services and aptitudes of the officers serving in Louisiana, ANC, D2C.50.63v.

10. "The Journal of M. Dabbadie, 1763–1764," trans. in Alvord and Carter, *Critical Period*, 1:189–90.

11. On Stirling, R. G. Caroon, *Broadswords and Bayonets: The Journals of the Expedition under the Command of Captain Thomas Stirling of the 42nd Regiment of Foot, Royal Highland Regiment (the Black Watch) to Occupy Fort Chartres in the Illinois Country, August 1765 to January 1766* (Kenilworth: Society of Colonial Wars in the State of Illinois, 1984), 45. On Eddington, ibid., 82–83.

12. For a full treatment of St. Ange's years in St. Louis, see Ekberg and Person, *St. Louis Rising*.

13. Ulloa entered the Spanish Navy as a young man, but more important, he was an intellectual and probably a genius. While still in his teens, he was appointed as a member of the French Academy of Sciences' French Geodesic Mission to South America to measure the diameter of the earth at the equator. While in South America, Ulloa became the codiscoverer of the element platinum. His ship was captured by the British as he returned to Europe but was soon released to return Spain through the influence of British intellectuals. In England, he was made a fellow of the Royal Society of London, and later he was elected to the Royal Swedish Academy of Sciences. He published several books on his work in South America; established the astronomical observatory at Cadiz, a natural history museum, and the first Spanish metallurgical laboratory; and returned to Peru, where he managed the vital mercury mines for six years. Mercury was required in quantity to extract silver and gold from ores. He had just retired to Havana when he was appointed to govern Louisiana.

14. Report of Don Pedro Piernas to Gov. O'Reilly Describing the Spanish Illinois Country, 31 October 1769, in L. Houck, ed., *The Spanish Regime in Missouri* (Chicago: R. R. Donnelley & Sons Co., 1909), 1:73; General Instructions

of O'Reilly to the Lieutenant-Governor (Piernas) of the Villages of St. Louis, San Genevieve, etc., 17 February 1770, in ibid., 1:83.

15. O. W. Collet, ed., "Will and Accompanying Documents of Louis St. Ange de Bellerive," *Magazine of Western History* 2 (1885): 64.

PART 3. PEOPLE OF FORT DE CHARTRES

Marie Rouensa-8cate8a: The Mother of French Illinois

1. C. J. Ekberg and A. J. Pregaldin, "Marie Rouensa-8cate8a and the Foundation of French Illinois," *Illinois Historical Journal* 84, no. 3 (Autumn 1991): 146–60. Before Ekberg and Pregaldin's article, Marie Rouensa-8cate8a was seldom mentioned in historical works and then given only short notice. Since then, she has become one of the most famous people of French Illinois. The degree to which she has come to play a dominant figure in discussions of the roles of women and relations among French and Indians may be seen, for example, in the large role she plays in S. White's *Wild Frenchmen and Frenchified Indians*. Recently, Ekberg has revisited Marie Rouensa-8cate8a as part of his broader study of the roles of Indian women in French Illinois, *Stealing Indian Women*. The sketch of her life in this chapter is essentially dependent on Ekberg's works, although any blunders or misinterpretations of events are, of course, my own.

2. Father Jacques Gravier to Father Jaque [*sic*] Joheneau, 15 February 1694, in Thwaites, *Jesuit Relations*, 64:231.

3. It is too simplistic to refer to Rouensa as the chief of the Kaskaskia, a European concept based on the European model of kingship. The social structure of the Kaskaskia, like most other tribes, was complex, with a number of levels and distinct roles of leadership often held by more than one individual at a time. Rouensa, however, seems to have been the preeminent chief, the *primus inter pares*.

4. The name Accault, as with most French names in the era, was spelled in a variety of ways, including Acco, Aco, and Ako.

5. Father Jacques Gravier to Father Jaque [*sic*] Joheneau, 15 February 1694, in Thwaites, *Jesuit Relations*, 64:193–95.

6. Ibid., 64:195–213.

7. Dean and Brown, Kaskaskia Manuscripts, 25.6.13.1; Ekberg and Pregaldin, "Marie Rouensa," 154.

8. Dean and Brown, Kaskaskia Manuscripts, 25.6.20.1; Ekberg and Pregaldin, "Marie Rouensa," 154.

9. One wonders whether Marie appreciated the irony in the parallel between her disapproval of a disobedient child in regard to marriage and her father's disapproval of her own years earlier.

10. R. M. Morrissey, "The Terms of Encounter: Language and Contested Visions of French Colonization in the Illinois Country, 1673–1702," in *French*

and Indians in the Heart of North America, 1630–1815, ed. R. Englebert and G. Teasdale (East Lansing: Michigan State University Press, 2013), 43–75.

11. The parallel of this conflict to the Chinese Rites controversy is obvious.

12. R. M. Morrissey, "I Speak It Well: Language, Communication, and the End of a Missionary Middle Ground in Illinois, 1673–1712," *Early American Studies* 9, no. 3 (September 2011): 646–48.

Étienne de Véniard de Bourgmont and Ignon Ouaconisen (Françoise Missouri): An Explorer and an Indian in Paris

1. "Relation de l'arrivée en France de quatre Sauvages du Missicipi, de leur sejour, & des audiences qu'ils ont euës du Roi, des Princes du Sang, de la Compagnie des Indes, avec les compliments qu'ils ont fait, les honneurs & les presens qu'ils ont reçûs, &c" [Account of the arrival in France of the four Indians of Mississippi, of their stay, and of the audiences they have had with the king, with the princes of the blood (sons of the monarch), with the East India Company, with the compliments they have made, the honors & the presents they received, etc.]. *Mercure de France* 1 (December 1725): 2828.

2. The standard biography of Bourgmont, containing basic information about Ignon Ouaconisen, is Norall, *Bourgmont*.

3. Vaudreuil to Minister, 4 November 1706, in C. M. Burton, ed., "Cadillac Papers," *Michigan Historical Collections* 33 (1904): 305–7. Norall gives a very summary account of the affair. *Bourgmont*, 8–11. A much fuller account can be found in S. Vincens, *Madame Montour et son temps* [Madame Montour and her time] (Montréal: Québec/Amérique, 1979), or in English, S. Vincens, *Madame Montour and the Fur Trade (1667–1752)*, trans. and ed. R. Bernstein (Bloomington, IN: Xlibris, 2011), 157–62.

4. Bourgmont's paramour at this juncture was Madame Tichenet, the daughter of a French man and an Indian woman. She was also known under a variety of other names, most commonly Madame Montour, but also Elizabeth Couc and La Chenette. Her brother's name was Louis Couc Montour. Cadillac disliked her and accused her of a variety of misdeeds, but he was routinely vituperative toward anyone to whom he had an aversion. Madame Montour eventually went over to the English and had a long and distinguished career as a translator and negotiator for officials and private traders in New York and Pennsylvania. She had mastered French, English, and a number of Indian languages from both the Algonquian and Iroquoian language families. Her career and even identity within her family are not totally clear, due at least in part to her own efforts to obscure her origins and events in her past. Vincens, *Madame Montour et son temps*; Vincens, *Madame Montour and the Fur Trade*; A. D. Hirsch, "'The Celebrated Madame Montour': Interpretess across Early American Frontiers," *Explorations in Early American Culture* 4 (2000): 81–112; J. Parmenter, "Isabel

Montour: Cultural Broker on the Eighteenth-Century Frontiers of New York and Pennsylvania," in *The Human Tradition in Colonial America*, ed. I. K. Steele and N. Rhoden (Wilmington, DE: Scholarly Resources, 1999), 141–59.

5. Norall, *Bourgmont*, 99–123 contains translations of Bourgmont's reports, ANC, 3JJ.277.2 and 13C.1.346–56.

6. Ibid., 125–61 contains a translation of Bourgmont's report of the journey to the Padouca and the establishment of peace among the tribes, ANC, 2JJ 55.26.1–44. For the role of Robert Groston de St. Ange and his sons, see the chapter on St. Ange and the literature cited there, particularly Ekberg and Person, *St. Louis Rising*.

7. "Relation de l'arrivée," 2828, reports that the group initially numbered twenty-two, but the article is frequently in error. An additional contemporary report of the visit, often ignored, is C. J[ordan], "Les Sauvages de l'Amerique ont audience du Roy et doivent s'en retourner en leur pays" [The American Indians have an audience with the king and have to return to their country], *Suite de la Clef, ou Journal historique sur les matières du temps* [Following the key, or Historical journal on materials of the time] 19 (February 1726): 209–10.

8. A tale, colorful but false, claimed it was the sinking of *La Bellone* that discouraged the larger group of Indians from proceeding to France, rather than the tightfistedness of the Superior Council of Louisiana. This may have been circulated purposely so that the Superior Council would not appear so miserly. The story appears already in "Relation de l'arrivée," 2828.

9. Brasseaux, "Dubois," *FFL*.

10. Louis Marin, captain of the militia, died on April 12, 1756. Dean and Brown, Kaskaskia Manuscripts, 56:5:15:1. Marin also served as an interpreter of Indian languages. Brown and Dean, *Village of Chartres*, K181. His name appears frequently elsewhere in the records of Chartres village.

11. Françoise died early in 1739, and her second husband, Marin, then requested guardians for their three children and the two children by her first marriage. Dean and Brown, Kaskaskia Manuscripts, 39:1:26:1; P. Weeks, "Princess of the Missouris," *Le Journal* 7, no. 3 (Fall 1991): 6–12. Concerning Ignon's marriages to Dubois and then Marin, and issues arising out of inheritances, H. P. Dart, "Decision Day in the Superior Council of Louisiana, March 5, 1746," *LHQ* 21, no. 4 (October 1938): 998–1020.

12. J.-F.-B Dumont de Montigny, *Mémoires historiques sur la Louisiane*, ed. J.-B. Le Mascrier, 2 vols. (Paris: C. J. B. Bauche, 1753). The title page contains the notation "Composés sur les Mémoires de M. Dumont par M. L' Abbé Le Mascrier."

13. Ibid., 2:75–78. For the recent edition of Dumont's manuscript, without the elaborations of Le Mascrier, see Dumont de Montigny, *Regards sur le monde atlantique, 1715–1747* [Views of the Atlantic world], ed. C. Zecher, G. M. Sayre, and S. L. Dawdy (Sillery, Québec: Septentrion, 2008), or the translation, J.-F.-B.

Dumont de Montigny, *The Memoir of Lieutenant Dumont, 1715–1747: A Sojourner in the French Atlantic*, trans. G. M. Sayre, ed. G. M. Sayre and C. Zecher (Chapel Hill: University of North Carolina Press, 2012).

14. For a fuller account of Bossu and his works, see the chapter on Jean-Bernard Bossu. Also see Bossu, *Nouveaux Voyages aux Indes Occidentales*, 1:161–62.

15. I thank particularly Patricia Weeks, a lineal descendant of Françoise Missouri, for her cordial aid and her excellent overview of her ancestor, "Princess of the Missouris."

Terrisse de Ternan: A Restless and Worrisome Personality

1. On Ternan as a privateer, M. Giraud, *A History of French Louisiana*, vol. 1, *The Reign of Louis XIV, 1698–1715*, trans. J. C. Lambert (Baton Rouge: Louisiana State University Press, 1974), 275 and sources cited there.

2. Vitrac de La Tour, whose name was also written as Vitral de La Tour, was a partisan of Bienville's and rival of Cadillac's. When La Tour married a relative of Bienville's without the required permission from Cadillac, the quarrel between La Tour and Cadillac became intensely personal. They exchanged insults, and Cadillac ordered La Tour's arrest.

3. Adjudication of the Council of the Marine of various letters of La Mothe Cadillac of 15, 23, 24, and 26 July and 9 October 1716, ANC, C13A.4.381–86; Adjudication of the Council of the Marine of a letter of Chastelain of 22 July and 9 October 1716, ANC, C13A.4.411–14; Adjudication of the Council of the Marine of a memoir of Crozat, 10 October 1716, ANC, C13A.4.417–18. Benoist survived and later twice became interim commandant of Fort de Chartres.

4. Adjudication of the Council of the Marine: the assignment of subaltern officers in the various companies of Louisiana, ANC, C13A.4.312.

5. [J.-B. Bénard de La Harpe and J. Chevalier de Beaurain], *Journal historique de l'établissement des Français à la Louisiane* (New Orleans: A. L. Boimare, 1831), 167. Although this work is commonly attributed simply to Jean-Baptiste Bénard de La Harpe, its origin is more complex. Much of the work is dependent on two works by La Harpe, a manuscript journal and a memoir, but the work may have been edited and supplemented by the French geographer Jean Chevalier de Beaurain (1696–1771) and finally published sixty years after Beaurain's death. Marc de Villiers du Terrage, "Un explorateur de la Louisiane, Jean-Baptiste Bénard de La Harpe (1683–1765)," *Société d'histoire et d'archéologie de Bretagne, Mémoires* 15 (1934; repr., Montréal: Bibliothèque nationale du Québec, 1988): 37.

6. Périer and La Chaise to Directors of the Company, 22 April 1726, ANC, C13.10.175v; translation in *MPA* 2:539.

7. For the depositions of the two men and the judgment in the case, see Dean and Brown, Kaskaskia Manuscripts, 30.12.22.1, 2, and 3; translation in Ekberg, Kilman, and Lebeau, *Code Noir*.

8. Dean and Brown, Kaskaskia Manuscripts, 30.12.22.3. Although Ternan wrote the decision in the name of the officers in general, the document is in his handwriting and bears his signature alone.

9. Officer evaluation, 6 March 1730, ANC, D2C.51.89v.

10. Terrisse de Ternan to Michel Rossard, 13 October 1729, in Cruzat, "Letters," 516, 531. Cruzat translated "L'arrest que l'en a envoye icy contre les jesuites" as "The decree sent here against the Jesuits" (516). "The complaint" seems to agree better with the context. In addition to the controversy about the church of Ste. Anne, the Jesuits at this time were quarreling with the Compagnie des Indes about finances, particularly in regard to the establishment of a new mission when the Compagnie moved the Indians out of Kaskaskia to a separate village a few miles away. The Compagnie felt the Jesuits' claims were excessive, and Ternan, of course, was only too glad to argue against the Jesuits.

11. Brown, *History*, 107–10; M. B. Palm, *The Jesuit Missions of the Illinois Country, 1673–1763* (Cleveland: St. Louis University, 1931), 56–61.

12. E.g., Palm, *Jesuit Missions.* Another source, C. E. O'Neill, *Church and State in French Colonial Louisiana: Policy and Politics to 1732* (New Haven, CT: Yale University Press, 1966), does not deal with the controversy at all. In Lower Louisiana, much greater disputes were occupying Jesuits, Capuchins, and representatives of the Compagnie des Indes.

13. Cruzat, "Letters," 509–42, has published eleven of Ternan's letters, in both the original French and English translation. The first was written in New Orleans, the others from Fort de Chartres or Kaskaskia. Another letter from Fort de Chartres and an overview of Ternan's life and character can be found in C. Ekberg, "Terrisse de Ternan, Epistoler and Soldier," *Louisiana History* 23, no. 4 (Fall 1982): 400–408.

14. Terrisse de Ternan to Michel Rossard, 13 October 1729, in Cruzat, "Letters," 516, 531.

15. In regard to flour, Cruzat, "Letters," 514, 529. The word as transcribed by Cruzat is *favines*, which appears in neither the 1762 French dictionary nor modern dictionaries. Cruzat somewhat hesitantly translated *favines* as okra. The letters *v* and *r* are difficult to distinguish in many eighteenth-century manuscripts, however, and the word is more likely to be *farines*, meaning flour. Thanks to M. Tourblanche for the suggestion. Flour became one of the major exports from the Illinois Country to New Orleans and on occasion even as far as France.

16. Bienville to Maurepas, 18 May 1733, ANC, C13.16.230v–231; translation in *MPA* 3:617. Oddly, Bienville, in a general review of officers, describes Ternan as an ensign, though he was listed earlier in 1733 as a second lieutenant in Illinois. ANC, D2C.50.35v. Perhaps some unrecorded incident led to another demotion and prompted his departure from Louisiana, but the apparent conflicts about Ternan's rank may reflect no more than the delay between the recommendation

of promotion and confirmation of the rank. Sometimes the royal government acted quickly, other times the wait might lengthen into years, and occasionally the royal government seems simply to have forgotten about a promotion and had to be reminded. On September 8, 1733, Ternan officially retired from active service in Louisiana, recorded in a general review of officers. ANC, D2C.50.41.

17. Avocat Léon, *Précis pour le sieur Point Marie de la Demoiselle Bourbosson légataire universelle du sieur Terrisse de Ternan son oncle, contre Demoiselle Marianne Terrisse, Veuve de Guillaume Carlet, etc. signé Léon, avocet* [Précis for Sieur Point Marie of the damsel Bourbosson, legatee of Sieur Terrisse de Ternan her uncle, against damsel Marianne Terrisse, widow of Guillaume Carlet, etc. signed Léon, lawyer]. (Grenoble: Impr. Cuchet J., 1759), accessed February 20, 2014, http://catalogue.bm-grenoble.fr/in/faces/details.xhtml?id=p::usmarcdef_0000396727&mozQuirk=?&highlight=Leon,%20avocat&posInPage=4&bookmark=c7e5b949–1626–4f36- 850a-e3a177ada9ae.

Claude Chetivau: The Man Who Wanted to Go to Canada

1. For another account of Claude Chetivau's misadventures, see Brown, *History*, 45–46. On Chetivau's transportation to Louisiana: "List of the company employees, concessionaries. Private passengers, tobacco smugglers, illicit salt dealers, vagabonds, deserters and others embarked on the *Deux Frères* commanded by M. Ferret bound for Louisiana from La Rochelle, 16 August 1719." G. R. Conrad, trans., *The First Families of Louisiana*, vol. 1 (Baton Rouge: Claitor's Publishing Division, 1970), 62. The account of Chetivau's attempted defection to Canada is based on the document edited and translated in Brown and Dean, *Village of Chartres*, K370.

2. "Monsieur de Lorene" is the most probable reading, but the name is otherwise unknown. It is possible that the semilegible scrawl represents "de Lorme," the director general of operations in Louisiana for the Compagnie des Indes, who served as sort of a head bookkeeper.

3. Brown and Dean, *Village of Chartres*, K17. A pot was a liquid measure equaling about a half gallon. The French pint contained a bit more than twice the English pint.

4. Ibid., K20.

5. Brochard's complaint and Chetivau's answer are found in ibid., K399.

(François-)Pierre Boucher de Boucherville: Escape to Fort de Chartres

1. "Boucher de Boucherville, Pierre (baptized François-Pierre)," *Dictionary of Canadian Biography*, accessed January 20, 2014, http://www.biographi.ca/en/bio/boucher_de_boucherville_pierre_3E.html.

2. The journey of the men from Fort Beauharnois is related in an account written by Boucherville and witnessed by five members of the group, published

initially as M. Bibaud, ed., "Relation des Aventures de M. de Boucherville, à son retour des Scioux, en 1728 et 1729, suivie d'Observations sur les moeurs, coutumes, &c. de ces Sauvages" [Account of the adventures of Mr. de Boucherville, on his return from the Sioux, in 1728 and 1729, followed by the manners, customs, etc. of the Indians], pts. 1 and 2, *La Bibliothèque Canadienne* 3, no. 1 (1826): 11–15; 3, no. 2 (1826): 46–50. An English translation is published in R. G. Thwaites, "1728–29: Narrative of de Boucherville," in *Collections of the State Historical Society of Wisconsin*, vol. 17, *The French Regime in Wisconsin—II: 1727–1748* (Madison: State Historical Society of Wisconsin, 1906), 36–57.

3. Edmunds and Peyser, *Fox Wars*, 100–103.

4. I follow the identifications of the rivers in Thwaites, "1728–29," 36–57.

5. Translation from ibid., 40.

6. Translation from ibid., 42–43.

7. For a list of the goods given to the Fox, Kickapoo, and other Indians during the escape, see E. D. Neill, *The Last French Post in the Valley of the Upper Mississippi* (St. Paul, MN: Pioneer Press Company, 1887), 8–9.

8. The Canadian governor Beauharnois to the Minister, 24 March 1729; Pierre-Noel le Gardeur de Tilly to the Minister, 30 April 1729; and Beauharnois to the Minister, 16 May 1729. English translations of the relevant parts are conveniently gathered in Thwaites, "1728–29," 58–62.

9. Translation from Thwaites, "1728–29," 48.

10. Beauharnois to Minister, 17 August and 1 September 1729. Translations from Thwaites, "1728–29," 65–70.

Claude-Alphonse de La Buissonnière and Marie-Thérèse Trudeau: Marriage Woes

1. A version of this essay was published as D. MacDonald, "Les tribulations nuptiales d'Alphonse de la Buissonnière et de Marie-Thérèse Trudeau," Hélène Trudeau, trans., *La Charpente* 6, no. 3 (December 2013): 3–10, and "Annexe: The Marriage Woes of Alphonse de la Buissonnière and Marie-Thérèse Trudeau," *La Charpente* 6, no. 3 (December 2013): 1–6.

2. Brasseaux, "La Buissonnière," *FFL*.

3. Brasseaux, ibid., noted that La Buissonnière was also the first cousin of Mme. Alexandrine-Ernestine Gourdan. She ran the most important bordello in Paris, patronized by the social elite: aristocrats, influential government officials, and even important members of the clergy. [Morande?], *Porte-feuille*. Her patrons included both men and women, and her husband petitioned for La Buissonnière's promotion to captain.

4. Service record, ca. 6 March 1730, ANC, D2C.51.91.

5. Service record, 1732, ANC, D2C.50.20v.

6. Me. E. Monty, "François Truteau," *Mémoires de la Société généalogique canadienne-française* 29, no. 3 (July–September 1978): 167.

7. Two of Marie-Thérèse's sisters, Marie-Josephte and Marie-Françoise, were married at fifteen. M. J. Trudeau, *The Trudeaus of Louisiana and Related Families* (N.p.: M. J Trudeau, 1996), 43–49. In Canada, women on the average seem to have been several years older at the time of their marriage than in Louisiana.

8. Bienville and Salmon to Minister, 22 September 1733, ANC, 13A.16.159.

9. The sister is not named in the letter but was probably Marie-Françoise, who married Pierre-Gabriel de Juzan, aide major at Mobile, on 29 April 1735. Brasseaux, "Juzan," *FFL*.

10. The Récollets, a branch of the Franciscans, were established in Illinois, where they too sometimes quarreled with the Jesuits over questions of jurisdiction.

11. See O'Neill, *Church and State*, 241, regarding tensions between the *gens d'épée* and *gens de plume* even before Bienville returned to Louisiana.

12. Ibid., 157–234. Before Beaubois came to New Orleans, he had served in Illinois, where there were no Capuchins. This may have influenced Bienville's choice to send La Buissonnière and Marie-Thérèse there.

13. Ibid., 170–74.

14. Such disobedience was no small matter. For a parallel case, see Council of Marine to Governor-General Vaudreuil, 14 June 1721, ANC, B.44.516–18; J. L. Peyser, trans., *Letters from New France: The Upper Country, 1686–1783* (Urbana: University of Illinois Press, 1992), 103–4. In Canada, a lieutenant married without permission, and although he was the nephew of the governor general, and the bishop of Quebec performed the marriage, the lieutenant escaped being dismissed from the service only by the intervention of the regent as a favor to the governor. Even then, the lieutenant was no longer permitted to serve in Canada and was shipped off to Isle Royale. The letter indicates that in the future, any officer marrying without permission would be cashiered, a fate that La Buissonnière escaped only because of the support of Bienville and perhaps the remoteness of the Illinois Post. A similar case arose in 1731 in Illinois, where Dutisné *fils*, a young *enseigne en pied*, married the recent widow of Giradot (Girardeau), a fellow officer. According to Terrisse de Ternan, a sublieutenant at Illinois, the marriage was done secretly by the Jesuit Fathers without the permission of the commandant, Dutisné having neither sought nor received advice about the matter. Terrisse de Ternan to Rossard, clerk of the Superior Council, 10 June 1731, in Cruzat, "Letters," 523–24. Périer was clearly annoyed by the marriage; in 1732, he characterized Dutisné as "a thoughtless (*étourdy*) young man who entered into a disadvantageous marriage without permission" (ANC, D2C.50. 21v), but that did not prevent Dutisné from being promoted to lieutenant that same year. Dutisné probably escaped severe censure chiefly because he was not involved in the factional disputes of Louisiana, but he also benefited from his station in distant Illinois and from the contemporary preoccupation with the Natchez War.

15. For a receipt dated 18 August 1736 by Marie-Thérèse to her father for her dowry, amounting to 6,493 livres, 16 sols, 4 deniers, and a detailed statement of slaves given at the time of the marriage by her father to Alphonse de La Buissonnière, whose value amounted to 6,059 livres, 65 sols, 45 deniers, see Cruzat, "Records of the Superior Council of Louisiana, XXVII, Supplement Index No. 4," *LHQ* 8, no. 3 (1925): 488. These were truly impressive sums. Belting indicated that what seems to have been the largest marriage settlement paid in the Illinois Country was less than half this amount. Belting, *Kaskaskia*, 77.

16. On the relationship to Bienville, L. Trudeau, "Page d'Histoire Onzième épisode: Le goût de la terre" [Page of history, eleventh episode: The flavor of the land], *La Charpente*, Vol. 4, no. 2 (June 2011), 6–10. On literacy, Bibliothèque et Archives nationales du Québec (BANQ), Notary Bénigne Basset, 25 September 1697, Agreement between François Trutau, Jacques Dain, and François Dumer; L. Trudeau, "Part One—Charles Laveau Trudeau, alias Don Carlos (1743–1816)," *La Charpente* 4, no. 4 (December 2011): 1–2.

17. Abstract of testimony concerning Bienville, 14–27 February 1708, ANC, C13.2.249–312; translation in *MPA* 3:78–85.

18. Narrative of events, 6 August–2 September 1719, ANC, C13.5.307–8; translation in *MPA* 3:248.

19. Subscription for providing materials to construct church, ANC, C13A.8.92–95; W. De Ville, ed., "Constructing a Future Cathedral, 1724," *Mississippi Valley Mélange* 3 (1998): 27–32.

20. Maduell, *Census Tables*, 115; Trudeau, "Page d'histoire," 6–10.

21. Trudeau was still recorded as captain of the militia on 29 April 1735 in the marriage contract of Pierre-Gabriel Juzan and Marie-Françoise Trudeau, in Cruzat, "Records of the Superior Council of Louisiana, XV," *LHQ* 5, no. 2 (1922): 264. Appointed to Superior Council 14 September 1735, *Alphabet Laffilard*, ANC, D2C.222.777.

22. De La Chase to the Directors of the Company of the Indies, 18 October 1723, ANC, 13.7.79–81v; translation in *MPA* 2:387–90.

23. Bienville and Salmon to Minister, 1 April 1734, ANC, 13A.18.38.

24. Bienville and Salmon to the Minister, 14 April 1735, ANC, 13A.20.47

25. Marriage contract of Pierre Gabriel Juzan and Marie-Françoise Trudeau, in Cruzat, "Records of the Superior Council of Louisiana XV," *LHQ* 5, no. 2 (1922): 264.

26. Cruzat, "Records of the Superior Council of Louisiana, XXVII, Supplement Index No. 4," *LHQ* 8, no. 3 (1925): 489. Dawdy mistakenly assumed the boat was to transport trade goods sent by Marie-Thérèse from Illinois rather than to transport her to Illinois so she could finally join her husband there. S. L. Dawdy, *Building the Devil's Empire: French Colonial New Orleans* (Chicago: University of Chicago Press, 2009), 106, 274 n15.

27. For the marriage contract of Louis de Portneuf de Robineau and Marie-Thérèse Trudeau, see Dean and Brown, Kaskaskia Manuscripts, 41:8:6:1. On reciprocal donation of all goods of new marriage partners, ibid., 41:8:9:1. For an inventory of the possessions of Portneuf and Thérèse Trudeau, see ibid., 49:4:2:2. On Portneuf's marriage to Madeleine Barrois, Brown and Dean, *Village of Chartres*, D-288. On Portneuf's military career, Brasseaux, "Robineau de Portneuf, Louis," *FFL*. On his service as commandant of the Missouri/Kansas Post, which was sometime attached to the Fort de Chartres command, Pease and Jenison, *Illinois on the Eve*, li n2. Also, Macarty to Vaudreuil, 20 January and 27 March 1752; Vaudreuil to Macarty, 25 April 1752, Vaudreuil Papers, 328, 339, 360. Translations in Jenison and Pease, *Illinois on the Eve*, 467, 548–50.

Jacques-Sernan Voisin: A Hero of the Chickasaw Wars?
1. For a general account of the 1736 campaign, see Atkinson, *Splendid Land*, 43–61. See also the chapter on Pierre d'Artaguiette d'Itouralde.
2. Maurepas to Bienville, 26 October 1736, ANC, B64.522–522v.
3. The April letter from Bienville to Maurepas apparently no longer exists.
4. On the Iroquois contingent, the anonymous "Account of the Battle Fought by d'Artaguiette with the Chickasaws," ANC, F3.24.258–63; text and translation in Dunn and Dunn, "Indiana's First War," 107–23. "Account of the March and of the Defeat of d'Artaguiette, by Parisien," ANC, F3.24.256–57; text and translation in ibid., 128–33. Bienville to Maurepas, 28 June 1736, ANC, C13A.21.207–212v; translation in Rowland and Sanders, *Mississippi*, 311–14. All agree that the Iroquois fought bravely during the retreat. They accompanied the survivors back to Illinois.
5. For an early private letter from Canada bearing news of the defeat, Toussaint Loizel to his brother, 13 April 1736, preserved in the *greffe* of Compearet, the *notaire* at Montréal, excerpt quoted in P.-G. Roy, "Jean Bissot de Vincennes," *Le Bulletin des Recherches Historiques* 6 (1900), 110. The letter contains a list of officers killed but does not discuss any details of the retreat. Two letters are concerned with the martyrdom of Father Senat but also offer no information about the retreat. Jesuit Father Mathurin Le Petit to the Very Reverend Father General Franciscus Retz, 29 June 1736 and 25 June 1738, in Thwaites, *Jesuit Relations*, 68:307–10, 69:27–29.
6. Bienville to Maurepas, 15 February 1737, ANC, C13A.22.72v–73; translation in Rowland and Sanders, *Mississippi*, 1:331–32. Bienville also accused the soldiers of cowardice in a previous letter. Bienville to Maurepas, 28 June 1736, ANC, C13.21.188–203v; translation in ibid., 1:297–314.
7. Charlevoix, *Histoire*, 2:501–2. The standard translation is Charlevoix, *History and General Description of New France*, trans. with notes by J. G. Shea, 6 vols. (1870; repr., New York: F. P. Harper, 1902). Charlevoix did not indicate his source for the account of Voisin's actions; Shea suggested that the source

was the account of Drouet de Richardville, which he had not been able to find (6:121 n1). Drouet de Richardville was captured before the events associated with Voisin, saw nothing of the retreat, and included nothing relevant in his account. ANC, F3.24.252–54; translation in Dunn and Dunn, "Indiana's First War," 132–43. Accounts of the distances of the retreat vary. Charlevoix's account of a fighting retreat of twenty-five leagues is exaggerated. Le Parisien's "Account," ANC, F3.24.256–57, claims they were pursued all day. The anonymous "Account," ANC, F3.24.258–63, gives the length of the fighting retreat as nearly four leagues, followed by a longer retreat during which the Chickasaw did not follow.

8. Brasseaux, "Voisin (Sometimes Voisin Le Jeune, Voysin, Voyssin), Jacques Fernan," *FFL*. Brasseaux gives Voisin's middle name as Fernan, but in the script of the period, the letters *f* and *s* were often rendered similarly, and Sernan is the reading to be preferred. Voisin was born at Ste. Sernan, Diocese Ste. Malo, Brittany, and was named after the local saint. Report of the ages, services, and aptitudes of the officers serving in Louisiana, 15 June 1740, ANC, C13A.25.90v, under the heading "Enseignes en second," "Voisin—Fils d'un marchand de ce pays. A reçu en 1737 une lettre d'enseigne. Bon sujet—23 ans." Ages listed in such governors' evaluations often differ from other records.

9. On Pierre Voisin as interim member of the Superior Council, acting on behalf of attorney for vacant estates, Brasseaux, Administrators: "Voisin, Pierre," *FFL*; Cruzat, "Records of the Superior Council of Louisiana, XLIV," *LHQ* 12, no. 4 (1929): 649 (5 January 1744); "XLV," *LHQ* 13, no. 1 (1930): 119, 123. Pierre Voisin frequently appears in the records of the Superior Council in regard to his business interests.

10. Cruzat, "Records of the Superior Council of Louisiana, XXIV," *LHQ* 7, no. 4 (1924): 702 (20 May 1734).

11. Ibid. On Jacques Voisin involved in the sale of slaves, Dean and Brown, Kaskaskia Manuscripts, 35:–:–:24; 35:–:–:25; 36:–:–:5. On Voisin trading the services of a male slave for those of female slave, ibid., 36:1:23:1. Otherwise, St. Pierre Laverdure guaranteed security for Voisin, ibid., 36:1:24:1. Voisin acknowledged a debt to Lapointe, ibid., 36:–:–:107. Another sale of a slave was conducted for Voisin by an agent exercising a power of attorney on 21 December 1737, ibid., 37:12:21:1. Two later Kaskaskia Manuscripts, 49:12:29:3 and 50:12:22:1, refer to the New Orleans merchant Pierre Voisin, Jacques Voisin's father. Brasseaux, "Voisin," *FFL*, noted that Jacques Voisin "reportedly served as a cadet in Saint-Domingue, 1736," but this was clearly an error.

12. Bienville to Minister, 29 June and 5 September 1736, ANC, C13A.21.181–86, C13A.21.218–218v. Translations in Rowland and Sanders, *Mississippi*, 1:331–32.

13. Bienville took Voisin on a second expedition against the Chickasaw. Louboey to Maurepas, 4 January 1740, ANC, C13A.25.209v; translation in Rowland and Sanders, *Mississippi*, 1:416.

14. On Voisin's marriage, A. D. Forsyth and G. Pleasonton, *Louisiana Marriage Contracts* (New Orleans: Polyanthos, 1980), 143; Cruzat, "Records of the Superior Council of Louisiana, L," *LHQ* 14, no. 2 (1931): 251. On his family, C. E. Nolan, *Sacramental Records of the Roman Catholic Church of the Archdiocese of New Orleans*, vol. 1, *1718–1750* (New Orleans: Archdiocese of New Orleans, 1987), 258–59. On January 29, 1762, Voisin sold his plantation along with fourteen slaves, twenty-five cattle, and five horses for 60,000 livres. G. Lugano, "Records of the Superior Council of Louisiana, LXXXIII," *LHQ*, Vol. 23, Issue 2 (1940), 604–5.

15. Brasseaux, "Voisin," *FFL*.

16. Jacques Voisin, who appears as Santiago Voisin in the Spanish records, was still alive on March 11, 1776. Porteous, "Index to the Spanish Judicial Records of Louisiana, XXII," *LHQ* 11, no. 3 (1928): 504–6. Notice of the death of Santiago Voisin and the order to make an inventory and appraisement of his estate was made on January 23, 1777. Porteous, "Index to the Spanish Judicial Records of Louisiana, XXIV," *LHQ* 12, no. 2 (1929): 348. Such notices and inventories were generally made within a day or two of the death.

17. Service record, 15 June 1740, ANC, C13A.25.90v; Service record, 1758: ANC, D2C.3.1.

Jean Ducoutray: The Chicken Thief of Kaskaskia

1. The documents recording Jean Ducoutray's chicken thievery and subsequent legal troubles are recorded in Cruzat, "Records of the Superior Council of Louisiana, LXXV," *LHQ* 21, no. 2 (1938), 587–604. For another account of Ducoutray's crime and punishment, see Brown, *History*, 47–48.

2. E. M. Scott and D. P. Heldman, "A French Descendant Community after the Fall of New France: Archaeology in Nouvelle Ste. Genevieve, 1780–1880," *Le Journal* 26, no. 1 (Winter 2010): 4; and M. Boyer, *Plantations by the River: Watercolor Paintings from St. Charles Parish, Louisiana by Father Joseph Paret, 1859* (Baton Rouge: Geoscience Publications, Louisiana State University Press, 2001), 67, cited by Scott and Heldman.

3. De Mazellières's name was, like those of so many of his contemporaries, also spelled in more than half a dozen different ways, but none of the documents give us his first name. He is recorded as captain *en second* of the Chasseurs of the colony in 1750, and in 1753 he commanded a detachment carrying supplies to the Ohio. Pease and Jenison, *Illinois on the Eve*, li n1. Ducoutray's name was also spelled several different ways, as was even his nickname "Poullailler."

4. Cruzat, "Records of the Superior Council of Louisiana, LXXV," *LHQ* 21, no. 2 (1938), 599.

5. Minister to Givery, 24 August 1753, ANC, B98.325.

Jean-Bernard Bossu: Officer and Travel Writer

1. On the Arkansas Post, Arnold, *Colonial Arkansas*.

2. Bossu, *Nouveaux voyages aux Indes Occidentales*, 1:128–30.

3. Ibid., 1:130–34. This incident is recounted in greater detail in the chapter on Jean-Jacques de Macarty Mactique.

4. Ibid., 1:148–52. See the chapter on Macarty for a detailed account of the events of 1751–52, noting the distortions of Bossu's accounts.

5. Ibid., 211–15.

6. The seminal study of the Kerlérec-Rochemore conflict is Villiers du Terrage, *Last Years*, 98–166. Villiers du Terrage was a relative of Kerlérec's, whose conduct he sought to vindicate. The work is nevertheless scholarly and of enduring value.

7. Bossu, *Nouveaux voyages aux Indes Occidentales*, 2:215–16.

8. Villiers du Terrage, *Last Years*, 378–406. More recent sources are A. P. Nasatir and J. R. Mills, *Commerce and Contraband in New Orleans during the French and Indian War: A Documentary Study of the Texel and Three Brothers Affairs* (Cincinnati: American Jewish Archives, 1968); and H. Gourmelon, *Le chevalier de Kerlérec: L'affaire de la Louisiane* [The Chevalier de Kerlérec: The Louisiana Affair], 2nd ed. (Saint-Jacques-de-la-Lande, France: Keltia graphic, 2004).

9. Bossu, *Nouveaux voyages aux Indes Occidentales*, 1:xii–xiii.

10. Ibid., 1:65–74.

11. Much has been written on the Villasur massacre in recent years, largely as a result of the discovery of the Segesser hide painting, a near-contemporary graphic representation of the battle. See Hotz, *Segesser Hide Paintings*; Chavez, *A Moment in Time*.

12. Bossu, *Nouveaux voyages aux Indes Occidentales* I, 175–76.

13. Charlevoix, *Histoire*, 3:246–51; Dumont, *Mémoires historiques*, 2:287–89; Le Page du Pratz, *Histoire*, 2:245–51.

14. On the Indian who saw LaSalle, Bossu, *Nouveaux voyages aux Indes Occidentales*, 1:80–81. On the trip up the Mississippi, ibid., 1:38. On honor, ibid., 1:121–23.

15. Ibid., 1:180.

16. Villiers du Terrage, *Last Years*, 395, 401.

Philippe-François de Rastel de Rocheblave: A Man of Many Flags

1. The number of children in the family and the number of sons who served in America vary in different modern accounts. Probably the most reliable is Seineke, *George Rogers Clark*, which concludes that there were twenty-three children, but the additional claim that seven served in America is less probable (43). Four seems more likely.

2. Pierre-Louis, ANC, D2C.59.43v; 94.47, 56; 127.67; 181.51.

3. There is testimony that Philippe-François specifically, rather than Pierre-Louis, was the Rocheblave at Braddock's defeat at Monongahela in 1755, but the testimony is a second-person account recorded a century after the event: A. Grignon, "Seventy-Two Years' Recollections of Wisconsin," in *Third Annual Report and Collections of the State Historical Society of Wisconsin*, vol. 3, ed. L. C. Draper (Madison, WI: Calkins & Webb, Printers, 1857), 213. Augustin Grignon was Charles de Langlade's grandson and heard accounts from his grandfather. It is possible that both Pierre-Louis and Philippe-François served in the area. The activities attributed to Rocheblave are sufficient for two individuals. If both brothers were active in the area, it would explain the confusion recorded below in note 7.

4. Villiers du Terrage, *Last Years*, 382; Seineke, *George Rogers Clark*, 46–47.

5. L. L. Porteous, "Trial of Pablo Rocheblave before Governor Unzaga, 1771," *LHQ* 8, no. 3 (July 1925): 372–81.

6. Rocheblave to Lord George Germaine, 28 February 1778, translation in E. G. Mason, "Rocheblave Papers," in *Early Chicago and Illinois*, ed. E. G. Mason, Chicago Historical Society's Collection, vol. 4 (Chicago: Fergus Printing Company, 1890), 407–8.

7. Confusion continues to reign, with some commentators (e.g., Mason) claiming that Philippe-François migrated to Canada, others (e.g., Seineke) that he migrated to Louisiana and was sent north to Fort de Chartres. E. G. Mason, "British Illinois—Philippe de Rocheblave," in *Early Chicago and Illinois*, ed. E. G. Mason, Chicago Historical Society's Collection, vol. 4 (Chicago: Fergus Printing Company, 1890), 360; Seineke, *George Rogers Clark*, 44. The evidence is ambiguous.

8. Grignon, "Seventy-Two Years' Recollections," 213–15. One wonders whether the story, recorded a century after the event, was remembered for its own sake or because of Philippe-François's later notoriety, or whether Philippe-François's dubious reputation may have caused his name rather than another Rocheblave's to be associated with the story. Seineke has argued that the story actually was about Pierre-Louis (*George Rogers Clark*, 45–46), although Grignon specifically attributed it to Philippe-François.

9. Seineke, *George Rogers Clark*, 44.

10. Rocheblave was back at Fort de Chartres signing as a witness to a wedding on January 7, 1761. Brown and Dean, *Village of Chartres*, D-298.

11. Ekberg, *Ste. Genevieve*.

12. Governor Don Antonio de Ulloa to the Marquis de Grimaldi, the Spanish First Secretary of State, 4 August 1768, Loyola University Spanish Documents Project, New Orleans, SD 2542-279-423, no. 20; translation in Seineke, *George Rogers Clark*, 121–22.

13. Ekberg, *Ste. Genevieve*, 341.

14. Seineke, *George Rogers Clark*, 208–10.

15. Rocheblave to Lieut.-Gov. Hamilton, May 8, 1777, translation in Mason, "Rocheblave Papers," 391.

16. P. L. Stevens, "'To Invade the Frontiers of Kentucky'? The Indian Diplomacy of Philippe de Rocheblave, Britain's Acting Commandant at Kaskaskia, 1776–1778," *Filson Club History Quarterly* 64, no. 2 (April 1990): 205–46.

17. Seineke, *George Rogers Clark*, 262–64.

18. Rocheblave specifically spoke about his feeling that the king of France had abandoned him. Mason, "British Illinois—Philippe de Rocheblave," 374, citing Madame de Rocheblave to Haldimand, 9 October 1780, from the Haldimand Papers (British Museum). Rocheblave would undoubtedly have seen his transference of loyalty from the French to the Spanish to the British monarchy as a matter of honor and duty, perhaps sharpened by his sense of underappreciation. Modern interpreters might be tempted to give a Freudian interpretation of Rocheblave's career as a recurring search for a surrogate father.

Lexicon

ȣ. A symbol used by the French to represent the sound "ou" or "w," which occurred in a number of Indian languages but had no equivalent in French.

à la façon du pays. A French term meaning "according to the fashion of the country," in this context referring to marriage between French traders and Indian women according to Indian custom but without the sanction of the church, heartily condemned by the clergy.

Arkansas Post. A small French fort and settlement on the lower Arkansas River. The post, whose location changed several times during the eighteenth century, was important as a midway station between New Orleans and Illinois where convoys could rest, resupply, and remain while river conditions did not permit travel.

arpent. An old French unit of both linear and area land measurement. As a linear measurement, an arpent was equal to approximately 192 feet; as an area measurement it was equal to approximately 0.85 acre.

arriviste. A person who has recently attained high rank, regarded with disdain by the traditional aristocracy.

bateau (pl. bateaux). The French word for "boat," in this context referring to a plank-built boat for river transportation and commerce. The early flat-bottomed bateaux were eventually largely replaced by keel boats, which were also often called bateaux. Bateaux varied greatly in size, with some capable of carrying as much as sixteen tons, and came in a number of styles, such as square or pointed prow and stern.

Baie des Puants. An early name for what today is Green Bay, Wisconsin, translating as the "Bay of Stinks" or "Bay of Stinkers.

La Belle Riviére. French name for the Ohio River. The French regarded the lower Ohio River as a tributary of the Wabash, although today the Wabash is considered a tributary of the Ohio.

cadet. A young man serving as a common soldier in anticipation of promotion to officer.

cadet de l'aiguillette. Literally, "cadet of the shoulder cord," so called for the distinctive symbol he wore. A *cadet de l'aiguillette* was of higher social status than a *cadet soldat* and generally received earlier promotion.

cadet soldat. A cadet often of bourgeois background and thus of lower social status than a *cadet de l'aiguillette.*

Cahokia. The northernmost of the French villages in the American Bottoms, on the eastern, Illinois side of the Mississippi, slightly south of modern St. Louis, and about forty miles north of Fort de Chartres.

Capuchins. The Order of Capuchin Friars Minor (Latin: Ordo Fratrum Minorum Capuccinorum) was a major offshoot of the Franciscan order. The Capuchins were vested with ministry to the French in New Orleans and settled areas of southern Louisiana, while the Jesuits were to be responsible for proselytizing Indians in most of the rest of Louisiana. The Jesuits, however, established their administrative center in New Orleans, and quarreling between the two orders became endemic.

Chartres (or Nouvelle Chartres). The village that grew up around Fort de Chartres. It was virtually abandoned at the end of the French regime, and many of the inhabitants migrated to Ste. Geneviève.

Code Noir de La Louisiane. Law code promulgated in 1724 regulating slavery in Louisiana.

commissaire-ordonnateur. The chief royal financial and judicial officer in Louisiana. He was assisted by subordinate district *commissaires.* The governor and *commissaire-ordonnateur* were frequently in conflict, at least in part because their respective roles were poorly defined and frequently overlapped. Such feuds were often bitter and destructive. Regional *commissaires* usually cooperated to a greater degree with regional commanders.

Compagnie des Indes. Formerly the Compagnie d'Occident, a French trading company that administered Louisiana (including le Pays de Illinois) as a proprietary colony from 1719 to 1731. The Compagnie des Indes retained certain trading privileges in French North America until the end of the French regime.

Compagnie d'Occident. A French trading company that administered Louisiana (including le Pays de Illinois) as a proprietary colony from 1717 to 1719, when it was reorganized as the Compagnie des Indes.

Compagnies Franches de la Marine. The troops stationed in Louisiana, including le Pays de Illinois, were members of the Compagnies Franches de la Marine, generally referred to as the French Marines. They were administered by the minister of the marine, who was also responsible for the French Navy and colonies.

coureurs des bois (sing. *coureur de bois*). Literally, "woods runners." Unlicensed individuals who traded European goods with the Indians for furs and hides, they were known for their independence and general immorality.

Coutume de Paris. Regional variations in law prevailed in France during the eighteenth century. The most important of these was the Coutume de Paris, which was the form of French law in use in colonial Louisiana, including le Pays des Illinois, and Canada.

fermier général (pl. *fermiers généraux*). Private individual who leased from the French royal government the right to collect royal taxes. These individuals often made great profits from the arrangement and exercised significant political influence. Not to be confused with the modern use of the term *ferme*, which means "farm."

filles du roi. Literally, "the king's daughters," young orphaned women whose migration to French America was sponsored and supported by the king.

fils. The French word for "son," the equivalent of the English "the Younger," attached to the name of a son who bore the same name as his father.

Fort Cavagnial. Fort established in 1744 on the Missouri River near what is now Fort Leavenworth and abandoned in 1764. It was initially named Fort de La Trinité.

Fort Cavendish. The English renamed Fort de Chartres as Fort Cavendish in 1765. The name never achieved general use.

Fort de Chartres. The military and administrative center of le Pays de Illinois, established in 1719–20 and ceded to the English in 1765. The fort was rebuilt in 1725, 1732, and 1752–54.

Fort de L'Assomption. Constructed at Ecorse à Prudhomme (modern-day Memphis), this fort served as Bienville's base during his unsuccessful campaign against the Chickasaw in 1739. The fort was abandoned and destroyed at the end of the campaign.

Fort de La Trinité. The original name of the fort established on the Missouri River near the site of modern Fort Leavenworth in 1744 and abandoned in 1764. It was later named Fort Cavagnial.

Fort d'Orléans. A post established on the Missouri River by Étienne de Véniard de Bourgmont in 1723. Despite rumors that the post was destroyed by Indians in 1728, it seems to have been occupied at least seasonally until 1736. Later, other posts were established on the Missouri River.

Fort Massiac. A French fort on the lower Ohio built in 1757, abandoned in 1763, and burnt by the Cherokee. It was rebuilt as the American Fort Massac in 1794 and again abandoned in 1814.

Fort St. Francis. This fort was constructed at the junction of the St. Francis and Mississippi Rivers early in Bienville's 1739 campaign against the Chickasaw. Considerable effort was expended in building the fort and transporting materials to it, but it soon became apparent that the fort was too far from the Chickasaw villages to be an effective base and it was abandoned.

franciser. To "Frenchify" or "Gallicize," referring to the policy of the Seminary of Foreign Missions priests to replace Indians' indigenous culture with French religion, language, and culture.

fusilier. An infantryman, named after the musket (or fusil) he bore. The term *fusil* was also applied to a smoothbore flintlock fowler. Both were long-barreled flintlock smoothbore shoulder-fired guns.

garde-magasin. The "storehouse guard," an important official, either military or civilian, charged with the administration of the government *magasin*. Military supplies and trade goods were received, stored, and dispersed at the storehouse, to the military, to the Indians as gifts or trade goods, and to civilians by sale or trade. Civilians could also deposit goods in the *magasin* in anticipation of shipment to New Orleans or some other destination for sale or trade.

génie. Military engineering.

gens d'épée. "People of the sword," men whose status derived from service as military officers. They were often in opposition to the *gens de plume*, the bureaucrats.

gens de plume. "People of the feather," a reference to the quill pens used by bureaucrats. These were men whose status derived from bureaucratic service. They were often in opposition to the *gens d'épée*, the military officers.

greffier. A court clerk charged with the responsibility of keeping the records of court proceedings.

habitant. A resident landowning farmer.

huissier. An assistant to a notary, who aided in the execution of legal matters.

Illinois. The native people of the American Bottoms and Illinois River. The term *Illinois* encompassed an alliance of four principal closely related tribes—the Cahokia, Michigamea, Kaskaskia, and Peoria—and a number of smaller tribes. The Illinois spoke a common Algonquian dialect and were related more distantly to other speakers of Algonquian dialects in the Midwest.

interprète. Translator of Indian languages. The post was usually held by a civilian, though occasionally by a trooper. The post was important, as the *interprète* had to serve as a cross-cultural intermediary as much as a simple translator.

Jesuits. Formally, the Society of Jesus (Latin: Societas Iesu). Charged with the chief responsibility for proselytizing Indians in Louisiana, the Jesuits, eager, aggressive, and at times overbearing, engaged in quarrels with the Seminary of Foreign Missions priests in Illinois, the Capuchins in southern Louisiana, and frequently the French military officers throughout the area.

Kaskaskia. The largest of the French villages in the American Bottoms, about eighteen miles south of Fort de Chartres, Kaskaskia became the first capital of the state of Illinois. It was washed away when the Mississippi changed course in the late nineteenth century.

le Pays d'en Haut. Meaning the "Upper Country," the term referred generally to a vast area including northwestern Québec, much of Ontario, the Great Lakes region, and west into the Canadian prairies.

le Pays des Illinois. The French term for the geographic region including, at its broadest, the middle Mississippi valley and the lower valleys of the Missouri, Illinois, Ohio, and Wabash Rivers.

Louisiana. René-Robert Cavelier de La Salle named the Mississippi River valley Louisiana in 1682 in honor of King Louis XIV. The first permanent French settlement was established in 1699. In 1717, le Pays des Illinois was attached to Louisiana.

marguillier. This person administered the material aspect of the local church parish, usually in cooperation with, but occasionally in opposition to, the local priest.

Métis. Literally, "mixed," used to indicate a person born of the union of French and Indian parents.

milice **(militia).** A locally raised quasimilitary force that might be employed for a local crisis or more broadly during time of war. Other than a few local officials, all physically able males between the ages of twelve and fifty were liable for militia duty.

Misère. Nickname for Ste. Geneviève during its early years, supposedly for the poverty of the early settlement, but the village seems to have prospered agriculturally, and the name may have been meant in an amusingly ironic sense.

notary. Lawyers were not allowed in French Louisiana. All legal work, such as contracts, bills of sale, and so on, were drawn up, signed, and registered by notaries. The notary was assisted by a *huissier*, who served subpoenas, aided with sales, and helped execute other legal matters.

Ouabache. French name for the Wabash River. The French considered the lower Ohio River to be a tributary of the Ouabache, while today the Wabash is considered a tributary of the Ohio. The French village of Vincennes was established on the Wabash.

Pain Court. "Short of Bread," the nickname for St. Louis in its early days. St. Louis was mainly a center for trade and for a long time lacked a sufficient agricultural base. The name probably developed because of early food shortages.

Pimetoui. Site of modern-day Peoria, on the Illinois River, home of the Peoria Indians, one of the Illinois tribes, and the location of a minor fort and trading post dependent on Fort de Chartres.

pirogue. A boat made from a hollowed-out tree trunk. Pirogues varied in size from small boats that could bear just one or two men to enormous vessels forty or fifty feet long that could carry several tons of merchandise.

Prairie du Rocher. A small French village several miles south of Fort de Chartres. Prairie du Rocher remains a vital community. Its old cemetery and Creole House attest to its French origins.

roturier. A commoner, as distinct from a person of aristocratic background. In the eighteenth century prosperous *roturiers* frequently attempted to elevate their status by marrying into families of the gentry or simply by adding apparently aristocratic elements to their names.

Seminary of Foreign Missions (Séminaire des Missions Étrangères). Founded in the seventeenth century and dedicated to proselytism, the seminary established a rich estate at Cahokia but seems to have had indifferent success in converting Indians. The seminary priests quarreled with the Jesuits about jurisdictional matters and the appropriate methods of proselytizing Indians.

Ste. Geneviève. Village established on the western, Missouri side of the Mississippi a few miles south of Fort de Chartres.

St. Louis. Founded on the western bank of the Mississippi after France had ceded its western holdings to Spain but before the cession was known in Illinois lands, St. Louis long retained its French character and culture.

St. Philippe. A small French village a few miles north of Fort de Chartres.

syndic. A local official who presided over village meetings on purely local concerns.

Vincennes. A French village on the Wabash River, today's Vincennes, Indiana. It was known by a variety of names, including Post au Ouabache, Post des Pianguichats, and Post St. Ange, before the name Vincennes became dominant.

Bibliography

ARCHIVAL AND MANUSCRIPT SOURCES

Alphabet Laffilard. Archives Nationales d'Outre-Mer. Secrétariat d'État à la Marine, Troupes et personnel civil (1650/1901), ANC, D2C.222. Accessed May 7, 2013. http://anom.archivesnationales.culture.gouv.fr/ark:/61561/tu245rsnme.num=20.geogname=Canada.

Archives Nationales d'Outre-Mer (formerly Archives Nationales Coloniales). Aix-en-Provence, France.

Bibliothèque et Archives nationales du Québec (BANQ). Montréal, Québec, Canada.

Dean, L. C., and M. K. Brown, comps. Kaskaskia Manuscripts, 1714–1816: A Calendar of Civil Documents in Colonial Illinois. Chester, IL: Randolph County Archives, 1981. Microfilm.

Gage, Thomas, Papers. Clements Library, Ann Arbor, MI.

Haldimand, Sir Frederick: Unpublished Papers and Correspondence, 1758–1784. London: World Microfilm Publications, 1977.

Kaskaskia Parish Records. Family Search Historical Record Collections. Accessed May 12, 2014. https://familysearch.org/search/collection/show#uri=http://familysearch.org/ searchapi/search/collection/1388122.

Louisiana Digital Library. Louisiana Purchase and Louisiana Colonial History. http://louisdl.louislibraries.org/cdm/landingpage/collection/LPC.

Vaudreuil Papers. Huntington Manuscripts, Loudoun Collection. Huntington Library, San Marino, CA.

PUBLISHED AND ONLINE SOURCES

Allain, M. "Louisiana Women Criminals during the French Colonial Period." *Le Journal* 16, no. 1 (Winter 1999). Reprinted in *French Colonial Studies: Le Pays des Illinois: Selections from Le Journal, 1983–2005*, edited by M. K. Brown and H. R. Williams, 103–8. Extended Publications Series, no. 6. Naperville, IL: Center for French Colonial Studies, 2006.

Alvord, C. W. *The Centennial History of Illinois*. Vol. 1, *The Illinois Country, 1673–1818*. Chicago: A. C. McClurg & Co., 1922.

Alvord, C. W., and C. E. Carter, eds. *The Critical Period, 1763–1765*. Collections of the Illinois State Historical Library, vol. 10; British Series, vol. 1. Springfield: Trustees of the Illinois State Historical Library, 1915.

Anderson, F. *Crucible of War: The Seven Years' War and the Fate of Empire in British North America, 1754–1766*. New York: Alfred A. Knopf, 2000.

Arnold, M. S. *Colonial Arkansas, 1686–1804: A Social and Cultural History*. Fayetteville: University of Arkansas Press, 1991.

Atkinson, J. R. *Splendid Land, Splendid People: The Chickasaw Indians to Removal*. Tuscaloosa: University of Alabama Press, 2004.

Baillardel, A., and A. Prioult. *Le Chevalier de Pradel*. Paris: Maisonneuve Frères, 1928.

Balvay, A. *L'Épée et la plume: Amérindiens et soldats des troupes de la marine en Louisiane et au Pays d'en Haut (1683–1763)* [The sword and the pen: American Indians and soldiers of the Troupes de la Marine in Louisiana and the Pays d'en Haut]. Québec: Les Presses de l'Université Laval, 2006.

———. "The French and the Natchez: A Failed Encounter." In *French and Indians in the Heart of North America, 1630–1815*, edited by R. Englebert and G. Teasdale, 144–47. East Lansing: Michigan State University Press, 2013.

Barron, B. *The Vaudreuil Papers: A Calendar and Index of the Personal and Private Records of Pierre de Rigaud de Vaudreuil, Royal Governor of the French Province of Louisiana, 1743–1753*. New Orleans: Polyanthos, 1975.

Belting, N. M. *Kaskaskia under the French Regime*. University of Illinois Studies in the Social Sciences, vol. 29, no. 3. Urbana: University of Illinois Press, 1948.

[Bénard de La Harpe, J.-B., and J. Chevalier de Beaurain]. *Journal historique de l'établissement des Français à la Louisiane* [Historical journal on the French settlement in Louisiana]. New Orleans: A. L. Boimare, 1831.

Berardinis, R. de, trans. "The 1732 French Census of Illinois." *Illinois State Genealogical Quarterly* 32, no. 3 (Fall 2000): 155–64.

———, trans. "The 1752 French Census of Illinois." *Illinois State Genealogical Quarterly* 32, no. 4 (Winter 2000): 195–203.

Bertet de La Clue-Sabran, J.-F. de. *A Voyage to Dauphin Island in 1720: The Journal of Bertet de la Clue*. Translated and edited by F. Escoffier and J. Higginbotham. Mobile, AL: Museum of the City of Mobile, 1974.

Bibaud, M., ed. "Relation des Aventures de M. de Boucherville, à son retour des Scioux, en 1728 et 1729, suivie d'Observations sur les moeurs, coutumes, &c. de ces Sauvages" [Account of the adventures of Mr. de Boucherville, on his return from the Sioux, in 1728 and 1729, followed by the manners, customs, etc. of the Indians]. Pts. 1 and 2. *La Bibliothèque Canadienne* 3, no. 1 (1826): 11–15; 3, no. 2 (1826): 46–50.

Blasingham, E. J. "The Depopulation of the Illinois Indians." Pts. 1 and 2. *Ethnohistory* 3, no. 3 (Summer 1956): 193–224; 3, no. 4 (Autumn 1956): 361–412.

Bossu, J.-B. *Jean-Bernard Bossu's Travels in the Interior of North America, 1751–1762.* Translated by S. Feiler. Norman: University of Oklahoma Press, 1962.

———. *New Travels in North America by Jean-Bernard Bossu, 1770–1771.* Translated and edited by S. D. Dickinson. Natchitoches, LA: Northwestern State University Press, 1982.

———. *Nouveaux voyage dans l'Amérique Septentrionale, contenant une collection de lettres écrites sur les lieux par l'auteur, à son ami M. Douin, chevalier, capitaine dans les troupes du roi, ci-devant son camarade dans le Nouveau Monde* [New travels in North America, containing a collection of letters written on location by the author, to his friend Mr. Douin, chevalier, captain in the king's troops, who was earlier his comrade in the New World]. Amsterdam: Chez Changuion, 1777.

———. *Nouveaux voyages aux Indes Occidentales; contenant une Relation des différens Peuples qui habitent les environs du grand Fleuve Saint-Louis, appellé vulgairement le Missisipi; leur Religion; leur gouvernement; leurs moeurs; leurs guerres et leur commerce* [Recent travels in the West Indies, containing a description of the various peoples who inhabit the vicinity of the great River Saint Louis, commonly called the Mississippi; their religion; their government; their customs; their wars; and their commerce]. 2 vols. Paris: Chez Le Jay, 1768.

———. *Nouveaux voyages en Louisiane, 1751–1768* [New travels in Louisiana]. Edited by P. Jacquin. Paris: Aubier Montaigne, 1994.

———. *Travels through That Part of North America Formerly Called Louisiana by Mr. Bossu, Captain of the French Marines.* Translated by J. R. Forester. 2 vols. London: Printed for T. Davies, 1771.

"Boucher de Boucherville, Pierre (baptized François-Pierre)." *Dictionary of Canadian Biography.* Accessed January 20, 2014. http://www.biographi.ca/en/bio/boucher_de_boucherville_pierre_3E.html.

Boyer, M. *Plantations by the River: Watercolor Paintings from St. Charles Parish, Louisiana by Father Joseph Paret, 1859.* Baton Rouge: Geoscience Publications, Louisiana State University Press, 2001.

Brasseaux, C. A. *France's Forgotten Legion: Service Records of French Military and Administrative Personnel Stationed in the Mississippi Valley and Gulf Coast Region, 1699–1769.* Baton Rouge: Louisiana State University Press, 2000. CD-ROM.

Brasseaux, C. A., and M. K. Le Blanc. "Franco-Indian Diplomacy in the Mississippi Valley, 1754–1763: Prelude to Pontiac's Uprising?" *Journal de la Société des Américanistes de Paris* 68, no. 1 (1982): 59–70.

Brown, M. K. "Allons, Cowboys!" *Journal of the Illinois State Historical Society* 76 (Winter 1983): 273–82.

———. *History as They Lived It: A Social History of Prairie du Rocher, Ill.* Tucson: Patrice Press, 2005.

———. "The Search for the Michigamea Indian Village." *Outdoor Illinois* (March 1972): 19, 26.

———. *The Voyageur in the Illinois Country: The Fur Trade's Professional Boatman in Mid America.* Extended Publication Series, no. 3. Naperville, IL: Center for French Colonial Studies, 2002.

Brown, M. K., and L. C. Dean. *The French Colony in the Mid-Mississippi Valley.* 2nd ed. St. Louis: Center for French Colonial Studies, 2012.

———. *The Village of Chartres in Colonial Illinois, 1720–1765.* 1977. Reprint, Baton Rouge, LA: Provincial Press, 2010.

Brown, M. K., and R. Mazrim. "Revisiting the Forts and Village at Chartres in the Illinois Country." *Illinois Archaeology* 22, no. 1 (2010): 134–47.

Brown, M. K., and H. R. Williams, eds. *French Colonial Studies: Le Pays des Illinois: Selections from Le Journal, 1983–2005.* Extended Publications Series, no. 6. Naperville, IL: Center for French Colonial Studies, 2006.

Burton, C. M., ed. "Cadillac Papers." *Michigan Historical Collections* 33 (1904): 36–715.

Caldwell, N. W. "The Chickasaw Threat to French Control of the Mississippi in the 1740s." *Chronicles of Oklahoma* 16, no. 4 (December 1938): 465–92.

Candler, A. D., ed. *The Colonial Records of the State of Georgia.* Vol. 21, *Original Papers, 1735–1737.* Atlanta: Chas. P. Byrd, State Printer, 1910.

Caroon, R. G. *Broadswords and Bayonets: The Journals of the Expedition under the Command of Captain Thomas Stirling of the 42nd Regiment of Foot, Royal Highland Regiment (the Black Watch) to Occupy Fort Chartres in the Illinois Country, August 1765 to January 1766.* Kenilworth: Society of Colonial Wars in the State of Illinois, 1984.

Charlevoix, P.-F.-X. de, S.J. *Histoire et description générale de la Nouvelle-France* [History and general description of New France]. 3 vols. Paris: Chez Rollin Fils, 1744.

———. *History and General Description of New France.* Translated with notes by J. G. Shea. 6 vols. 1870. Reprint, New York: F. P. Harper, 1902.

Chavez, T. E. *A Moment in Time: The Odyssey of New Mexico's Segesser Hide Paintings.* Los Ranchos, NM: Rio Grande Books, 2012.

Coker, W. S., ed. *Proceedings of the Gulf Coast History and Humanities Conference.* Vol. 7, *The Military Presence on the Gulf Coast.* Pensacola, FL: Gulf Coast History and Humanities Conference, 1978.

Collet, O. W., ed. "Will and Accompanying Documents of Louis St. Ange de Bellerive." *Magazine of Western History* 2 (1885): 60–64.

Conrad, G. R. "Administration of the Illinois Country: The French Debate." *Louisiana History* 36, no. 1 (Winter 1995): 31–53.

———, trans. *The First Families of Louisiana*. Vol. 1. Baton Rouge, LA: Claitor's Publishing Division, 1970.

———, ed. *The Louisiana Purchase Bicentennial Series in Louisiana History*. Vol. 1, *The French Experience in Louisiana*. Lafayette: Center for Louisiana Studies, University of Southwestern Louisiana, 1995.

Costa, D. J. "On the Origins of the Name 'Illinois.'" *Society for the Study of the Indigenous Languages of the Americas Newsletter* 25, no. 4 (2007): 9–12.

Cruzat, H. H. "Letters of Sieur Terrisse de Ternan." *Louisiana Historical Quarterly* 3, no. 4 (1920): 509–42 (hereafter cited as *LHQ*).

———. "Records of the Superior Council of Louisiana, XV." *LHQ* 5, no. 2 (1922): 239–76; "XXIV," *LHQ* 7, no. 4 (1924): 676–705; "XXVII," *LHQ* 8, no. 3 (1925): 478–507; "XLIV," *LHQ* 12, no. 4 (1929): 647–74; "XLV," *LHQ* 13, no. 1 (1930): 119–60; "XLVIII," *LHQ* 13, no. 4 (1930): 660–82; "L," *LHQ* 14, no. 2 (1931): 245–70; "LIII," *LHQ* 15, no. 1 (1932): 120–55; "LIV," *LHQ* 15, no. 3 (1932): 508–31; "LV," *LHQ* 15, no. 4 (1932): 659–74; "LXIV," *LHQ* 18, no. 3 (1935): 696–726; "LXX," *LHQ* 20, no. 1 (1937): 212–44; "LXXI," *LHQ* 20, no. 2 (1937): 486–517; "LXXIV," *LHQ* 21, no. 1 (1938): 282–318; "LXXV," *LHQ* 21, no. 2 (1938): 564–609; "LXXVI," *LHQ* (1938) 21, no. 3 (1938): 875–908.

Dart, H. P. "Decision Day in the Superior Council of Louisiana, March 5, 1746." *LHQ* 21, no. 4 (1938): 998–1020.

D'Artaguiette Family Tree. *Amitiés Vendée-Louisiane*. Accessed June 16, 2013. http://www.vendeelouisiane.fr/images/stories/famille%20dartaguiette%20%20des%20cars.pdf.

Dawdy, S. L. *Building the Devil's Empire: French Colonial New Orleans*. Chicago: University of Chicago Press, 2009.

Deliette, Pierre. "Memoir of De Gannes Concerning the Illinois Country." In *The French Foundations, 1680–1693*, edited by T. C. Pease and R. C. Werner, 302–95. Collections of the Illinois State Historical Library, vol. 23; French Series, vol. 1. Springfield: Illinois State Historical Library, 1934.

De Ville, W., ed. "Constructing a Future Cathedral, 1724." *Mississippi Valley Mélange* 3 (1998): 27–32.

———. *Mississippi Valley Mélange* 7 (2012).

Dictionary of Canadian Biography/Dictionnaire biographique du Canada. Toronto and Laval: University of Toronto and Université Laval, 1959–. http://www.biographi.ca.

Dictionnaire de l'Académie française. 4th ed. Paris: Chez la Vve B. Brunet, 1762.

Din, G. C. "François Coulon de Villiers: More Light on an Illusive [*sic*] Historical Figure." *Louisiana History* 41, no. 3 (Summer 2000): 345–57.

Diron d'Artaguiette, [Bernard]. "Journal of Diron d'Artaguiette, Inspector General of Louisiana, 1722–1723." In *Travels in the American Colonies*, edited by N. D. Mereness, 15–92. New York: Macmillan, 1916.

Dumont de Montigny, J.-F.-B. *The Memoir of Lieutenant Dumont, 1715–1747: A Sojourner in the French Atlantic.* Translated by G. M. Sayre. Edited by G. M. Sayre and C. Zecher. Chapel Hill: University of North Carolina Press, 2012.

———. *Mémoires historiques sur la Louisiane* [Historical memoirs of Louisiana]. Edited by J.-B. Le Mascrier. 2 vols. Paris: C. J. B. Bauche, 1753.

———. *Regards sur le monde atlantique, 1715–1747* [Views of the Atlantic world]. Edited by C. Zecher, G. M. Sayre, and S. L. Dawdy. Sillery, Québec: Septentrion, 2008.

Dunn, C., and E. Dunn, trans. "Indiana's First War." *Indiana Historical Society Publications* 8, no. 2 (1924): 73–143.

Dunnigan, B. L. *Siege—1759: The Campaign against Niagara.* Rev. ed. Youngstown, NY: Old Fort Niagara Association, 1996.

Edmunds, R. D., and J. L. Peyser. *The Fox Wars: The Mesquakie Challenge to New France.* Norman: University of Oklahoma Press, 1993.

Ekberg, C. J. "Black Slavery in Illinois, 1720–1765." *Western Illinois Regional Studies* 12, no. 1 (Spring 1989): 5–19.

———. *Colonial Ste. Genevieve: An Adventure on the Mississippi Frontier.* 2nd ed. Tucson, AZ: Patrice Press, 1996.

———. "The Exclusive Maxent-Laclède Trading Grant." *Missouri Historical Review* 106 (July 2012): 185–97.

———. *French Roots in the Illinois Country: The Mississippi Frontier in Colonial Times.* Urbana: University of Illinois Press, 1998.

———. *Stealing Indian Women: Native Slavery in the Illinois Country.* Urbana: University of Illinois Press, 2007.

———. "Terrisse de Ternan, Epistoler and Soldier." *Louisiana History* 23, no. 4 (Fall 1982): 400–408.

Ekberg, C. J., G. Kilman, and P. Lebeau, trans. and eds. *Code Noir: The Colonial Slave Laws of French Mid-America.* Extended Publication no. 4. Naperville, IL: Center for French Colonial Studies, 2005.

Ekberg, C. J., and S. Person. *St. Louis Rising: The French Regime of Louis St. Ange de Bellerive.* Urbana: University of Illinois Press, 2015.

Ekberg, C. J., and A. J. Pregaldin. "Marie Rouensa-8cate8a and the Foundations of French Illinois." *Illinois Historical Journal* 84, no. 3 (Autumn 1981): 146–60.

Englebert, R. "Beyond Borders: Mental Mapping and the French River World in North America, 1763–1805." PhD diss., University of Ottawa, 2010.

Englebert, R., and G. Teasdale, eds. *French and Indians in the Heart of North America, 1630–1815.* East Lansing: Michigan State University Press, 2013.

Faye, S. "The Arkansas Post of Louisiana: French Domination." *LHQ* 26, no. 3 (1943): 633–721.

Forsyth, A. D., and G. Pleasonton. *Louisiana Marriage Contracts*. New Orleans: Polyanthos, 1980.

"Fort de Chartres." From Kaskaskia to Sangamo: Dispatches from the Archaeological History of the Illinois Country, 1600–1850. Accessed October 14, 2013. http://illinoiscountryarchaeology.blogspot.com/search/label/Fort%20de%20Chartres.

Fortier, B. "New Light on Fort Massac." In *Frenchmen and French Ways in the Mississippi Valley*, edited by J. F. McDermott, 57–71. Urbana: University of Illinois Press, 1969.

Gagné, J. F. "'Fidèle à Dieu, à la France, et au Roi': Les retraites militaires de La Chapelle et de Beaujeu vers la Louisiane après la perte du Canada, 1760–1762" ["Faithful to God, to France, and to the king": Military retreats of La Chapelle and Beaujeu toward Louisiana after the loss of Canada]. Master's thesis, Université Laval, 2014. http://www.theses.ulaval.ca/2014/30241/30241.pdf.

Giraud, M. *Histoire de la Louisiane Française* [A history of French Louisiana]. 5 vols. Paris: Presses Universitaires de France, 1953–87.

———. *A History of French Louisiana*. Vol. 1, *The Reign of Louis XIV, 1698–1715*. Translated by J. C. Lambert. Baton Rouge: Louisiana State University Press, 1974.

———. *A History of French Louisiana*. Vol. 2, *Years of Transition, 1715–1717*. Translated by B. Pearce. Baton Rouge: Louisiana State University Press, 1993.

———. *A History of French Louisiana*. Vol. 5, *The Company of the Indies, 1723–1731*. Translated by B. Pearce. Baton Rouge: Louisiana State University Press, 1991.

Good, M. E. *Guebert Site: An 18th Century Historic Kaskaskia Indian Village in Randolph County, Illinois*. Wood River, IL: Central States Archaeological Societies, 1972.

Gourmelon, H. *Le chevalier de Kerlérec: L'affaire de la Louisiane* [The Chevalier de Kerlérec: The Louisiana Affair]. 2nd ed. Saint-Jacques-de-la-Lande, France: Keltia graphic, 2004.

Grignon, A. "Seventy-Two Years' Recollections of Wisconsin." In *Third Annual Report and Collections of the State Historical Society of Wisconsin*, vol. 3, edited by L. C. Draper, 195–295. Madison, WI: Calkins & Webb, Printers, 1857.

Hardcastle, D. "The Military Organization of French Colonial Louisiana." In *Proceedings of the Gulf Coast History and Humanities Conference*. Vol. 7, *The Military Presence on the Gulf Coast*, edited by W. S. Coker, 1–20. Pensacola, FL: Gulf Coast History and Humanities Conference, 1978. Reprinted in *The Louisiana Purchase Bicentennial Series in Louisiana History*. Vol. 1, *The French Experience in Louisiana*, edited by G. R. Conrad, 345–59. Lafayette: Center for Louisiana Studies, University of Southwestern Louisiana, 1995.

Hauser, R. E. "The Fox Raid of 1752: Defensive Warfare and Decline of Illinois Indian Tribe." *Illinois Historical Journal* 86 (1993): 210–24.

Hirsch, A. D. "'The Celebrated Madame Montour': Interpretess across Early American Frontiers." *Explorations in Early American Culture* 4 (2000): 81–112.

Hotz, G. *The Segesser Hide Paintings: Masterpieces Depicting Spanish Colonial New Mexico*. Translated by J. Malthaner. Santa Fe: Museum of New Mexico Press, 1991.

Houck, L., ed. *The Spanish Regime in Missouri*. Vol. 1. Chicago: R. R. Donnelley & Sons Co., 1909.

J[ordan], C. "Les Sauvages de l'Amérique ont audience du Roy et doivent s'en retourner en leur pays" [The American Indians have an audience with the king and have to return to their country]. *Suite de la Clef, ou Journal historique sur les matières du temps* [Following the key, or Historical journal on materials of the time] 19 (February 1726): 209–10.

Kellogg, L. P. "La Chapelle's Remarkable Retreat through the Mississippi Valley, 1760–61." *Mississippi Valley Historical Review* 22 (1935): 63–81.

———. "Passerat de La Chapelle in the American Revolution." *Mississippi Valley Historical Review* 25, no. 4 (March 1939): 535–38.

Kernion, G. C. H. "The Chevalier de Pradel." *LHQ* 12, no. 2 (1929): 238–54.

LeJeune, R. P. L. *Dictionnaire Général de biographie, histoire, littérature, agriculture, commerce, industrie et des arts, sciences, mœurs, coutumes, institutions politiques et religieuses du Canada* [General dictionary of biography, history, literature, agriculture, commerce, industry and the arts, sciences, mores, customs, political and religious institutions of Canada]. Vol. 2. Ottawa: Université d'Ottawa, 1931.

Lemieux, D. J. "Some Legal and Practical Aspects of the Office of *Commissaire-Ordonnateur* of French Louisiana." *Louisiana Studies* 14 (1975): 379–93. Reprinted in *The Louisiana Purchase Bicentennial Series in Louisiana History*. Vol. 1, *The French Experience in Louisiana*, edited by G. R. Conrad, 395–407. Lafayette: Center for Louisiana Studies, University of Southwestern Louisiana, 1995.

Léon, avocat. *Précis pour le sieur Point Marie de la Demoiselle Bourbosson légataire universelle du sieur Terrisse de Ternan son oncle, contre Demoiselle Marianne Terrisse, Veuve de Guillaume Carlet, etc. signé Léon, avocat* [Précis for Sieur Point Marie of the damsel Bourbosson, legatee of Sieur Terrisse de Ternan her uncle, against damsel Marianne Terrisse, widow of Guillaume Carlet, etc. signed Léon, lawyer]. Grenoble: Impr. Cuchet J., 1759. Accessed February 20, 2014. http://catalogue.bm-grenoble.fr/in/faces/details.xhtml?id=p::usmarcdef_0000396727&mozQuirk=?&highlight=Leon,%20avocat&posInPage=4&bookmark=c7e5b949-1626-4f36- 850a-e3a177ada9ae.

Le Page du Pratz, A.-S. *Histoire de la Louisiane* [History of Louisiana]. 3 vols. Paris: De Bure, 1758.

Löfling, P. *Iter Hispanicum, eller resa til Spanska Länderna uti Europa och America, 1751 til 1756* [Iter Hispanicum, or Travels through Spain and Cumana in South America, 1751–1756]. Stockholm: Tryckt på direct. L. Salvii, 1758.

Long, C. M. *Madame Lalaurie: Mistress of the Haunted House*. Gainesville: University Press of Florida, 2012.

Lugano, G. "Records of the Superior Council of Louisiana, LXXXIII," *LHQ* 23, no. 2 (1940): 589–634; "LXXXVII," *LHQ* 24, no. 2 (1941): 544–600; "XCIV," *LHQ* 26, no. 1 (1943): 169–256.

MacDonald, D. "Annexe: The Marriage Woes of Alphonse de la Buissonnière and Marie-Thérèse Trudeau." *La Charpente* 6, no. 3 (December 2013): 1–6.

———. "Les tribulations nuptiales d'Alphonse de la Buissonnière et de Marie-Thérèse Trudeau." Hélène Trudeau, trans. *La Charpente* 6, no. 3 (December 2013): 3–10.

Maduell, C. R., Jr., ed. and trans. *The Census Tables for the French Colony of Louisiana from 1699 through 1732*. Baltimore: Genealogical Pub. Co., 1972.

Mason, E. G. "British Illinois—Philippe de Rocheblave." In *Early Chicago and Illinois*, edited by E. G. Mason, 360–82. Chicago Historical Society's Collection, vol. 4. Chicago: Fergus Printing Company, 1890.

———. "Rocheblave Papers." In *Early Chicago and Illinois*, edited by E. G. Mason, 382–419. Chicago Historical Society's Collection, vol. 4. Chicago: Fergus Printing Company, 1890.

McCarthy, W. P. "The Chevalier Macarty Mactigue." *Journal of the Illinois State Historical Society* 61, no. 1 (Spring 1968): 41–57.

McDermott, J. F. *Frenchmen and French Ways in the Mississippi Valley*. Urbana: University of Illinois Press, 1969.

Menier, M.-A., É. Taillemite, and G. de Forges. *Inventaire des archives colonials: Correspondance à l'arrivée en provenance de la Louisiane* [Inventory of the colonial archives: Correspondence on arrival from Louisiana]. 2 vols. Paris: Archives Nationales, 1976–83.

Mereness, N. D. *Travels in the American Colonies*. New York: Macmillan Company, 1916.

Miller Surrey, N. M. *The Commerce of Louisiana during the French Regime, 1699–1763*. New York: Columbia University Press, 1916.

Mills, E. S. "Parallel Lives: Philippe de La Renaudière and Philippe (de) Renault, Directors of the Mines, Company of the Indies." *Natchitoches Genealogist* 22 (April 1998): 3–18.

Monty, Me. E. "François Truteau." *Mémoires de la Société généalogique canadienne-française* 29, no. 3 (July–September 1978): 167.

[Morande, Charles Théveneau de?] *Le Porte-feuille de Madame Gourdan dite la Comtesse* [The portfolio of Madame Gourdan, called the countess]. Spa, 1783.

Morgan, M. J. *Land of Big Rivers: French and Indian Illinois, 1699–1778.* Carbondale: Southern Illinois University Press, 2010.

Morrissey, R. M. "I Speak It Well: Language, Communication, and the End of a Missionary Middle Ground in Illinois, 1673–1712." *Early American Studies* 9, no. 3 (September 2011): 617–48.

———. "The Terms of Encounter: Language and Contested Visions of French Colonization in the Illinois Country, 1673–1702." In *French and Indians in the Heart of North America, 1630–1815*, edited by R. Englebert and G. Teasdale, 43–75. East Lansing: Michigan State University Press, 2013.

Mumford, H. W. *The French Governors of Illinois, 1718–1765.* Evanston, IL: National Society of the Colonial Dames of American in the State of Illinois, 1963.

Nasatir, A. P., and J. R. Mills. *Commerce and Contraband in New Orleans during the French and Indian War: A Documentary Study of the Texel and Three Brothers Affairs.* Cincinnati: American Jewish Archives, 1968.

Neill, E. D. *The Last French Post in the Valley of the Upper Mississippi.* St. Paul, MN: Pioneer Press Company, 1887.

Nolan, C. E. *Sacramental Records of the Roman Catholic Church of the Archdiocese of New Orleans.* Vol. 1, *1718–1750.* New Orleans: Archdiocese of New Orleans, 1987.

Norall, F. *Bourgmont, Explorer of the Missouri, 1698–1725.* Lincoln: University of Nebraska Press, 1988.

Norton, M. C. *Illinois Census Returns, 1810, 1818.* Collections of the Illinois State Historical Library, vol. 24; Statistical Series, vol. 2. Springfield: Trustees of the Illinois State Historical Library, 1935.

Nye, R. A. *Masculinity and Male Codes of Honor in Modern France.* New York: Oxford University Press, 1993.

O'Neill, C. E. *Church and State in French Colonial Louisiana: Policy and Politics to 1732.* New Haven, CT: Yale University Press, 1966.

Orser, C. E., Jr. "The Kolmer Site: An Eighteenth Century Michigamea Village." Master's thesis, Wayne State University, Detroit, 1975.

Palm, M. B. *The Jesuit Missions of the Illinois Country, 1673–1763.* Cleveland: St. Louis University, 1931.

Parkman, F. *Montcalm and Wolfe*, Vol. 1. 1884. Reprint, Boston: Little, Brown and Co., 1914.

Parmenter, J. "Isabel Montour: Cultural Broker on the Eighteenth-Century Frontiers of New York and Pennsylvania." In *The Human Tradition in Colonial America*, edited by I. K. Steele and N. Rhoden, 141–59. Wilmington, DE: Scholarly Resources, 1999.

Passerat de La Chapelle, P. "Le Baron Pierre Passerat de La Chapelle. Conférence faite à la Société d'Histoire du Canada par M. le Baron de La Chapelle." Pts. 1 and 2. *Nova Francia* 7, no. 1 (January–June 1932): 81–135; 7, no. 2 (July–December 1932): 178–210.

Pease, T. C. *Anglo-French Boundary Disputes in the West, 1749–1763*. Collections of the Illinois State Historical Library, vol. 27; French Series, vol. 2. Springfield: Trustees of the Illinois State Historical Library, 1936.

Pease, T. C., and E. Jenison. *Illinois on the Eve of the Seven Years' War, 1747–1755*. Collections of the Illinois State Historical Library, vol. 29; French Series, vol. 3. Springfield: Trustees of the Illinois State Historical Library, 1940.

Pénicaut, A. *Fleur de Lys and Calumet: Being the Pénicaut Narrative of French Adventure in Louisiana*. Translated and edited by R. G. McWilliams. 1953. Reprint, Tuscaloosa: University of Alabama Press, 1988.

Peyser, J. L., trans. *Letters from New France: The Upper Country, 1686–1783*. Urbana: University of Illinois Press, 1992.

Piper, M. "Tarnished Galahad: The Short and Dynamic Career of Claude-Charles DuTisné." *Journal of the Early Americas* 2, no. 3 (June–July 2012): 26–31.

Pittman, P. *The Present State of the European Settlements on the Mississippi*. London: J. Nourse, 1770.

Porteous, L. L. "Index to the Spanish Judicial Records of Louisiana, XXII." *LHQ* 11, no. 3 (1928): 503–29; "XXIV," *LHQ* 12, no. 2 (1929): 331–58; "LXXX," *LHQ* 28, no. 2 (1945): 573–673.

———. "Trial of Pablo Rocheblave before Governor Unzaga, 1771." *LHQ* 8, no. 3 (July 1925): 372–81.

Pouchot, P. *Mémoires sur la dernière guerre de l'Amérique Septentrionale entre la France et l'Angleterre* [Memoirs on the last war in North America between the French and the English]. Vol. 3. Yverdon, 1781.

Pusch, D. E. "Founders of Louisiana: The First Two Ship Lists of 1699." *Mississippi Valley Mélange* 7 (2012): 2–31.

"Relation de l'arrivée en France de quatre Sauvages du Missicipi, de leur sejour, & des audiences qu'ils ont euës du Roi, des Princes du Sang, de la Compagnie des Indes, avec les compliments qu'ils ont fait, les honneurs & les presens qu'ils ont reçûs, &c" [Account of the arrival in France of the four Indians of Mississippi, of their stay, and of the audiences they have had with the king, with the princes of the blood (sons of the monarch), with the East India Company, with the compliments they have made, the honors & the presents they received, etc.]. *Mercure de France* 1 (December 1725): 2827–59.

Rowland, D., and A. G. Sanders. *Mississippi Provincial Archives*. Vols. 1–3. Jackson: Press of the Mississippi Department of Archives and History, 1927–32.

———. *Mississippi Provincial Archives*. Vol. 4. Revised and edited by P. K. Galloway. Baton Rouge: Louisiana State University Press, 1984.

Roy, P.-G. "Jean Bissot de Vincennes." *Le Bulletin des Recherches Historiques* 6 (1900): 109–14.

Ruddy, D. D. "Louis Liénard de Beaujeu de Villemonde." *Dictionary of Canadian Biography*. Accessed December 9, 2013. http://www.biographi.ca/en/bio.php?id_nbr=2507.

Russ, C. J. "Dutisné." *Dictionary of Canadian Biography*. Accessed February 27, 2014. http://www.biographi.ca/en/bio/dutisne_claude_charles_2E.html.

———. "Liettes, Pierre-Charles de (di Lietto, Deliette, Desliettes)." *Dictionary of Canadian Biography*. Accessed October 7, 2013. http://www.biographi.ca/en/bio/liette_pierre_charles_de_2E.html.

———. "Tonty de Liette (Deliette, Desliettes), Charles-Henri-Joseph de." *Dictionary of Canadian Biography*. Accessed October 7, 2013. http://www.biographi.ca/en/bio/tonty_de_liette_charles_henri_joseph_de_3E.html.

Scott, E. M., and D. P. Heldman. "A French Descendant Community after the Fall of New France: Archaeology in Nouvelle Ste. Genevieve, 1780–1880." *Le Journal* 26, no. 1 (Winter 2010): 1–7.

Scott, J. *The Illinois Nation.* Pt. 1. Streator, IL: Streator Historical Society, 1973.

Seineke, K. W. *The George Rogers Clark Adventure in the Illinois and Selected Documents of the American Revolution at the Frontier Posts.* New Orleans: Polyanthos, 1981.

Steele, I. K., and N. Rhoden, eds. *The Human Tradition in Colonial America.* Wilmington, DE: Scholarly Resources, 1999.

Stevens, P. L. "'To Invade the Frontiers of Kentucky?' The Indian Diplomacy of Philippe de Rocheblave, Britain's Acting Commandant at Kaskaskia, 1776–1778." *Filson Club History Quarterly* 64, no. 2 (April 1990): 205–46.

Thwaites, R. G., ed. *The Jesuit Relations and Allied Documents: Travels and Explorations of the Jesuit Missionaries in New France, 1610–1791.* 73 vols. Cleveland: Burrows, 1896–1901.

———. "1728–29: Narrative of de Boucherville." In *Collections of the State Historical Society of Wisconsin*, vol. 17, *The French Regime in Wisconsin—II, 1727–1748*, 36–70. Madison: State Historical Society of Wisconsin, 1906.

Trudeau, L. "Page d'histoire, Onzième épisode: Le goût de la terre" [Page of history, eleventh episode: The flavor of the land]. *La Charpente* 4, no. 2 (June 2011): 6–10.

———. "Part One: Charles Laveau Trudeau, alias Don Carlos (1743–1816)." *La Charpente* 4, no. 4 (December 2011): 1–2.

Trudeau, M. J. *The Trudeaus of Louisiana and Related Families.* N.p.: M. J Trudeau, 1996.

Verge-Franceschi, M. *Le Lieutenant général des Armées navales Jean-François de Bertet de La Clue-Sabran (1696–1764)*. Accessed March 10, 2013. https://www.departemento6.fr/documents/Import/decouvrir-les-am/rr90-1985-04.pdf.

Villiers du Terrage, M. de. *Un Explorateur de la Louisiane, Jean-Baptiste Bénard de La Harpe (1683–1765)*. 1934. Reprint, Montréal: Bibliothèque nationale du Québec, 1988.

———. *The Last Years of French Louisiana*. Edited by C. A. Brasseaux and G. R. Conrad. Annotated by C. A. Brasseaux. Translated by Hosea Phillips. Lafayette: Center for Louisiana Studies, University of Southwestern Louisiana, 1982.

———. "Le massacre de l'expédition espagnole du Missouri (11 août 1720)" [The massacre of the Spanish expedition in Missouri (11 August 1720)]. *Journal de la Société des Américanistes de Paris*, n.s., 13 (1921): 239–55.

Vincens, S. *Madame Montour and the Fur Trade (1667–1752)*. Translated and edited by R. Bernstein. Bloomington, IN: Xlibris, 2011.

———. *Madame Montour et son temps* [Madame Montour and her time]. Montréal: Québec/Amérique, 1979.

Walczynski, M. *Massacre 1769: The Search for the Origin of the Legend of Starved Rock*. William L. Potter Publication Series, no. 10. St. Louis: Center for French Colonial Studies, 2013.

Wallace, J. "Fort de Chartres: Its Origin, Growth and Decline." *Transactions of the Illinois State Historical Society* (1903): 105–17.

Wedel, M. M. "Claude-Charles Dutisné: A Review of His 1719 Journeys." Pts. 1 and 2. *Great Plains Journal* 11, no. 1 (1972): 4–25; 12, no. 2 (1973): 147–73.

Weeks, P. "Princess of the Missouris." *Le Journal* 7, no. 3 (Fall 1991): 6–12.

White, S. *Wild Frenchmen and Frenchified Indians: Material Culture and Race in Colonial Louisiana*. Philadelphia: University of Pennsylvania Press, 2012.

Index

Italicized page numbers indicate figures.

A Shawnee Book